Edexcel Certificate/International GCSE
Physics

This book covers the **Edexcel Level 1/Level 2 Certificate in Physics** and the **Edexcel International GCSE in Physics**.

It's also great for the Edexcel Certificate/International GCSE in **Science (Double Award)** — but you won't need to learn the Paper 2 material if you're doing this course.

How to get your free Online Edition

This book includes a **free** Online Edition you can read on your computer or tablet wherever you have an internet connection.

To get it, just go to **cgpbooks.co.uk/extras** and enter this code...

4209 8535 1735 1931

This code only works for one person. If somebody else has used this book before you, they might have already claimed the Online Edition.

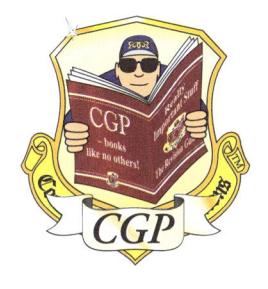

Complete Revision and Practice

Contents

Section 1 — Forces and Motion

Speed and Velocity 1
Acceleration 2
Distance-Time Graphs 3
Velocity-Time Graphs 4
Mass, Weight and Gravity 5
   Warm-Up and Exam Questions 6
Forces 8
Friction 9
Investigating Motion 10
Terminal Velocity 11
Investigating Falling Objects 12
   Warm-Up and Exam Questions 13
The Three Laws of Motion 15
Combining Forces 17
Stopping Distances 18
Momentum and Collisions 19
   Warm-Up and Exam Questions 21
Turning Forces and Centre of Gravity 23
Principle of Moments 25
Hooke's Law 26
Gravity and the Universe 28
Orbital Speed 29
   Warm-Up and Exam Questions 30
Revision Summary for Section 1 32

Section 2 — Electricity

Safe Plugs 33
Fuses and Circuit Breakers 34
Energy and Power in Circuits 35
Circuits — The Basics 37
Resistance and V = I × R 39
LDRs, Thermistors and LEDs 41
   Warm-Up and Exam Questions 42
Series Circuits 44
Parallel Circuits 45
Charge, Voltage and Energy Change 46
Static Electricity 47
Static Electricity — Examples 50
   Warm-Up and Exam Questions 51
Revision Summary for Section 2 53

Section 3 — Waves

Waves — The Basics 54
Wave Behaviour and EM Waves 56
Uses of Electromagnetic Waves 57
Dangers of Electromagnetic Waves 60
   Warm-Up and Exam Questions 61
Reflection of Waves 63
Refraction of Waves 65
Refractive Index and Snell's Law 66
Snell's Law and Critical Angles 68
   Warm-Up and Exam Questions 69
Analogue and Digital Signals 71
Sound Waves 72
   Warm-Up and Exam Questions 75
Revision Summary for Section 3 76

Section 4 — Energy Resources and Energy Transfer

Conservation of Energy 77
Efficiency 78
Energy Transfers 79
Sankey Diagrams 81
   Warm-Up and Exam Questions 82
Heat Transfer 84
Heat Conduction and Convection 85
Examples of Heat Convection 86
Reducing Energy Transfers 87
   Warm-Up and Exam Questions 88
Work 89
Power 90
Kinetic and Gravitational
   Potential Energy 91
   Warm-Up and Exam Questions 92
Non-Renewable Energy
   and Power Stations 93
Nuclear and Geothermal Energy 94
Wind and Wave Energy 95
Solar Energy 96
Generating Electricity Using Water 97
Pumped Storage 98
   Warm-Up and Exam Questions 99
Revision Summary for Section 4 101

Contents

Section 5 — Solids, Liquids and Gases

Density 102
Pressure 103
Changes of State 104
Evaporation 105
Particle Theory and Temperature
    in Gases 106
Particle Theory and Pressure in Gases 107
    Warm-Up and Exam Questions 108
Revision Summary for Section 5 110

Section 6 — Magnetism and Electromagnetism

Magnets and Magnetic Fields 111
Electromagnetism 112
The Motor Effect 113
Electric Motors and Loudspeakers 114
Electromagnetic Induction 115
Transformers 117
    Warm-Up and Exam Questions 119
Revision Summary for Section 6 122

Section 7 — Radioactivity and Particles

Atoms and Isotopes 123
Radioactivity 124
The Three Kinds of Radioactivity 125
Radioactivity and Nuclear Equations 126
Alpha Scattering 127
    Warm-Up and Exam Questions 128

Half-Life 130
Uses of Nuclear Radiation 132
More Uses of Nuclear Radiation 133
Risks from Nuclear Radiation 134
Nuclear Fission 135
    Warm-Up and Exam Questions 136
Revision Summary for Section 7 138

Describing Experiments

Experimental Know-How 139
Drawing Graphs and
    Interpreting Results 141
Planning Experiments and
    Evaluating Conclusions 142

Practice Papers

Practice Paper 1 143
Practice Paper 2 167
Useful Equations 182

Answers 183
Working Out Your Grade 194
Index 195

Edexcel Certificate Exam Information

1) You have to do two exams for the Edexcel Certificate in Physics — Paper 1 and Paper 2.
2) Paper 1 is 2 hours long and worth 120 marks. *If you're doing the International GCSE in Physics, it works*
3) Paper 2 is just 1 hour long, and it's worth 60 marks. *in exactly the same way — so you'll do two papers too.*
4) Some material in the specification will only be tested in Paper 2. The Paper 2 material in this book is marked with a burgundy 'Paper 2' border. The 'Warm-Up Questions' that cover Paper 2 material are printed in burgundy and the 'Exam Questions' are marked with this stamp: PAPER 2

Remember, if you're doing the Edexcel Certificate/International GCSE in
Science (Double Award) you don't need to learn the Paper 2 material.

Published by CGP

From original material by Paddy Gannon.

Editors:
Rachel Kordan, David Maliphant, Sarah Pattison, Sophie Scott, Camilla Simson, Hayley Thompson.

Contributors:
Jason Howell

ISBN: 978 1 78294 184 2

With thanks to Glenn Rogers for the proofreading.
With thanks to Laura Jakubowski for the copyright research.

Data used to construct stopping distance diagrams on pages 18 and 151 from the Highway Code.
© Crown Copyright re-produced under the terms of the Open Government licence
http://www.nationalarchives.gov.uk/doc/open-government-licence/

Printed by Elanders Ltd, Newcastle upon Tyne.
Clipart from Corel®

Based on the Classic CGP style created by Richard Parsons.

Text, design, layout and original illustrations © Coordination Group Publications Ltd. (CGP) 2014
All rights reserved.

Photocopying more than one chapter of this book is not permitted. Extra copies are available from CGP.
0870 750 1242 • www.cgpbooks.co.uk

Section 1 — Forces and Motion

Speed and Velocity

Speed and velocity aren't the same thing, you know. There's more to velocity than meets the eye.

Speed and Velocity are Both How Fast You're Going

Speed and velocity are both measured in m/s (or km/h or mph).
They both simply say how fast you're going, but there's a subtle difference between them which you need to know:

> **SPEED** is just how fast you're going (e.g. 30 mph or 20 m/s) with no regard to the direction.

> **VELOCITY** however must also have the direction specified, e.g. 30 mph north or 20 m/s, 060°.

Seems kinda fussy I know, but they expect you to remember that distinction, so there you go.

Speed, Distance and Time — the Formula:

$$\text{Speed} = \frac{\text{Distance}}{\text{Time}}$$

If you're not sure how to use formula triangles, have a look inside the front cover.

You really ought to get pretty slick with this very easy formula.
The formula triangle version makes it all a bit of a breeze.
You just need to try and think up some interesting word for remembering the order of the letters in the triangle, $s^d t$. Errm... sedit, perhaps... well, you think up your own.

Example

A cat skulks 20 m in 35 s. Find:
   a) its average speed,   b) how long it takes to skulk 75 m.

ANSWER: Using the formula triangle:
   a) s = d ÷ t = 20 ÷ 35 = <u>0.57 m/s</u> (to 2 d.p.)
   b) t = d ÷ s = 75 ÷ 0.57 = 132 s = <u>2 min 12 s</u>

A lot of the time we tend to use the words "speed" and "velocity" interchangeably.
For example, to calculate velocity you'd just use the above formula for speed instead.

Velocity is like speed, but with a bit more direction

It's easy to get speed and velocity mixed up — they both tell you how fast something's going and even have the same units. Remember that velocity also tells you what direction something's travelling in.

Acceleration

If something is speeding up, we say that it is accelerating.
Now don't you accelerate too much through this page. It's important stuff you know.

Acceleration *is* How Quickly Velocity *is* Changing

Acceleration is definitely not the same as velocity or speed.

1) Acceleration is how quickly the velocity is changing.
2) This change in velocity can be a CHANGE IN SPEED or a CHANGE IN DIRECTION or both.
   (You only have to worry about the change in speed bit for calculations.)

Velocity is a simple idea. Acceleration is altogether more subtle, which is why it's confusing.

Acceleration — The Formula:

$$\text{acceleration} = \frac{\text{change in velocity}}{\text{time taken}}$$

Well, it's just another formula.
And it's got a formula triangle like all the others.

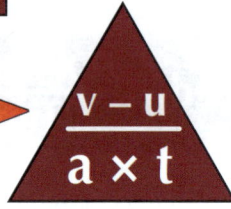

Formula triangle: $\frac{v - u}{a \times t}$

Here 'v' is the final velocity and 'u' is the initial velocity.

Mind you, there are two tricky things with this one.

1) First there's the '(v – u)', which means working out the 'change in velocity', as shown in the example below, rather than just putting a simple value for velocity or speed in.
2) Secondly there's the unit of acceleration, which is m/s². Not m/s, which is velocity, but m/s².

Example

A skulking cat accelerates from 2 m/s to 6 m/s in 5.6 s. Find its acceleration.

ANSWER: Using the formula triangle:
$a = (v - u) \div t = (6 - 2) \div 5.6 = 4 \div 5.6 = \underline{0.71 \text{ m/s}^2}$

Acceleration measures how quickly the velocity is changing

Remember, the units for acceleration are m/s², NOT m/s. So if you're ever doing an acceleration calculation, make sure you stick the correct units onto the end of your answer. You've been warned...

SECTION 1 — FORCES AND MOTION

Distance-Time Graphs

Distance-time (D-T) graphs tell you how fast an object is moving and what direction it's travelling in. Simple as that really. Make sure you get them straight in your head before turning over...

Distance-Time Graphs

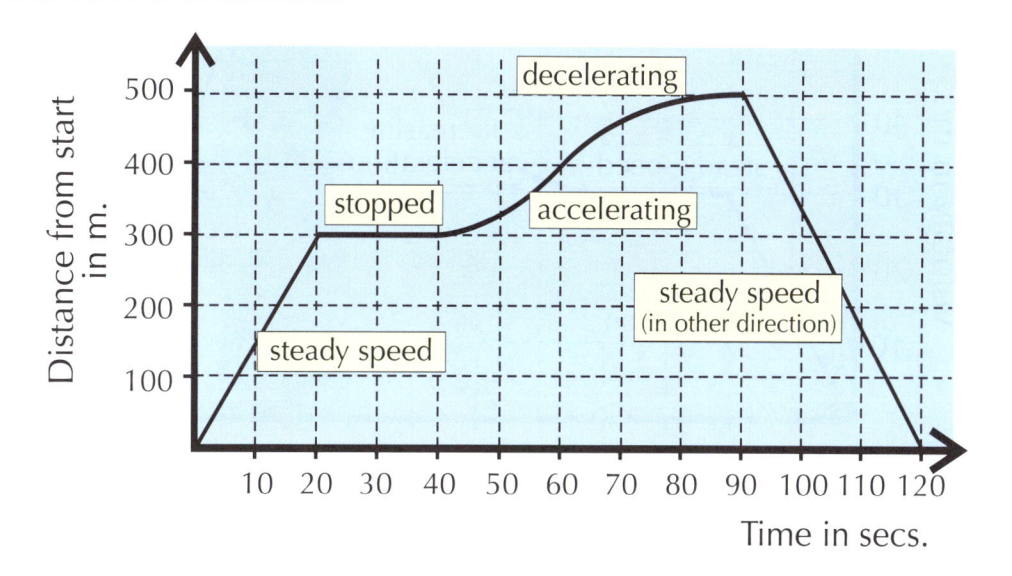

[Graph showing Distance from start in m. (y-axis, 0 to 500) vs Time in secs. (x-axis, 0 to 120) with labels: steady speed, stopped, accelerating, decelerating, steady speed (in other direction)]

Very Important Notes:

1) Gradient = speed.
2) Flat sections are where it's stopped.
3) The steeper the graph, the faster it's going.
4) Downhill sections mean it's going back toward its starting point.
5) Curves represent acceleration or deceleration.
6) A steepening curve means it's speeding up (increasing gradient).
7) A levelling off curve means it's slowing down (decreasing gradient).

Calculating Speed from a Distance-Time Graph

To calculate the speed from a distance-time graph, just work out the gradient.

For example, the speed of the return section of the graph is:

$$\text{Speed} = \text{gradient} = \frac{\text{vertical}}{\text{horizontal}} = \frac{500}{30} = 16.7 \text{ m/s}$$

Don't forget that you have to use the scales of the axes to work out the gradient. Don't measure in cm!

SECTION 1 — FORCES AND MOTION

Velocity-Time Graphs

Here's the distance-time graph's big brother — the velocity-time (V-T) graph.

Velocity-Time Graphs

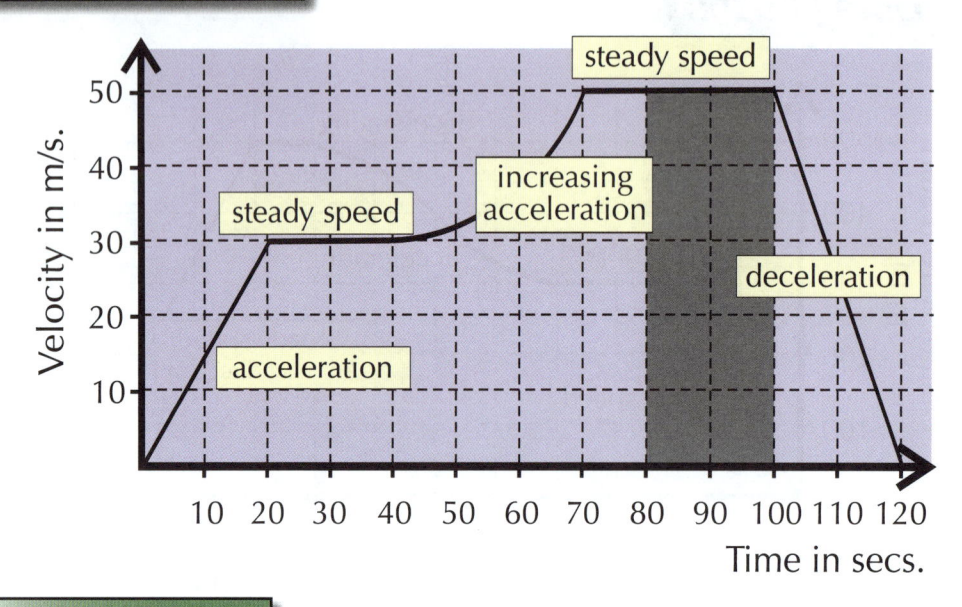

[Graph: Velocity in m/s vs Time in secs. Shows acceleration from 0 to 30 m/s over 0-20s, steady speed at 30 m/s from 20-50s, increasing acceleration curve from 50-70s up to 50 m/s, steady speed at 50 m/s from 70-100s (shaded area between 80-100s), deceleration from 100-120s down to 0.]

Very Important Notes:

1) <u>Gradient</u> = <u>acceleration</u>.
2) <u>Flat</u> sections represent <u>steady</u> speed.
3) The <u>steeper</u> the graph, the <u>greater</u> the <u>acceleration</u> or deceleration.
4) <u>Uphill</u> sections (/) are <u>acceleration</u>.
5) <u>Downhill</u> sections (\) are <u>deceleration</u>.
6) The <u>area</u> under any section of the graph (or all of it) is equal to the <u>distance</u> travelled in that <u>time</u> interval.
7) A <u>curve</u> means <u>changing acceleration</u>.

Calculating Acceleration, Speed and Distance from a V-T Graph

1) The <u>acceleration</u> represented by the <u>first section</u> of the graph is:

$$\underline{\text{Acceleration}} = \text{gradient} = \frac{\text{vertical}}{\text{horizontal}} = \frac{30}{20} = \underline{1.5 \text{ m/s}^2}$$

2) The <u>speed</u> at any point is simply found by <u>reading the value</u> off the <u>velocity axis</u>.
3) The <u>distance travelled</u> in any time interval is equal to the <u>area</u> under the graph. For example, the distance travelled between t = 80 s and t = 100 s is equal to the <u>shaded area</u>, which is equal to <u>1000 m</u> (50 m/s × 20 s).

Don't get velocity-time and distance-time graphs mixed up

The tricky thing about <u>velocity-time graphs</u> and <u>distance-time graphs</u> is that they can look pretty much the same but represent <u>totally different</u> kinds of motion. If you're given one of these graphs in the exam, make sure you check the <u>axis labels</u> carefully so you know which type of graph it is.

SECTION 1 — FORCES AND MOTION

Mass, Weight and Gravity

Gravity is the Force of Attraction Between All Masses

Gravity attracts all masses, but you only notice it when one of the masses is really really big, e.g. a planet. Anything near a planet or star is attracted to it very strongly.
This has three important effects:

1) On the surface of a planet, it makes all things accelerate towards the ground (all with the same acceleration, g, which is about 10 m/s^2 on Earth).
2) It gives everything a weight.
3) It keeps planets, moons and satellites in their orbits. The orbit is a balance between the forward motion of the object and the force of gravity pulling it inwards (see pages 28-29).

Weight and Mass are Not the Same

To understand this you must learn all these facts about mass and weight:

1) Mass is just the amount of 'stuff' in an object.
   For any given object this will have the same value anywhere in the Universe.
2) Weight is caused by the pull of gravity. In most questions the weight of an object is just the force of gravity pulling it towards the centre of the Earth.
3) An object has the same mass whether it's on Earth or on the Moon — but its weight will be different. A 1 kg mass will weigh less on the Moon (about 1.6 N) than it does on Earth (about 10 N), simply because the force of gravity pulling on it is less.
4) Weight is a force measured in newtons. It's measured using a spring balance or newton meter. Mass is not a force. It's measured in kilograms with a mass balance (an old-fashioned pair of balancing scales).

The Very Important Formula Relating Mass, Weight and Gravity

weight = mass × gravitational field strength

$$W = m \times g$$

1) Remember, weight and mass are not the same. Mass is in kg, weight is in newtons.
2) The letter "g" represents the strength of the gravity and its value is different for different planets. On Earth g ≈ 10 N/kg. On the Moon, where the gravity is weaker, g is only about 1.6 N/kg.
3) This formula is hideously easy to use:

> Example: What is the weight, in newtons, of a 5 kg mass, both on Earth and on the Moon?
> Answer: "W = m × g".   On Earth: W = 5 × 10 = 50 N   (The weight of the 5 kg mass is 50 N.)
>   On the Moon: W = 5 × 1.6 = 8 N   (The weight of the 5 kg mass is 8 N.)

See what I mean. Hideously easy — as long as you've learnt what all the letters mean.

Warm-Up and Exam Questions

You lucky thing. As if all that exciting stuff about speed and velocity wasn't enough — here are some marvellous questions about it. Make sure you do them all.

Warm-Up Questions

1) How are speed and velocity different?
2) Samuel runs 125 metres at an average speed of 6.5 m/s. How long does this take Samuel?
3) What are the units of acceleration?
4) What is represented by the gradient of a velocity-time graph?
5) What are the units of mass? And of weight?

Exam Questions

1. A cyclist travels 1500 m from his house to his local shops in 300 seconds.

   a) State the equation linking average speed, distance moved and time taken.
   (1 mark)

   b) Calculate the cyclist's average speed during his journey.
   (2 marks)

   c) On the return home, the cyclist accelerates from 2.0 m/s with a steady acceleration of 2.4 m/s^2. Calculate the time it takes the cyclist to reach 10 m/s.
   (4 marks)

2. A student walks to football training but finds she has left her boots at home. She turns around and walks back home, where she spends 50 seconds looking for the boots. Below is a distance-time graph for her journey.

   a) Use the graph to find the time it took for the student to walk to training.
   (1 mark)

   b) State whether the student walked to training at a steady speed. Explain how you know.
   (2 marks)

   c) Use the graph to calculate the student's average speed as she walked to football training.
   (3 marks)

   d) The student returns home after training in a car. During the journey, the car constantly accelerates for 10 s to overtake another vehicle and then travels at a constant speed for a further 30 s. Sketch a velocity-time graph to show the motion of the car during this time.
   (3 marks)

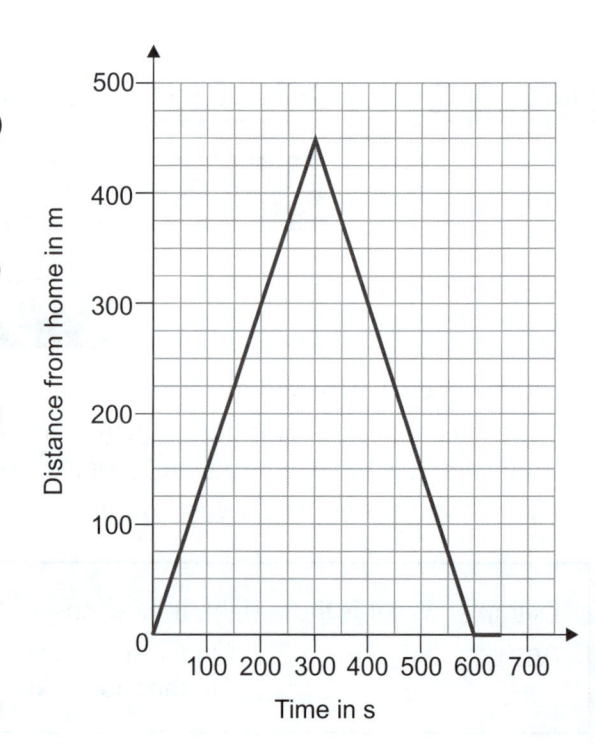

Exam Questions

3   The diagram shows a velocity-time graph for a car during a section of a journey.

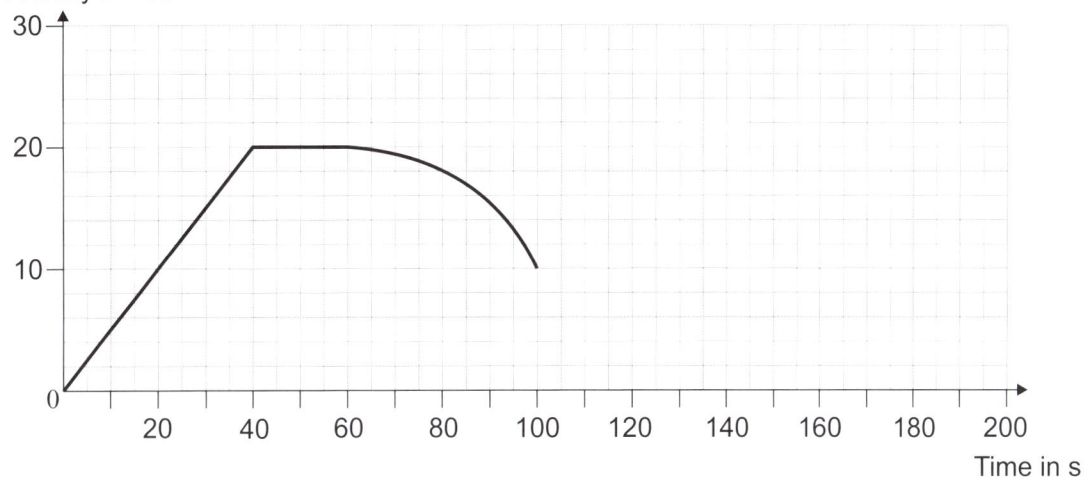

   a) Describe the motion of the car during the following parts of the journey.
       i)   Between 40 and 60 seconds.
       ii) Between 60 and 100 seconds.
       (2 marks)

   b) Calculate the distance travelled by the car between 40 and 60 seconds.
       (3 marks)

   c) Calculate the acceleration of the car between 0 and 40 seconds.
       (3 marks)

   d) After 100 seconds, the car accelerates steadily for 40 seconds until it reaches a steady velocity of 30 m/s, which it maintains for 60 seconds. Copy and complete the graph to show this motion.
       (2 marks)

4   A student is measuring gravitational field strength, g, in a classroom experiment. He takes an object with a mass of 2 kg and suspends it from a newton meter held in his hand. He takes multiple readings of the object's weight and calculates an average value of 19.6 N.

   a) i)   State the equation linking weight, mass and gravitational field strength.
            (1 mark)

       ii) Calculate the gravitational field strength in the student's classroom and give the unit.
            (3 marks)

   b) State how the student's measurement for the object's weight would differ if he performed the same experiment on the Moon. Explain your answer.
       (2 marks)

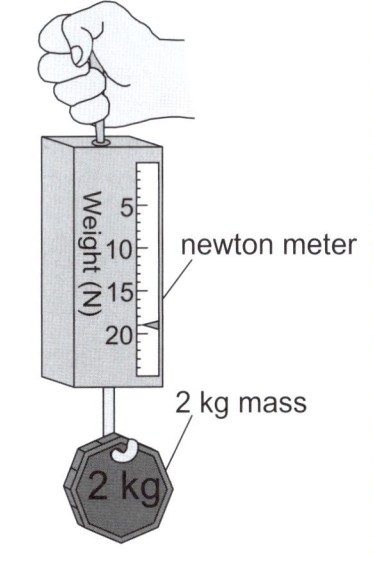

SECTION 1 — FORCES AND MOTION

Forces

Forces are our friends — without them, you'd never get anywhere, and movement would be impossible.

There are Loads of Different Types of Force

A force is simply a push or a pull. There are lots of different types of force you need to know about:

1) GRAVITY or WEIGHT (see page 5) always acting straight downwards.

2) REACTION FORCE from a surface, usually acting straight upwards.

3) ELECTROSTATIC FORCE between two charged objects. The direction depends on the type of the charge (like charges repel, opposite charges attract) (see page 48).

4) THRUST or PUSH or PULL due to an engine or rocket speeding something up.

5) DRAG or AIR RESISTANCE or FRICTION which is slowing the thing down (see next page).

6) LIFT due to an aeroplane wing.

7) TENSION in a rope or cable.

You Can Draw the Forces Acting on a Body

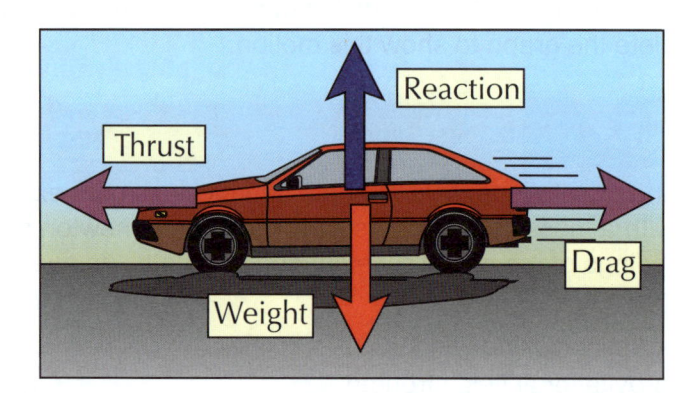

1) Chances are, there are loads of forces acting on you right now that you don't even know about. You don't notice them because they all balance out.

2) Any object with a weight feels a reaction force back from the surface it's on. Otherwise it would just keep falling.

3) When an object moves in a fluid (air, water, etc.) it feels drag in the opposite direction to its motion.

I'm not forcing you to learn this, but I really think you should
The reaction force of a surface works against your weight, otherwise you'd just sink into everything you stood on. Makes sure you learn that and all the different types of forces listed above.

SECTION 1 — FORCES AND MOTION

Friction

Friction is found nearly everywhere, slowing down and stopping moving objects. Sometimes this is just a nuisance, but other times it's very useful.

Friction is Always There to **Slow Things Down**

1) If an object has no force propelling it along, it will always slow down and stop because of friction (unless you're out in space where there's no friction). Friction is a force that opposes motion.
2) To travel at a steady speed, things always need a driving force to counteract the friction.
3) Friction occurs in three main ways:

a) **Friction** Between **Solid Surfaces** Which are **Gripping**

This is known as static friction.

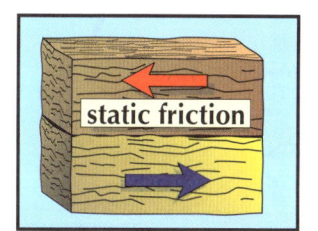

b) **Friction** Between **Solid Surfaces** Which are **Sliding** Past Each Other

This is known as sliding friction.

You can reduce both static friction and sliding friction by putting a lubricant like oil or grease between the surfaces. Friction between solids can often cause wear of the two surfaces in contact.

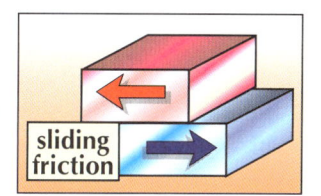

c) **Resistance** or **"Drag"** from **Fluids** (**Liquids** or **Gases**, e.g. Air)

1) The most important factor by far in reducing drag in fluids is keeping the shape of the object streamlined, like boat hulls or sports cars.

- Lorries and caravans have "deflectors" on them to make them more streamlined and reduce drag.
- Roof boxes on cars spoil their streamlined shape and so slow them down.

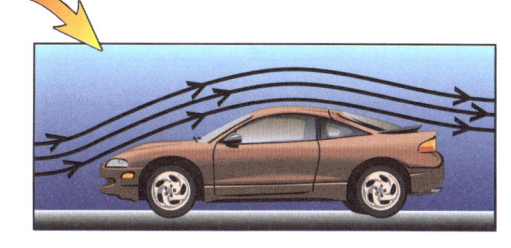

2) For a given thrust, the higher the drag, the lower the top speed of the car.
3) The opposite extreme to a sports car is a parachute which is about as high drag as you can get — which is, of course, the whole idea.
4) In a fluid, FRICTION ALWAYS INCREASES AS THE SPEED INCREASES.

Friction is really annoying when it's slowing you down...

...think how much faster cars or boats or lorries could go if friction wasn't there holding them back. But friction's good for other stuff — e.g. without it, you wouldn't be able to walk or run or skip or write.

SECTION 1 — FORCES AND MOTION

Investigating Motion

There's no use in knowing about speed, velocity and acceleration if you don't know how they can be used to describe an object's motion. Here's a simple toy car experiment you can try out yourself.

You can Investigate the Motion of a Toy Car on a Ramp

1) Set up your apparatus like in the diagram below, holding the car still just before the first light gate.

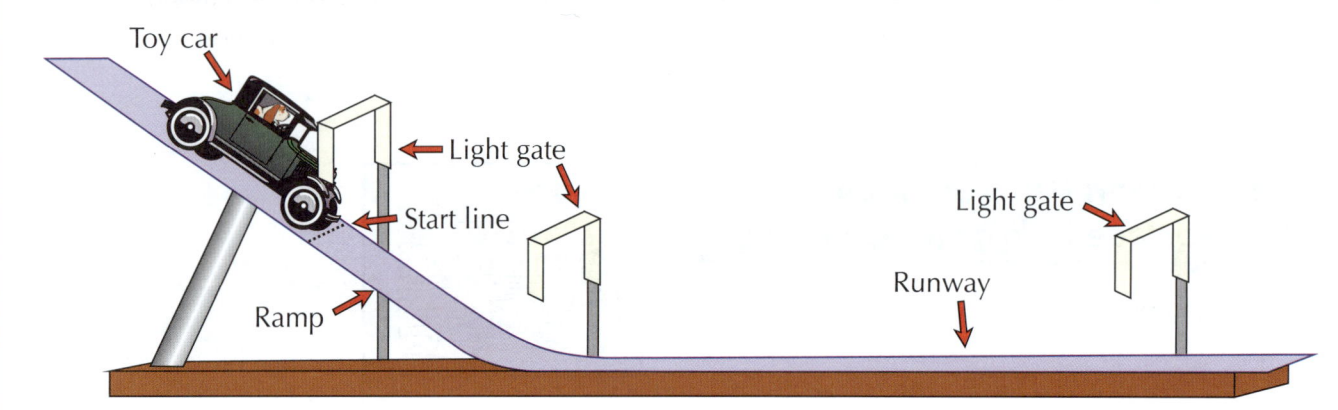

2) Mark a line on the ramp — this is to make sure the car starts from the same point each time.

3) Measure the distance between each light gate — you'll need this to find the car's average speed.

4) Let go of the car just before the light gate so that it starts to roll down the slope.

5) The light gates should be connected to a computer. When the car passes through each light gate, a beam of light is broken and a time is recorded by data-logging software.

If you don't have light gates, you could use a stopwatch with a lap function.

6) Repeat this experiment several times and get an average time it takes for the car to reach each light gate. This will make your results more reliable (see page 139).

7) Using these times and the distances between light gates you can find the average speed of the car on the ramp and the average speed of the car on the runway — just divide the average time taken for the car to travel between light gates by the distance between the gates (page 1).

You Could Play Around with the Experimental Set-up

You could change different things in this experiment to investigate other factors that might affect the car's motion. Just make sure that if you do change something, every other part of the experiment stays the same.

1) You could try seeing if the mass of the car affects its average speed — just load weights onto it (but make sure you don't overload it so that the wheel axles grind).

2) To see how friction affects the motion of the car you could try placing different materials on the ramp. If you do this, make sure they're laid flat and they don't change the angle of the ramp in any way.

3) You could investigate the acceleration of the car due to gravity by starting it off higher up the ramp and seeing how this affects its average speed between the gates.

4) You could change the angle of the ramp to see how that affects the car's speed down the slope.

5) You could even try it with different cars — see how the size, shape and weight of the car affects how fast it goes down the ramp.

You'd expect the more streamlined cars to go quicker — see page 9.

SECTION 1 — FORCES AND MOTION

Terminal Velocity

Frictional forces increase with speed — but only up to a certain point. Read on...

Moving Objects Can Reach a Terminal Velocity

1) When objects first set off they have much more force accelerating them than resistance slowing them down.
2) As the velocity increases the resistance builds up.
3) This gradually reduces the acceleration until eventually the resistance force is equal to the accelerating force and then it won't be able to accelerate any more. It will have reached its maximum velocity or terminal velocity.

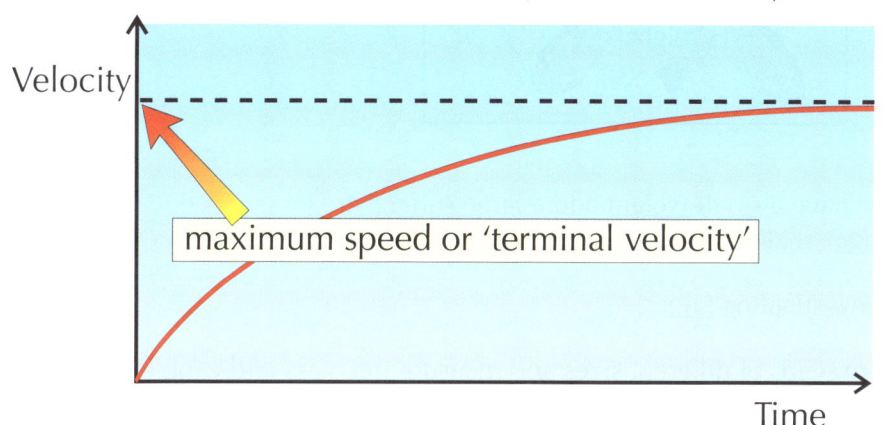

This whole terminal velocity thing is explained by Newton's laws of motion (see pages 15 and 16).

Terminal Velocity of Falling Objects Depends on Shape and Area

1) The accelerating force acting on all falling objects is gravity and it would make them all accelerate at the same rate, if it wasn't for air resistance.

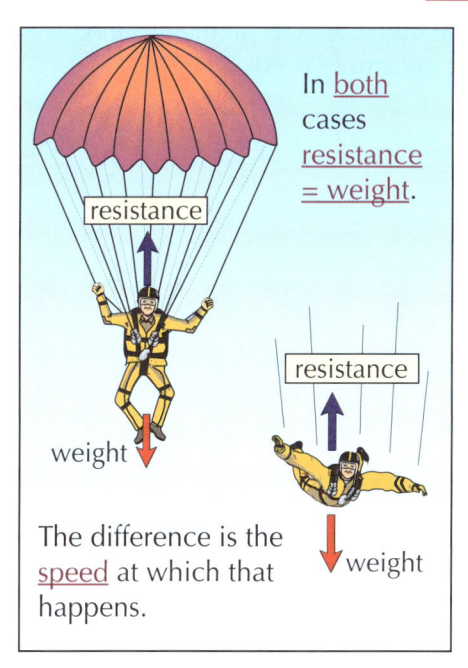

In both cases resistance = weight.

The difference is the speed at which that happens.

2) To prove this, on the Moon, where there's no air, hamsters and feathers dropped simultaneously will hit the ground together.
3) However, on Earth, air resistance causes things to fall at different speeds, and the terminal velocity of any object is determined by its drag compared to its weight.
4) The drag depends on its shape and area.
5) The most important example is the human skydiver.
6) Without his parachute open he has quite a small area and a force equal to his weight pulling him down.
7) He reaches a terminal velocity of about 120 mph.
8) But with the parachute open, there's much more air resistance (at any given speed) and still only the same force pulling him down.
9) This means his terminal velocity comes right down to about 15 mph, which is a safe speed to hit the ground at.

Terminal velocity is different for different objects

Just remember — the terminal velocity of an object is related to its weight and drag. Objects with a smaller weight generally have a smaller terminal velocity and so will take longer to fall long distances.

Investigating Falling Objects

Sorry to make all this terminal velocity stuff drag on, but it's really important you suss out how weight, surface area and drag are all related to how quickly something falls.

You Can Use Sycamore Seeds to Investigate Falling Objects

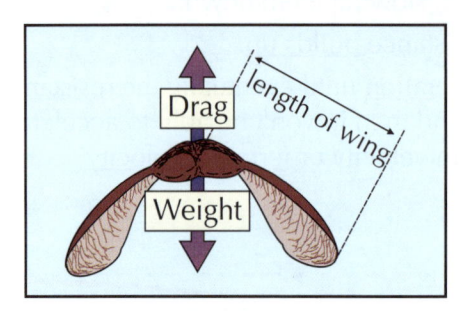

1) Sycamore seeds (see above) have a small weight and a large surface area, so they reach terminal velocity really quickly and fall slowly.

2) This makes them great for investigating falling.

3) Collect a bunch of sycamore seeds of different sizes and measure the mass and wing lengths of each one. Use an accurate ruler (or callipers) and repeat each measurement several times to make sure it's accurate. Use all the seeds that have a similar mass but different wing lengths.

4) Drop each of the seeds from the same height and use a stopwatch to find how long each one takes to fall to the ground. The higher you drop them from the better — it gives a larger measurement and so improves the accuracy of the measurement (see page 140).

5) Repeat the experiment for each seed and find an average time.

6) You can then plot a graph of the length of the wings against the time taken to hit the ground. This will tell you if there is a relation between the shape of the sycamore seeds and their terminal velocity.

7) You should get something that looks like the graph below.

Bigger wings means bigger surface area, and so higher drag.

Higher drag means lower terminal velocity, and so slower free fall.

A larger surface area means a higher drag

Having large wings gives sycamore seeds a large surface area and so a high drag. This (combined with the fact that they're very light) gives them a low terminal velocity, so they fall slowly from trees.

Warm-Up and Exam Questions

That terminal velocity stuff was a bit tricky. It's a good thing I've got some exam questions for you to have a go at — doing them will make sure that the past few pages have really sunk in.

Warm-Up Questions

1) Give the name of the force that pulls objects towards the centre of the Earth.
2) What are electrostatic forces?
3) Name a force that opposes motion.
4) When does a falling object reach terminal velocity?

Exam Questions

1 The diagram below shows a truck moving forwards at a steady speed.
   The thrust (driving force) acting on the truck is shown.

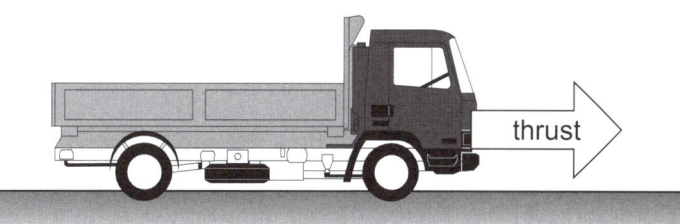

   a) i) As the truck moves, it experiences resistance from drag and friction.
           State the direction in which the resistance acts.
           (1 mark)

      ii) Describe how the speed of the truck affects the
           resistance force it experiences.
           (1 mark)

   b) Name **one** more force that acts on the truck and state the direction in which it acts.
      (2 marks)

2 A student investigates how high a ball bounces
   after being dropped from different heights.
   She does this by dropping the ball from each
   height onto a hard surface next to a ruler.
   She records the highest point the ball reached
   after hitting the surface for the first time.
   The table below shows the student's results.

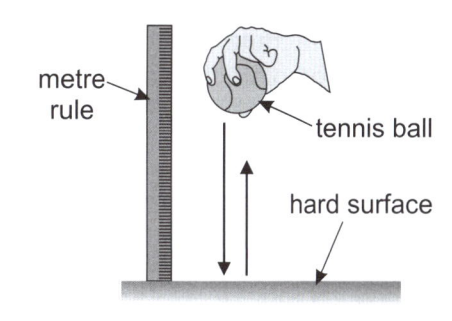

Initial height (cm)	20	30	40	50	60	70
Bounce height (cm)	13	21	27	35	41	49

   a) Describe the relationship between the initial
      height and the bounce height of the ball.
      (1 mark)

   b) Describe how the student could alter the experiment to investigate how the height
      reached by the ball will change with each successive bounce.
      (2 marks)

SECTION 1 — FORCES AND MOTION

Exam Questions

3   Dirk and Jenny are discussing the forces acting on an object falling at terminal velocity.

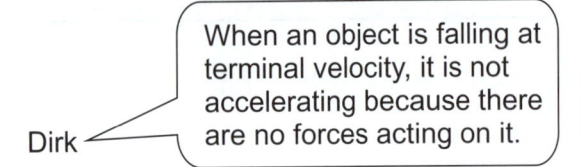

Dirk: When an object is falling at terminal velocity, it is not accelerating because there are no forces acting on it.

Jenny: When an object is falling at terminal velocity, the force of its weight is still pulling it down.

a)   State whose argument is **not** correct — Dirk's or Jenny's. Explain why.
(2 marks)

b)   Explain why a falling object reaches terminal velocity.
(2 marks)

c)   Dirk takes two balls of the same size but with different weights and drops them off a high balcony. Which of the two balls will have a lower terminal velocity? Explain your answer.
(3 marks)

4   The students in a class are investigating how the area of an object's parachute affects the forces acting on it as it falls. They do this by attaching parachutes of varying sizes to a steel ball and dropping it from a fixed height, timing how long it takes to hit the ground.

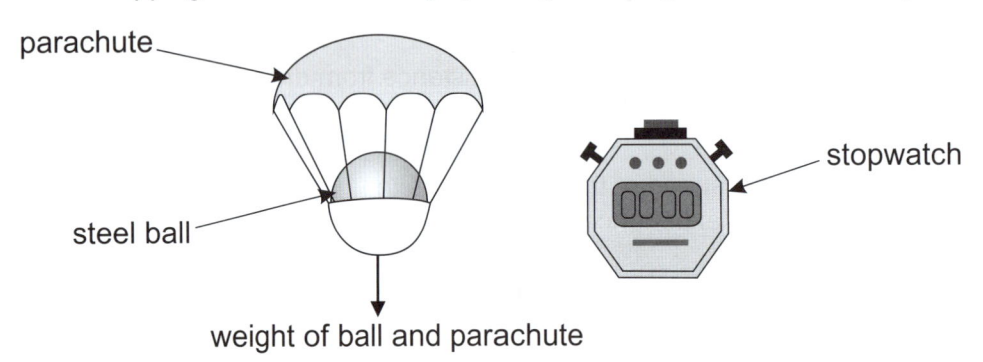

a)   For each parachute, the steel ball initially accelerates before reaching terminal velocity. Copy and complete the sentences using words from the box.

| larger | slowly | quickly | smaller |

i)   The ball with the largest parachute will be travelling more .... than the other balls travelling at terminal velocity.
(1 mark)

ii)   The resistive forces due to air resistance are .... for larger parachutes.
(1 mark)

b)   Describe how the experiment could be altered to investigate how the mass of an object affects the forces acting on it as it falls.
(2 marks)

The Three Laws of Motion

Around about the time of the Great Plague in the 1660s, a chap called Isaac Newton worked out the Three Laws of Motion. At first they might seem kind of obscure or irrelevant, but to be perfectly blunt, if you can't understand these three simple laws then you'll never understand forces and motion:

First Law — Balanced Forces Mean No Change in Velocity

So long as the forces on an object are all balanced, then it'll just stay still, or else if it's already moving it'll just carry on at the same velocity — so long as the forces are all balanced.

1) When a train or car or bus or anything else is moving at a constant velocity then the forces on it must all be balanced.
2) Never let yourself entertain the ridiculous idea that things need a constant overall force to keep them moving — NO NO NO NO NO NO!
3) To keep going at a steady speed, there must be zero resultant force — and don't you forget it.

Second Law — A Resultant Force Means Acceleration

If there is an unbalanced force, then the object will accelerate in that direction.

1) An unbalanced force will always produce acceleration (or deceleration).
2) This "acceleration" can take five different forms: Starting, stopping, speeding up, slowing down and changing direction.
3) On a force diagram, the arrows will be unequal:

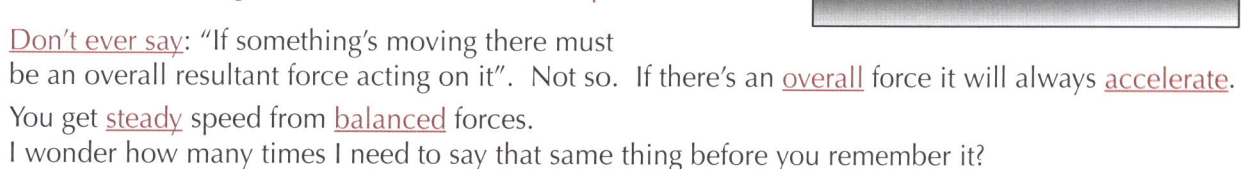

Don't ever say: "If something's moving there must be an overall resultant force acting on it". Not so. If there's an overall force it will always accelerate.
You get steady speed from balanced forces.
I wonder how many times I need to say that same thing before you remember it?

Three Points Which Should be Obvious:

1) The bigger the force, the greater the acceleration or deceleration.
2) The bigger the mass, the smaller the acceleration.
3) To get a big mass to accelerate as fast as a small mass it needs a bigger force. Just think about pushing heavy trolleys and it should all seem fairly obvious, I would hope.

The Overall Unbalanced Force is Often Called the Resultant Force

Any resultant force will produce acceleration, and this is the formula for it:

$$F = ma \quad \text{or} \quad a = F/m$$

m = mass, a = acceleration, F is always the resultant force.

The Three Laws of Motion

You can use Newton's second law to find an object's acceleration. All you need to know is the object's mass and the resultant force acting on it. You might have to rearrange the equation first though...

Resultant Force is Real Important — Especially for "F = ma"

The notion of resultant force is a really important one for you to get your head round. It's not especially tricky, it's just that it seems to get kind of ignored.

1) In most real situations there are at least two forces acting on an object along any direction. The overall effect of these forces will decide the motion of the object — whether it will accelerate, decelerate or stay at a steady speed.

2) If the forces act along the same line, the "overall effect" is found by just adding or subtracting them (see next page). The overall force you get is called the resultant force. And when you use the formula "F = ma", F must always be the resultant force.

Example: A car of mass of 1750 kg has an engine which provides a resultant driving force of 5200 N. Find the car's acceleration.

ANSWER: First draw a force diagram for the car. This will make the situation easier to understand:

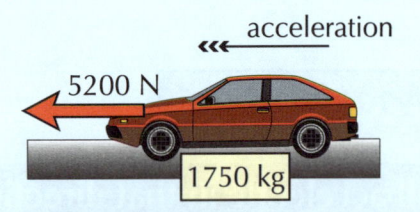

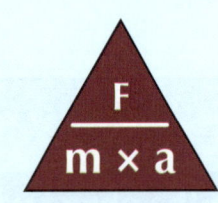

Apply "F = ma" using the formula triangle:

a = F/m = 5200 ÷ 1750 = 3.0 m/s²

The Third Law — Reaction Forces

If object A exerts a force on object B then object B exerts the exact opposite force on object A.

This is called Newton's third law of motion.

1) That means if you push something, say a shopping trolley, the trolley will push back against you, just as hard.

2) And as soon as you stop pushing, so does the trolley. Kinda clever really.

3) So far so good. The slightly tricky thing to get your head round is this — if the forces are always equal, how does anything ever go anywhere? The important thing to remember is that the two forces are acting on different objects. Think about a pair of ice skaters:

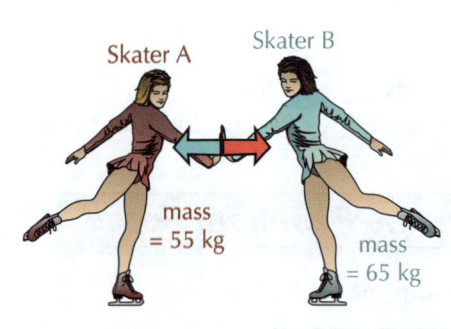

When skater A pushes on skater B (the 'action' force), she feels an equal and opposite force from skater B's hand (the 'reaction' force). Both skaters feel the same sized force, in opposite directions, and so accelerate away from each other.

Skater A will be accelerated more than skater B, though, because she has a smaller mass — remember F = ma.

4) It's the same sort of thing when you go swimming. You push back against the water with your arms and legs, and the water pushes you forwards with an equal-sized force in the opposite direction.

Combining Forces

When you're talking about the forces acting on an object, it's not enough to just talk about the size of each force. You need to know their direction too so you know which way the object will accelerate.

Vectors Have Size and Direction — Scalar Quantities Only Have Size

1) When there are multiple forces acting on an object, it's often useful to know the resultant force acting on the object (see previous page). To do this you need to know the size of all the different forces acting on the object and their direction.
2) Force is a vector quantity — vector quantities have a size and a direction.
3) Lots of physical quantities are vector quantities:

Vector quantities are usually represented by arrows.

> Vector quantities: force, velocity, displacement, acceleration, momentum, etc.

4) Some physical quantities only have size and no direction. These are called scalar quantities:

> Scalar quantities: mass, temperature, time, length, etc.

To Work Out Resultant Force — You Need To Combine Vectors

You can find the resultant force or forces acting along the same line by adding them end to end.

> Example: What's the resultant force of a 220 N force north, a 180 N force south and a 90 N force south?
>
> Start by choosing a direction as the positive — let's say north. This means you add any forces in the north direction and subtract any forces in the south direction.
> Resultant force = 220 − 180 − 90 = −50 N, so 50 N south.

> Example: a) The jets on the plane are producing a thrust of 22 000 N east, and the friction from the air is 8000 N west at this speed. What is the resultant force acting on the plane? 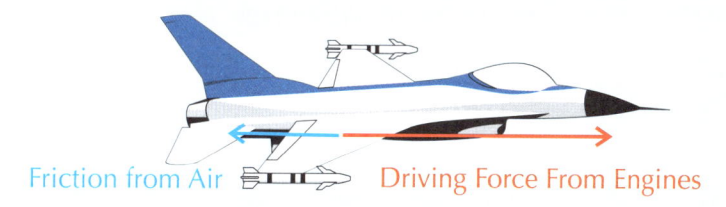
>
> Friction from Air   Driving Force From Engines
>
> Draw the vectors end to end: Engine thrust 22 000 N east + Friction 8000 N west = Resultant Force 14 000 N east
>
> b) Find the acceleration of the plane in part a) if it has a mass of 10 000 kg.
> Rearrange F = ma (page 15) using the formula triangle to give:
> a = F/m = 14 000 ÷ 10 000 = 1.4 m/s²

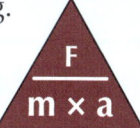

SECTION 1 — FORCES AND MOTION

Stopping Distances

If you need to stop in a given distance then the faster you're going, the bigger braking force you'll need. But in real life it's not quite that simple — there are loads of other factors too...

Many Factors Affect Your Total Stopping Distance

1) The stopping distance of a car is the distance covered in the time between the driver first spotting a hazard and the car coming to a complete stop. They're pretty keen on this for exam questions, so make sure you learn it properly.
2) The distance it takes to stop a car is divided into the thinking distance and the braking distance.

1) Thinking Distance

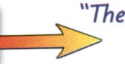

→ *"The distance the car travels in the time between the driver noticing the hazard and applying the brakes."*

It's affected by two main factors:

a) How fast you're going — obviously. Whatever your reaction time, the faster you're going, the further you'll go.

b) How dopey you are — This is affected by things like tiredness, drugs, alcohol and old age. Inexperience can also affect your reaction time.

2) Braking Distance

→ *"The distance the car travels during its deceleration whilst the brakes are being applied."*

It's affected by four main factors:

a) How fast you're going — The faster you're going the further it takes to stop.

b) The mass of the vehicle — with the same brakes, the larger the mass of a vehicle, the longer it takes to stop. A car won't stop as quickly when it's full of people and luggage or towing a caravan.

c) How good your brakes are — all brakes must be checked and maintained regularly. Worn or faulty brakes will let you down catastrophically just when you need them the most, i.e. in an emergency.

d) How good the grip is — this depends on three things:
   1) road surface,   2) weather conditions,   3) tyres.

The figures below for typical stopping distances are from the Highway Code.

- 30 mph: 9 m thinking, 14 m braking — 6 car lengths
- 50 mph: 15 m thinking, 38 m braking — 13 car lengths
- 70 mph: 21 m thinking, 75 m braking — 24 car lengths

So even at 30 mph, you should drive no closer than 6 or 7 car lengths away from the car in front — just in case. This is why speed limits are so important, and some residential areas are now 20 mph zones.

Bad visibility can also be a major factor in accidents — lashing rain, thick fog, bright oncoming lights, etc. might mean that a driver doesn't notice a hazard until they're quite close to it — so they have a much shorter distance available to stop in.

Stop right there — and learn this page

Wet or icy roads are more slippy than dry roads, but you may only discover this when you try to brake. Tyres should have a minimum tread depth (1.6 mm). This is essential for getting rid of water in wet conditions. Without tread, a tyre will ride on a layer of water and skid easily. This is "aquaplaning".

Momentum and Collisions

A large rugby player running very fast is going to be a lot harder to stop than a scrawny one out for a Sunday afternoon stroll — that's momentum for you.

Momentum = Mass × Velocity

Momentum (kg m/s) = Mass (kg) × Velocity (m/s)

1) The greater the mass of an object and the greater its velocity, the more momentum the object has.
2) Momentum is a vector quantity (page 17) — it has size and direction (like velocity, but not speed).

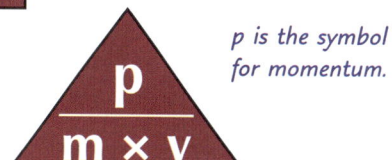

p is the symbol for momentum.

Momentum Before = Momentum After

Momentum is conserved when no external forces act.
The total momentum after is the same as it was before.

Example 1: Two skaters approach each other, collide and move off together as shown. At what velocity do they move after the collision?

ANSWER
1) Choose which direction is positive.
   I'll say "positive" means "to the right".
2) Total momentum before collision
   = momentum of Ed + momentum of Sue
   = {80 × 2} + {60 × (–1.5)} = 70 kg m/s
3) Total momentum after collision
   = momentum of Ed and Sue together
   = 140 × v
4) So 140v = 70, i.e. v = 0.5 m/s to the right

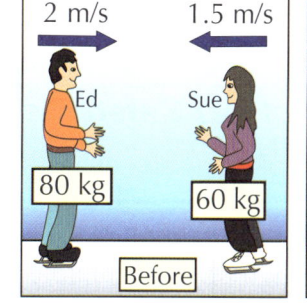

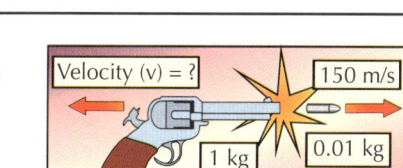

Example 2: A gun fires a bullet as shown. At what speed does the gun move backwards?

ANSWER
1) Choose which direction is positive.
   Again, I reckon "positive" means "to the right".
2) Total momentum before firing
   = 0 kg m/s
3) Total momentum after firing
   = momentum of bullet + momentum of gun
   = (0.01 × 150) + (1 × v)
   = 1.5 + v
4) So 1.5 + v = 0, i.e. v = –1.5 m/s
   So the gun moves backwards at 1.5 m/s.   *This is the gun's recoil.*

This makes sense if you think about Newton's third law of motion (page 16).
In example 2, the gun 'pushes' on the bullet, giving it a forward momentum.
The bullet 'pushes back', giving the gun a backward momentum. The size of the force on each object is the same, but the gun has a higher mass, so it has a lower acceleration (a = F ÷ m).

SECTION 1 — FORCES AND MOTION

Momentum and Collisions

Momentum doesn't just stay the same — that would just be far too easy...

Forces Cause Changes in Momentum

When a force acts on an object, it causes a change in momentum.

$$\text{Force acting (N)} = \frac{\text{Change in momentum (kg m/s)}}{\text{Time taken for change to happen (s)}}$$

1) A larger force means a faster change of momentum (and so a greater acceleration — see page 16).

2) Likewise, if someone's momentum changes very quickly (like in a car crash), the forces on the body will be very large, and more likely to cause injury.

This is why cars are designed to slow people down over a longer time when they have a crash — the longer it takes for a change in momentum, the smaller the force (and so the less severe the injuries are likely to be).

Examples of Car Safety Features

AIR BAGS slow you down more gradually.

CRUMPLE ZONES at the front and back of the car crumple up on impact. This increases the time taken for the car to stop.

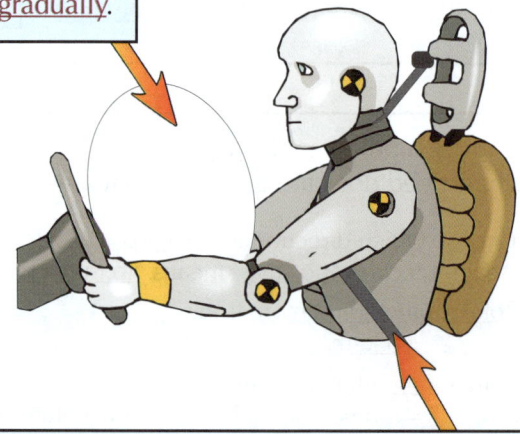

SEAT BELTS stretch slightly, increasing the time taken for the wearer to stop. This reduces the forces acting in the chest.

Learn this stuff — it'll only take a moment... um

Momentum's a big deal in physics — it's always conserved in collisions and explosions with no external forces acting. If a car hits a wall, all that momentum needs to go somewhere.

SECTION 1 — FORCES AND MOTION

Warm-Up and Exam Questions

Yep, you guessed it... more questions. Get into the swing of things with the Warm-Ups, then try your hand at the Exam Questions. Better get cracking...

Warm-Up Questions

1) What is Newton's first law of motion?
2) Explain why a car takes longer to stop when it's full of passengers. State two additional factors that increase stopping distance.
3) What does "conservation of momentum" mean?

Exam Questions

1   A camper van has a mass of 2500 kg. It is driven along a straight, level road at a constant speed of 90 kilometres per hour.

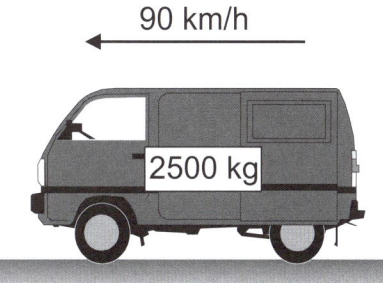

90 km/h

2500 kg

    a)   A headwind begins blowing with a force of 200 N, causing the van to slow down. Calculate the van's deceleration.

(3 marks)

    b)   The van begins travelling at a steady speed before colliding with a stationary traffic cone with a mass of 10 kg. The traffic cone accelerates in the direction of the van's motion with an acceleration of 29 m/s^2.

        i)   Calculate the force applied to the traffic cone by the van.

(2 marks)

[PAPER 2]

        ii)   State the force applied by the cone to the van during the collision.

(1 mark)

        iii)   Calculate the deceleration of the van during the collision. Assume all of the force applied by the cone to the van causes the deceleration.

(2 marks)

2   Two students have fitted their scooters with the same engine. Student A and his scooter have a combined mass of 127.5 kg and a maximum acceleration of 2.40 m/s^2. Student B has a maximum acceleration of 1.70 m/s^2 on her scooter.

    a)   State the equation linking force, mass and acceleration.

(1 mark)

    b)   Show that the combined mass of student B and her scooter is 180 kg.

(4 marks)

SECTION 1 — FORCES AND MOTION

Exam Questions

PAPER 2

3   Most quantities can be divided into two groups: scalars and vectors.

   a)   Describe the difference between a scalar and a vector quantity.
   (2 marks)

   b)   Which of the following is a **vector**?

   | distance | mass | speed | force |

   (1 mark)

   c)   Which of the following is a **scalar** quantity?

   | 14 kg | 300 kN down | 24 m/s west | 1 m/s² up |

   (1 mark)

PAPER 2

4   Two jam jars are placed on a table. The forces acting on each jar are shown.

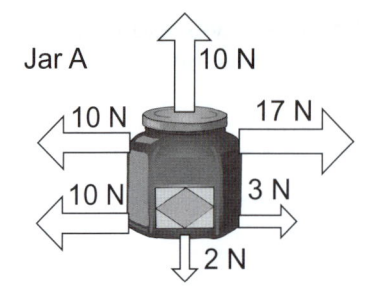

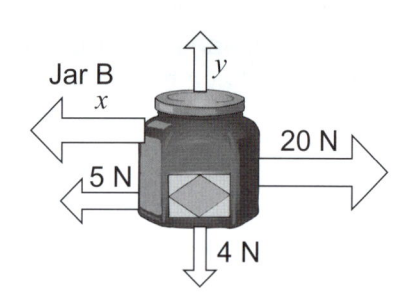

   Jar A: 10 N up, 10 N left, 17 N right, 10 N left, 3 N right, 2 N down

   Jar B: y up, x left, 20 N right, 5 N left, 4 N down

   a)   Calculate the resultant force acting on Jar A and give its direction.
   (2 marks)

   b)   The resultant force acting on Jar B is zero. Calculate the size of forces x and y.
   (2 marks)

PAPER 2

5   A 1200 kg car is travelling at 30 m/s along a motorway. It crashes into the barrier of the central reservation and is stopped in a period of 1.2 seconds (after which its momentum is zero).

   a)   i)   State the equation linking momentum, mass and velocity.
   (1 mark)

        ii) Calculate the momentum of the car before the crash and give the unit.
   (3 marks)

   b)   i)   State the equation linking force, change in momentum and time taken.
   (1 mark)

        ii) Calculate the size of the average force acting on the car during the collision.
   (2 marks)

PAPER 2

6   In a demolition derby, cars drive around an arena and crash into each other.

   a)   One car has a mass of 650 kg and a velocity of 15 m/s.
        Calculate the momentum of the car and give the unit.
   (4 marks)

   b)   The car collides head-first with another car with a mass of 750 kg. The two cars stick together. Calculate the combined velocity of the two cars immediately after the collision if the other car had a velocity of 10 m/s before the collision.
   (4 marks)

   c)   The cars have crumple zones at the front of the car that crumple on impact.
        Explain how a crumple zone reduces the forces acting on a driver during a collision.
   (2 marks)

SECTION 1 — FORCES AND MOTION

Turning Forces and Centre of Gravity

Turning forces — full of good ol' spanners and levers. Not very difficult... not very exciting either. Expect to be royally sick of pivots and centre of gravity by the time you've finished these pages.

A *Moment* is the *Turning Effect* of a Force

MOMENT = FORCE × perpendicular DISTANCE from the line of action of the force to the pivot

1) The force on the spanner causes a turning effect or moment on the nut. A larger force would mean a larger moment.

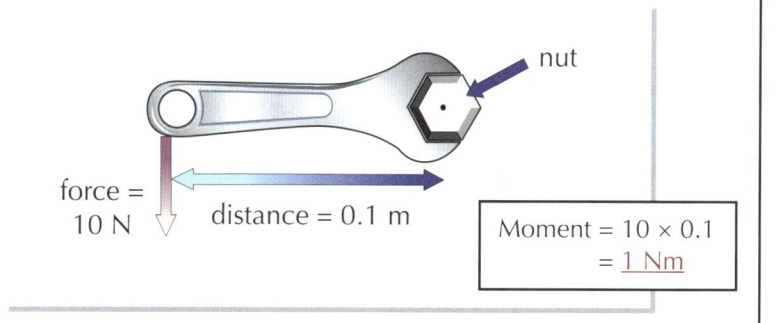

   force = 10 N, distance = 0.1 m
   Moment = 10 × 0.1 = 1 Nm

2) Using a longer spanner, the same force can exert a larger moment because the distance from the pivot is greater.

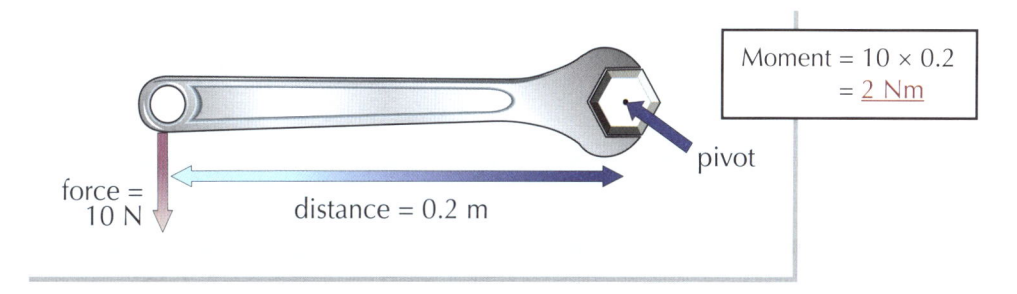

   force = 10 N, distance = 0.2 m
   Moment = 10 × 0.2 = 2 Nm

3) To get the maximum moment (or turning effect) you need to push at right angles (perpendicular) to the spanner.

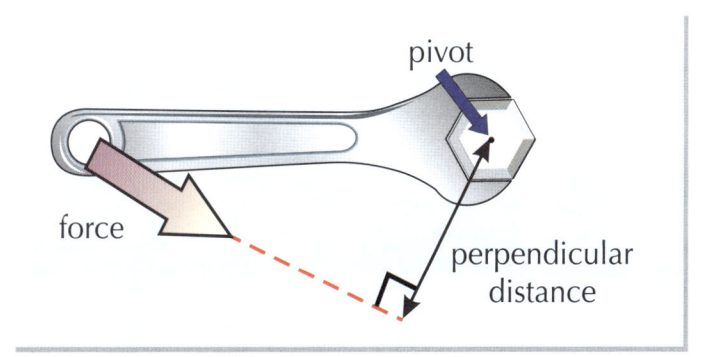

4) Pushing at any other angle means a smaller moment because the perpendicular distance between the line of action and the pivot is smaller.

Make sure you've mastered moments before turning the page

Think of the extra force you need to open a door by pushing it near the hinge compared to at the handle — the distance from the pivot is less, so you need more force to get the same moment.

SECTION 1 — FORCES AND MOTION

Turning Forces and Centre of Gravity

All this centre of gravity stuff turns my stomach a bit, but let's see what you make of it...

The Centre of Gravity Hangs Directly Below the Point of Suspension

1) You can think of the centre of gravity of an object as the point through which the weight of a body acts.

2) A freely suspended object will swing until its centre of gravity is vertically below the point of suspension.

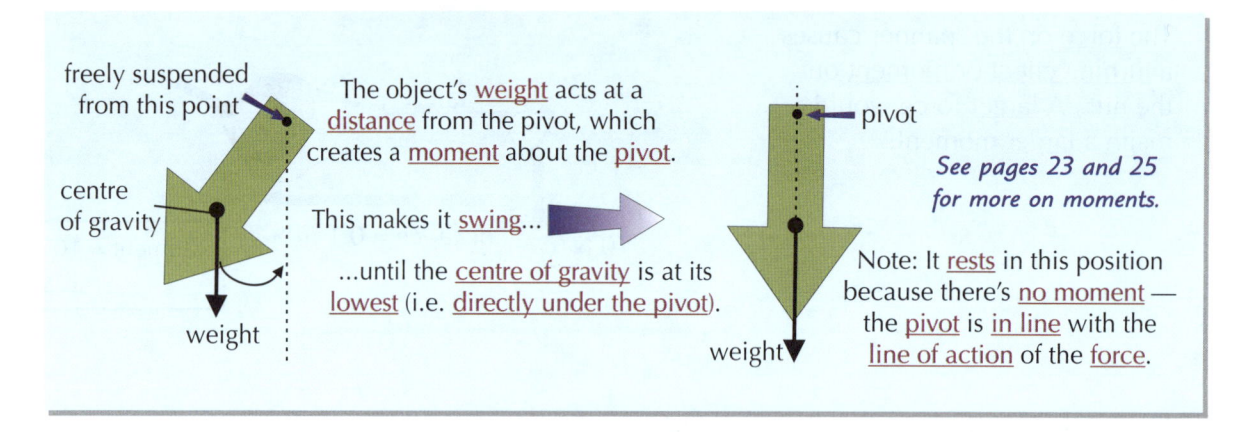

freely suspended from this point

The object's weight acts at a distance from the pivot, which creates a moment about the pivot.

centre of gravity

This makes it swing...

...until the centre of gravity is at its lowest (i.e. directly under the pivot).

weight

pivot

See pages 23 and 25 for more on moments.

Note: It rests in this position because there's no moment — the pivot is in line with the line of action of the force.

weight

3) This means you can find the centre of gravity of any flat shape like this:

1) Suspend the shape and a plumb line from the same point, and wait until they stop moving.
2) Draw a line along the plumb line.
3) Do the same thing again, but suspend the shape from a different pivot point.
4) The centre of gravity is where your two lines cross.

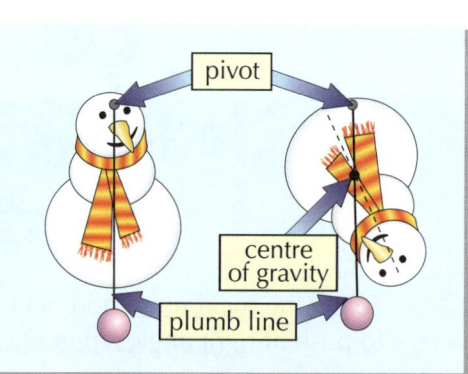

pivot

centre of gravity

plumb line

4) But you don't need to go to all that trouble for simple shapes. You can quickly guess where the centre of gravity is by looking for lines of symmetry.

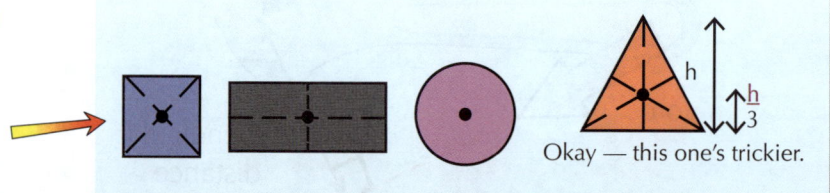

h, $\frac{h}{3}$

Okay — this one's trickier.

A suspended object swings until its centre of gravity is below the pivot

So there you go — now you know how to find the centre of gravity of any irregularly-shaped piece of paper in a few easy steps — why not practise finding the centre of gravity for lots of different shapes.

SECTION 1 — FORCES AND MOTION

Principle of Moments

Once you can calculate moments, you can work out if a seesaw is balanced. Useful thing, Physics.

A Question of Balance — Are the Moments Equal?

The principle of moments says:

If an object is balanced then: Total Anticlockwise Moments = Total Clockwise Moments

You can use this idea to help solve problems where forces are acting on a balanced object.

Example: Your younger brother weighs 300 N and sits 2 m from the pivot of a seesaw. If you weigh 700 N, where should you sit to balance the seesaw?

Answer: For the seesaw to balance:
Total anticlockwise moments = total clockwise moments

Ignore the weight of the seesaw — its centre of gravity is on the pivot, so it doesn't have a turning effect.

anticlockwise moment = clockwise moment
$300 \times 2 = 700 \times y$
$y = 0.86$ m

Forces are Not Always Equal Across All Supports

1) If a light rod is being supported at both ends, the upwards force provided by each support won't always be the same.
2) If a heavy object is placed on the rod, the support closest to the object will provide a larger force.

"Light" means you can ignore the weight in your calculations. In general, if they don't tell you the weight, you can ignore it.

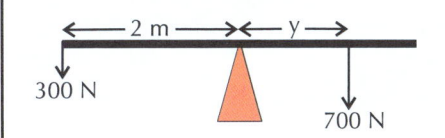

Example: A 6 m long light rod is suspended by two cables (A and B) at its ends. A 900 N weight is placed 4 m from one end, as shown below. Work out the tension in cable A, T_A, and the tension in cable B, T_B.

Answer:
The weight is balanced by the tension forces in the cables. To work out the forces, start at one end and treat that end as a pivot, so you can work out the upward force at the other end:

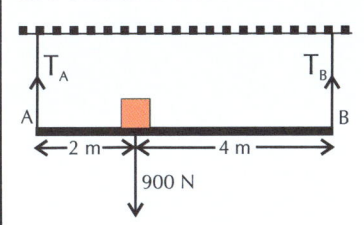

clockwise moment around B = anticlockwise moment around B
$T_A \times 6 = 900 \times 4$ so $T_A = 3600/6 = 600$ N

Then you can work out the force in B as we know the vertical forces balance:

$900\ N = T_A + T_B$
So $T_B = 900 - T_A = 900 - 600 = 300$ N

And if the Moments are Not Equal...

If the Total Anticlockwise Moments do not equal the Total Clockwise Moments, there will be a Resultant Moment

...so the object will turn.

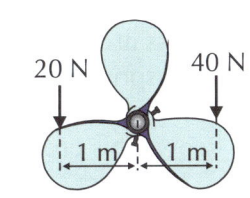

clockwise moments = $40 \times 1 = 40$ Nm
anticlockwise moments = $20 \times 1 = 20$ Nm
so the propellor will turn clockwise.

SECTION 1 — FORCES AND MOTION

Hooke's Law

Applying a force to an object can cause it to change shape temporarily... or even permanently.

Hooke's Law Says that Extension is Proportional to Force

1) The length of an unstretched metal wire is called its natural length, l.

2) If a metal wire (see right) is supported at the top and then a weight attached to the bottom, it stretches. The weight pulls down with force F, producing an equal and opposite force at the support.

3) This will also happen to helical springs and any object that will stretch without immediately snapping or deforming.

4) Robert Hooke discovered in 1676 that the extension of a stretched wire is proportional to the load, or force. This relationship is now called Hooke's law.

5) A metal spring (or other object) will also obey Hooke's law if a pair of opposite forces are applied to each end.

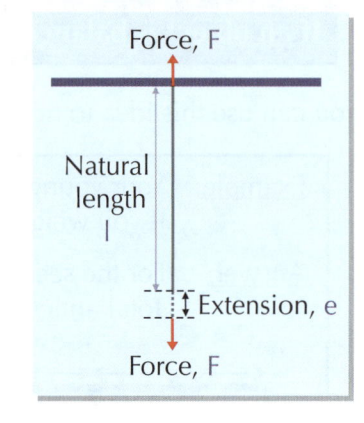

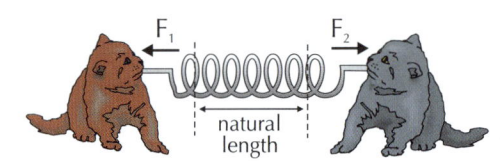

You Can Investigate Hooke's Law with a Spring

1) Set up the apparatus as shown below. Make sure you have plenty of extra masses, and measure the weight of each (with a balance).

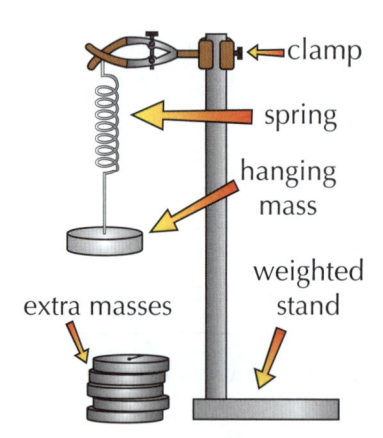

2) Measure the length of the spring (e.g. with an accurate mm ruler) when no load is applied. Ensure the ruler is vertical (e.g. with a set square) and measure the spring at eye level. (This is the spring's natural length.)

3) Add one mass at a time and allow the spring to come to rest, then measure the new length of the spring. The extension is the change in length from the original length. Adding a marker to the top and bottom of the spring might make measuring lengths easier. Repeat this process until you have enough measurements (no fewer than 6).

4) Once you're done, repeat the experiment and calculate an average value for the length of the spring for each applied weight. This will make your results more reliable (see page 139).

SECTION 1 — FORCES AND MOTION

Hooke's Law

Hooke's law is all well and good, but if you stretch something lots, some crazy Physics happens.

Hooke's law Stops Working when the Force is Great Enough

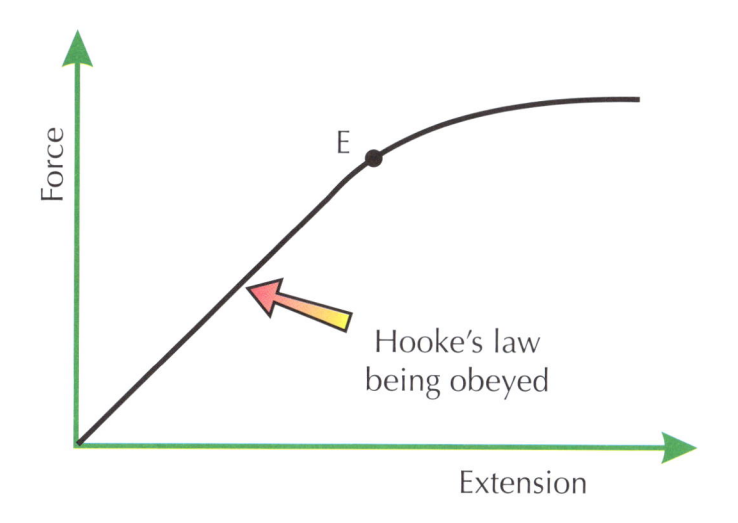

[Graph showing Force (y-axis) against Extension (x-axis). The curve rises linearly then bends over. Point E is marked near the top of the linear section. An arrow points to the linear portion labelled "Hooke's law being obeyed".]

1) There's a <u>limit</u> to the force you can apply for Hooke's law to stay true. The graph shows <u>force against extension</u> for a typical <u>metal wire</u>.

2) The <u>first part</u> of the graph shows <u>Hooke's law</u> being <u>obeyed</u> — there's a <u>straight-line relationship</u> between force and extension.

3) When the force becomes great enough, the graph starts to <u>curve</u>.

4) The point <u>marked E</u> on the graph is called the <u>elastic limit</u>.

5) If you <u>increase</u> the force <u>past</u> the elastic limit, the material will be <u>permanently stretched</u>. When all the force is removed, the material will be <u>longer</u> than at the start.

6) Some materials, like <u>rubber</u>, only obey Hooke's law for really <u>small extensions</u>.

A Material Can Return to its Original Shape After an Elastic Deformation

1) If a material returns to its <u>original shape</u> once the forces are removed, it displays <u>elastic behaviour</u>.

2) Metals display elastic behaviour as long as <u>Hooke's law</u> is obeyed.

Learn it — it could be in the exam

Okay, so this isn't the most riveting stuff in the world — but at least it's fairly simple. I promise you, Physics does get more interesting than this. You always get the boring stuff near the beginning of a book. Wait till page 106 — you'll be longing for a bit of elastic-based tedium then.

Gravity and the Universe

There's loads of exciting stuff in the Universe — our whole Solar System is just part of a huge galaxy. And there are billions and billions of galaxies. You should be realising now that the Universe is huge.

Our Solar System is in the Milky Way Galaxy

1) A galaxy is a large collection of stars.
2) Our Sun is just one of many billions of stars which form the Milky Way galaxy. Our Sun is about halfway along one of the spiral arms of the Milky Way.
3) The distance between neighbouring stars in the galaxy is often millions of times greater than the distance between planets in our Solar System.
4) The force which keeps the stars together in a galaxy is gravity, of course. And like most things in the Universe, galaxies rotate — a bit like a Catherine wheel.

The Universe is a Large Collection of Billions of Galaxies

1) Galaxies themselves are often millions of times further apart than the stars are within a galaxy.
2) So even the slowest among you will have worked out that the Universe is mostly empty space and is really really BIG.

Gravity Provides the Force That Causes Orbits

1) If an object is travelling in a circle it is constantly changing direction, which means there must be a force acting on it.
2) An orbit is a balance between the forward motion of the object and a force pulling it inwards.
3) The planets move around the Sun in almost circular orbits. The forces that make this happen are provided by the gravity between each planet and the Sun.
4) Gravity is also responsible for other types of orbits that exist in the Solar System:

The planet is trying to move in this direction...
... but the force is always towards the centre of the circle.

- The Moon orbits the Earth. Rather confusingly, other planets also have 'moons' orbiting them. These moons have their own names, but we just call the Earth's moon — 'Moon'.
- Artificial satellites that are made by man and put into space by rockets also orbit the Earth (e.g. those that are used for satellite navigation systems).
- Comets are small lumps of icy rock which orbit the Sun.

Moons are known as natural satellites of planets.

The next page has more about the orbits of comets, moons and planets.

SECTION 1 — FORCES AND MOTION

Orbital Speed

I think that this page has quite a cool title — could even be the name of a blockbuster movie.

Gravity Decreases Quickly as You Get Further Away

1) With very large masses like stars and planets, gravity is very big and acts a long way out.
2) The closer you get to a star or a planet, the stronger the force of attraction.
3) Because of this stronger force, planets nearer the Sun move faster and cover their orbit quicker.
4) Moons and artificial satellites are also held in orbit by gravity (see previous page). The further out from Earth they orbit, the slower they move.

There are Different Types of Orbit

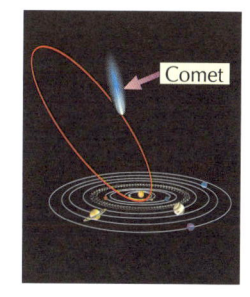

1) The orbits of moons and planets are usually slightly elliptical.
2) Comets orbit the Sun, but have very elliptical (elongated) orbits with the Sun at one focus (near one end of the orbit).
3) Comets have orbital periods much longer than the Earth, as they travel from the outer edges of the Solar System. A comet travels much faster when it's nearer the Sun than it does in the more distant parts of its orbit. That's because the increased pull of gravity makes it speed up the closer it gets to the Sun.
4) Some artificial Earth satellites have an orbital period of exactly one day. They're called geostationary satellites, and are useful in communications because they're always over the same part of the planet.

You can Work Out the Speed of an Orbiting Object

1) You can calculate the speed of an orbit using the formula:

$$\text{Speed} = \frac{\text{Distance}}{\text{Time}}$$

2) For a circular orbit, the distance travelled is the circumference of the orbit, which is given by the formula:

   distance = 2 × π × radius of orbit   *2πr is the circumference of a circle.*

3) So the formula for the speed of an orbit is:

$$\text{Orbital speed} = \frac{2 \times \pi \times \text{orbital radius}}{\text{Time period}} \qquad v = \frac{2\pi r}{T}$$

Remember that 'r' is the distance between the centre of the planet or star and the object that is orbiting around it.

Example: Calculate the speed of a satellite that is orbiting above the Earth's surface at an altitude of 600 km. The radius of the Earth is 6400 km and the satellite takes 200 min to orbit the Earth once.

ANSWER: First you need to calculate r = 6400 + 600 = 7000 km
Then find the time period in seconds: T = 200 × 60 = 12 000 s
Then you can work out the orbital speed:

$$v = \frac{2 \times \pi \times 7000}{12\,000} = 3.7 \text{ km/s (or 3700 m/s)}$$

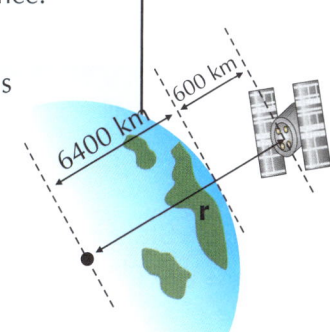

Warm-Up and Exam Questions

That's it — you're almost at the end of the section. Just these last few pages of questions...

Warm-Up Questions

1) Describe an experiment you could use to investigate Hooke's law, using a spring.
2) Give the name used to describe any body that orbits a planet and the force that keeps them in orbit.
3) What is the Universe?

Exam Questions

1 A door has a horizontal door handle.
   To open the door, its handle needs to be rotated clockwise.

   a) Pictures A, B, C and D show equal forces being exerted on the handle.

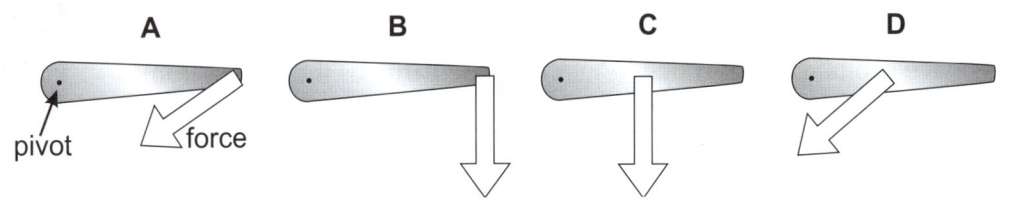

   State which picture shows the largest moment on the handle. Explain your answer.
   (2 marks)

   b) Copy and complete the sentences below using words from the box.

   | moment | gravity | balance | force | velocity |

   i) The turning effect of a .... is called its moment.
   (1 mark)

   ii) The weight of a body acts through its centre of ....
   (1 mark)

   c) i) State the equation linking the moment, force and the perpendicular distance from the line of action of the force to the pivot.
   (1 mark)

   ii) A force of 45 N is exerted vertically downwards on the door handle at a distance of 0.1 m from the pivot. Calculate the moment about the pivot and give the unit.
   (3 marks)

PAPER 2

2 A light beam is suspended horizontally by two ropes, one at either end, and a heavy box is placed on the beam in two different positions.

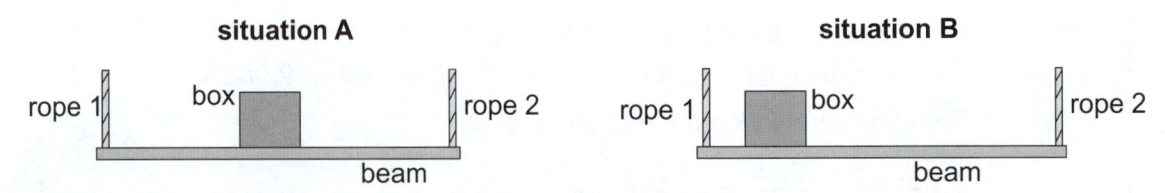

   situation A   situation B

   State in which situation, A or B, rope 1 is applying more force to the beam. Explain your answer.
   (2 marks)

SECTION 1 — FORCES AND MOTION

Exam Questions

3 A student wants to investigate how a type of rope extends when a force is applied to it.

He plots this graph of force against extension using the results from his experiment. He then writes a summary of his results. Copy and complete the passage below, using appropriate words to fill in the gaps.

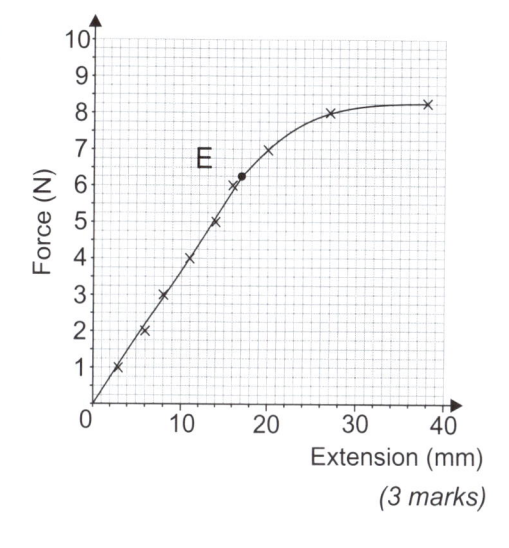

Applying a force to the rope causes it to change .... Up to the point E shown on the graph, the extension of the rope is directly .... to the applied force, i.e. it obeys Hooke's law. In this region the rope also returns to its original shape every time a weight is removed. This is known as .... behaviour.

(3 marks)

PAPER 2

4 The diagram shows three weights on a light wooden plank, resting on a pivot. Weight A is 2 N and sits 20 cm to the left of the pivot. Weight B exerts an anticlockwise moment of 0.8 Nm.

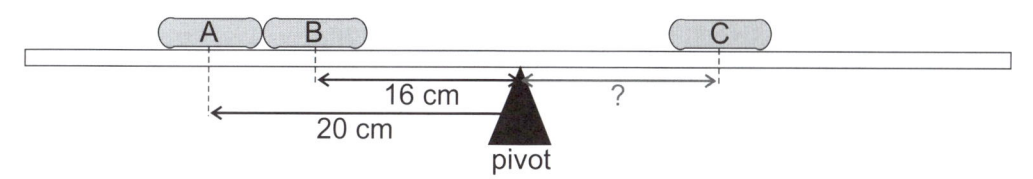

a) Calculate the anticlockwise moment exerted by weight A.

(3 marks)

b) The system is currently balanced. Weight C has a weight of 8 N. Calculate the distance of weight C from the pivot.

(4 marks)

5 These diagrams represent the orbits of four different objects in space.

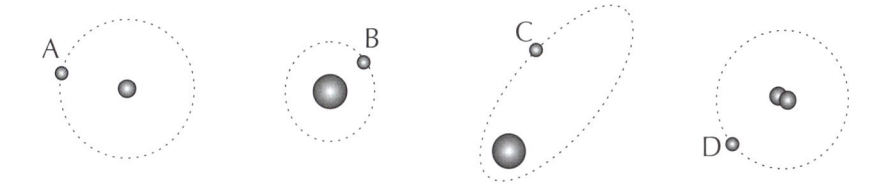

a) Which of the objects, A, B, C or D, is most likely to be a comet? Explain your answer.

(2 marks)

b) Objects A and D have the same time period and orbital radius. Object A has an orbital speed of 1.2 km/s. What is the orbital speed of object D? Give a reason for your answer.

(1 marks)

c) Object B has an orbital radius of 42 000 km and a time period of 1 day. Calculate the orbital speed of object B and give the unit.

(3 marks)

SECTION 1 — FORCES AND MOTION

Revision Summary for Section 1

Had enough of forces and motion yet? Well, tough! Here are some questions to tackle before tea break.

1) What's the relationship between the average speed, distance moved and the time taken for a moving object?
2)* How long would a robot take to reach 2.7 m/s from rest if it had an acceleration of 0.5 m/s²?
3) What does a straight, horizontal line show on a distance-time graph?
4) What does a straight, horizontal line show on a velocity-time graph?
5) How can you find the acceleration of an object from its velocity-time graph?
6) How could you find the distance travelled by an object from its velocity-time graph?
7) What's the force that acts between all masses called?
8) What's the difference between mass and weight?
9)* The value of g on the moon is 1.6 N/kg. How much does my 25 kg kitten weigh on the Moon?
10) In what direction does friction always act, and how does friction change with the speed of an object?
11) Describe a simple experiment you could carry out to investigate the motion of a toy car.
12) Why does a falling object reach a terminal velocity? Name two ways you can lower its terminal velocity.
13) Describe an experiment to see how the surface area of an object affects its terminal velocity.
14) What will happen to a moving object if all the forces on it are balanced?
15) What will happen to a moving object if there is an unbalanced force on it?
16) What's the relationship between force, mass and acceleration?
17)* A 25 kg kitten is hurled with a force of 25 000 N. What will its acceleration be?
18) What is Newton's third law of motion?
19) Is a force a vector or a scalar quantity? Explain your answer.
20)* What's the resultant force on a train with a driving force of 19 000 N and a drag of 13 500 N?
21) State four factors that could affect a vehicle's stopping distance.
22)* What's the mass of a car that has a momentum of 14 700 kg m/s when moving at 15 m/s?
23) How do crumple zones in cars reduce the risk of injury to the passengers in a crash?
24)* A 25 kg kitten collides with a stationary 37 kg puppy at 5 m/s and sticks. Find their speed after the collision.
25)* A car's brakes apply a force of 230 N for 10 seconds. Find its change in momentum.
26)* What's the moment produced by a 290 N force acting at a perpendicular distance of 7.5 m from a pivot?
27) What name is given to the point through which all of an object's weight acts?
28)* How far from the pivot should a 27 N anticlockwise force be applied to balance a 108 Nm clockwise moment?
29) A light rod is held up by two bricks. One brick is at each end of the rod. Which brick feels more force when a mass is placed on one end?
30) Describe a simple experiment you could use to investigate Hooke's law using a metal wire.
31) What does a force-extension graph demonstrating Hooke's law look like?
32) What does elastic behaviour mean?
33) What's a galaxy? How many galaxies are in the Universe? What's the name of our galaxy?
34) What force causes the orbits of moons, planets, comets and satellites?
35) How do the orbits of comets differ from the orbits of moons and planets?
36)* The Earth is an average distance of 150 million km from the Sun. Find its orbital speed (assuming the orbit is circular).

*Answers on page 184.

Section 2 — Electricity

Safe Plugs

Now then, did you know... electricity is dangerous. It can kill you. Well just watch out for it, that's all.

Plugs and Cables — Learn the Safety Features

Plugs must be wired correctly...

1) The right coloured wire is connected to each pin, and firmly screwed in.
2) No bare wires are showing inside the plug.
3) The cable grip is tightly fastened over the cable outer layer.

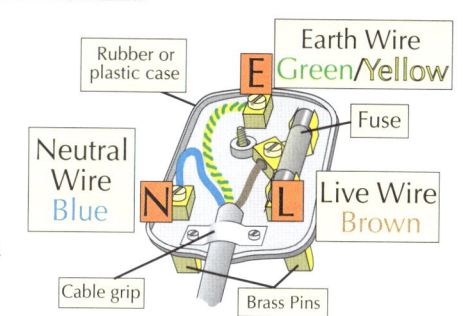

...and made of the right stuff

1) The metal parts are made of copper or brass because these are very good conductors.
2) The case, cable grip and cable insulation are made of rubber or plastic because they're really good insulators. The plastic or rubber used for the cable insulation is flexible too.

Appliances must be Earthed or Insulated

1) As you've seen — there are three wires in a plug. Only the live and neutral wires are usually needed, but if something goes wrong, the earth wire stops you getting hurt.
2) The LIVE WIRE alternates between a HIGH +VE AND −VE VOLTAGE of about 230 V.
3) The NEUTRAL WIRE is always at 0 V.
4) Electricity normally flows in through the live wire and out through the neutral wire.
5) The EARTH WIRE and fuse (or circuit breaker) are just for safety and work together — see next page.

Positive can be written as +ve and negative as −ve.

- All appliances with metal cases must be "earthed" to reduce the danger of electric shock. "Earthing" just means the case must be attached to an earth wire. An earthed conductor can never become live.

- If the appliance has a plastic casing and no metal parts showing then it's said to be double insulated.

- The plastic is an insulator, so it stops a current flowing — which means you can't get a shock.

- Anything with double insulation doesn't need an earth wire — just a live and neutral.

You Should Take Safety Precautions When Using Plugs

Plugs have their own safety features — but you've got to make sure you're using them safely too.

1) Check the plug isn't damaged, e.g. a missing, cracked or broken case. If the plug's damaged, live parts could be exposed and you could get a shock.
2) Check the cable isn't frayed, e.g. wires exposed. If the cable's frayed, live parts might be uncovered.
3) Check the cables aren't too long for the appliance — they could be a trip hazard.
4) Check there's no water near electrical objects. Water is a very good conductor.
5) Never push a metal object into a plug socket (unless it's the pins of a plug). Metal conducts electricity so you could get a shock.

Fuses and Circuit Breakers

If an appliance needs to be earthed then you'll need a fuse or circuit breaker too.
They work with the earth wire to prevent appliances from giving you a shock or causing a fire.

Earthing and *Fuses* Prevent *Fires* and *Shocks*

1) If a fault develops in which the live somehow touches the metal case, then because the case is earthed, a big current flows in through the live, through the case and out down the earth wire.

2) This surge in current 'blows' (melts) the fuse (or trips the circuit breaker — see below), which cuts off the live supply.

3) This isolates the whole appliance, making it impossible to get an electric shock from the case. It also prevents the risk of fire caused by the heating effect of a large current.

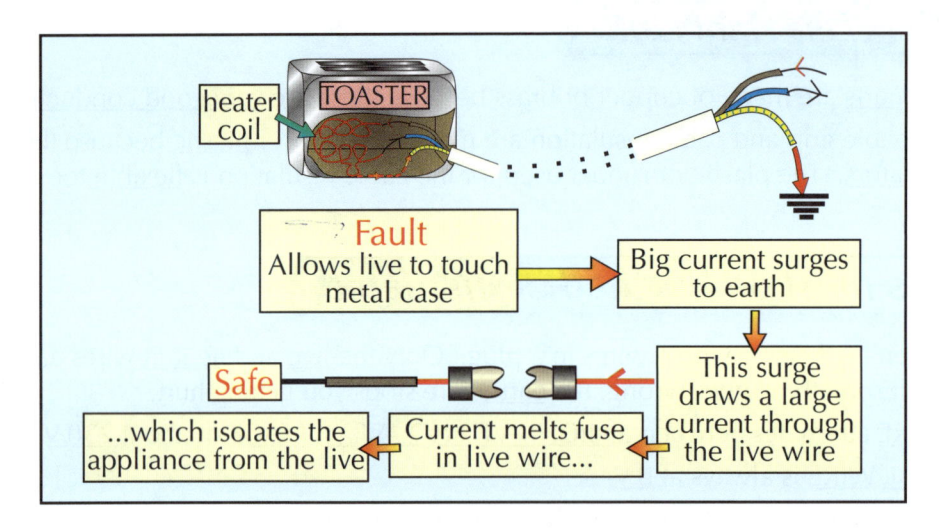

Circuit Breakers Have Some *Advantages* Over *Fuses*

1) Circuit breakers are an electrical safety device used in some circuits. Like fuses, they protect the circuit from damage if too much current flows.

2) When circuit breakers detect a surge in current in a circuit, they break the circuit by opening a switch.

3) A circuit breaker (and the circuit they're in) can easily be reset by flicking a switch on the device. This makes them more convenient than fuses — which have to be replaced once they've melted.

4) One type of circuit breaker used instead of a fuse and an earth wire is a Residual Current Circuit Breaker (RCCB):

You'll probably have a circuit breaker in your house somewhere — sometimes they 'trip' if you have too many appliances on at once.

   a) Normally exactly the same current flows through the live and neutral wires. If somebody touches the live wire, a small but deadly current will flow through them to the earth. This means the neutral wire carries less current than the live wire. The RCCB detects this difference in current and quickly cuts off the power by opening a switch.

   b) They also operate much faster than fuses — they break the circuit as soon as there is a current surge — no time is wasted waiting for the current to melt a fuse. This makes them safer.

   c) RCCBs even work for small current changes that might not be large enough to melt a fuse. Since even small current changes could be fatal, this means RCCBs are more effective at protecting against electrocution.

Energy and Power in Circuits

This page is all about how to cook toast... well, maybe not... but it's just as useful.

Resistors Get Hot When Electric Current Passes Through Them

1) When there is an electric current in a resistor there is an energy transfer which heats the resistor.
2) This heating effect increases the resistor's resistance — so less current will flow, or a greater voltage will be needed to produce the same current.
3) This heating effect can cause components in the circuit to melt — which means the circuit will stop working, or not work properly. Fuses use this effect to protect circuits — they melt and break the circuit if the current gets too high.
4) The heating effect of an electric current can have other advantages. For example, it's ace if you want to heat something. Toasters contain a coil of wire with a really high resistance. When a current passes through the coil, its temperature increases so much that it glows and gives off infrared (heat) radiation which cooks the bread. Old-style light bulbs work in a similar way.

Electrical Power and Fuse Ratings

1) Electrical power is the rate at which an appliance transfers energy.
2) An appliance with a high power rating transfers a lot of energy in a short time.
3) This energy comes from the current flowing through it. This means that an appliance with a high power rating will draw a large current from the supply.
4) Power is measured in watts (W). The formula for electrical power is:

Electrical Power = Current × Voltage

$$\frac{P}{I \times V}$$

5) Most electrical goods show their power rating and voltage rating.
6) Fuses should be rated as near as possible but just higher than the normal operating current.
7) To work out the fuse needed, you need to work out the current that the item will normally use.

EXAMPLE: A hair dryer is rated at 230 V, 1 kW. Find the fuse needed.

ANSWER: 1 kW = 1000 W
I = P/V = 1000/230 = **4.3 A**. Normally, the fuse should be rated just a little higher than the normal current, so a **5 amp fuse** is ideal for this one.

The most common fuse ratings in the UK are 3 A, 5 A and 13 A.

Choose the right fuse for the job

You need to make sure your fuse is rated as close as possible to the normal operating current. If it's too low, the fuse will keep blowing for no reason. If it's too high, the fuse won't blow when it needs to.

Energy and Power in Circuits

If you know what current is flowing through a device, what voltage is supplied to it and how long the device is on for, you can work out the total energy transferred by the device.

Electrical Appliances Transfer Electrical Energy

When a current flows through a component, energy is transferred.

> For example, when a current goes through a light bulb, electrical energy is transferred to light energy (and heat energy).

The energy transferred by an appliance depends on the current through it, the voltage supplied to it and how long it is on for (measured in seconds, s). The formula for energy transferred is:

Energy transferred = Current × voltage × time

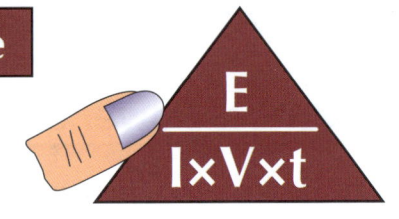

$$\frac{E}{I \times V \times t}$$

Examples

EXAMPLE 1: The motor in an electric toothbrush is attached to a 3 V battery. If a current of 0.8 A flows through the motor for 3 minutes, calculate the energy transferred by the motor.

ANSWER: Use E = I × V × t
= 0.8 × 3 × (3 × 60)
= 432 J

Time needs to be in seconds.

EXAMPLE 2: The energy transferred by a light bulb in a torch over 20 minutes is 1800 J. If the voltage of the battery in the torch is 5 V, then what is the current that flows through the bulb?

ANSWER: $I = \frac{E}{V \times t}$

$I = \frac{1800}{5 \times (20 \times 60)} = 0.3 A$

'A' stands for 'amp'. It's the unit for current. You'll read more about it on the next page.

Another useful triangle

You not only need to remember the equation for energy transferred, but you may need to rearrange it to find current, voltage or time. The triangle shows you how to do this, so remember it well.

SECTION 2 — ELECTRICITY

Circuits — The Basics

Isn't electricity great. Mind you it's pretty bad news if the words don't mean anything to you...
Hey, I know — learn them now!

Some Important Terms

Current — is the rate of flow of charge round the circuit.
Current will only flow through a component
if there is a voltage across that component.
Unit: ampere (amp for short), A.

Voltage — is the driving force that pushes the
current round. Kind of like "electrical pressure".
Unit: volt, V.

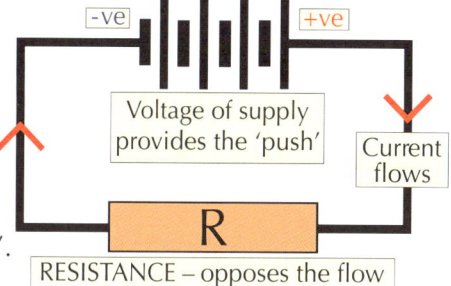

Resistance — is anything in the circuit which slows the flow down.
If you add more components to the circuit (one after
the other) there will be a higher overall resistance.
Unit: ohm, Ω.

Voltage of supply provides the 'push'
Current flows
RESISTANCE – opposes the flow

There's balance — the voltage is trying to push the current round the circuit, and the resistance is opposing it — the relative sizes of the voltage and resistance decide how big the current will be:

> **If you increase the voltage — then more current will flow.**
> **If you increase the resistance — then less current will flow**
> **(or more voltage will be needed to keep the same current flowing).**

Circuit Symbols You Should Know:

You will need these for the exam — so learn them now.

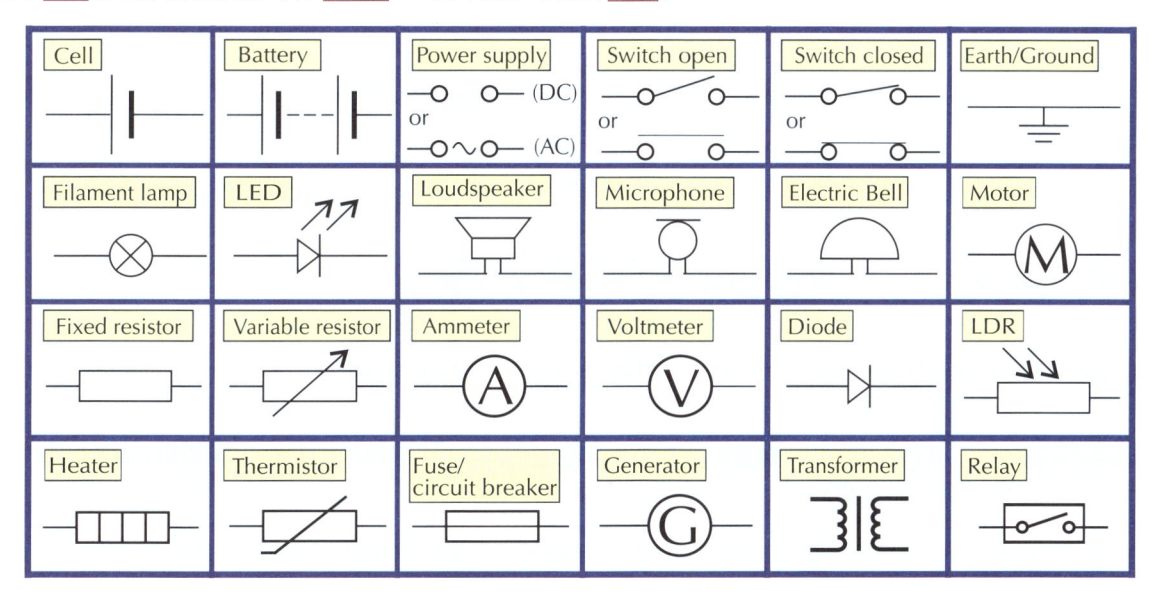

Cell	Battery	Power supply	Switch open	Switch closed	Earth/Ground
Filament lamp	LED	Loudspeaker	Microphone	Electric Bell	Motor
Fixed resistor	Variable resistor	Ammeter	Voltmeter	Diode	LDR
Heater	Thermistor	Fuse/circuit breaker	Generator	Transformer	Relay

---

Current, voltage and resistance — three exciting terms to learn
Get them clear in your head now — it'll save you a lot of confusion over the next few pages.

SECTION 2 — ELECTRICITY

Circuits — The Basics

The standard test circuit is really useful — you can use it to test different components.
You can also use it to take readings, which allow you to plot I-V graphs. But more on them later...

The Standard Test Circuit

This is without doubt the most totally bog-standard circuit the world has ever known. So know it.

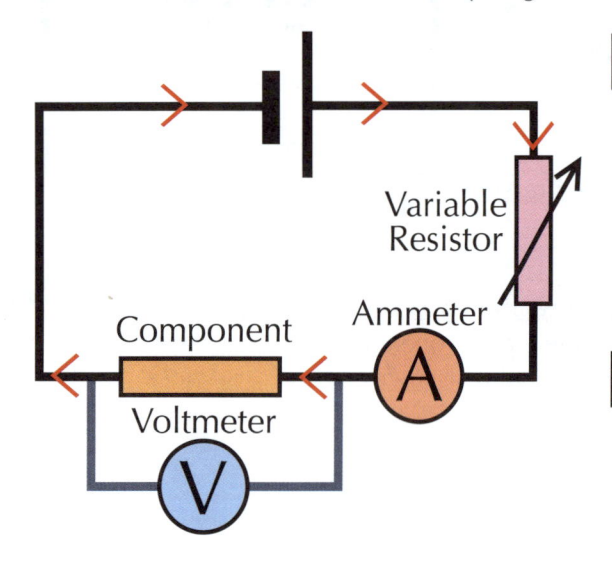

The Ammeter

1) Measures the current (in amps) flowing through the component.
2) Must be placed in series (see page 44) anywhere in the main circuit, but never in parallel like the voltmeter.

The Voltmeter

1) Measures the voltage (in volts) across the component.
2) Must be placed in parallel (see page 45) around the component under test — NOT around the variable resistor or the battery!

Five Important Points

1) This very basic circuit is used for testing components, and for getting V-I graphs for them.
2) The component, the ammeter and the variable resistor are all in series, which means they can be put in any order in the main circuit. The voltmeter, on the other hand, can only be placed in parallel around the component under test, as shown. Anywhere else is a definite no-no.
3) As you vary the variable resistor it alters the current flowing through the circuit.
4) This allows you to take several pairs of readings from the ammeter and voltmeter.
5) You can then plot these values for current and voltage on an I-V graph (see next page).

Mains Supply is a.c., Battery Supply is d.c.

1) The UK mains electricity supply is approximately 230 volts.
2) It is an a.c. supply (alternating current), which means the current is constantly changing direction.
3) By contrast, cells and batteries supply direct current (d.c.). This just means that the current keeps flowing in the same direction.

Learn the standard test circuit

Because mains power is a.c., its current can be increased or decreased using something called a transformer. This is done before electricity goes through power lines — the lower the current, the less energy is wasted as heat. No one likes waste, so it's good news for everyone.

Resistance and V = I × R

The voltage across and current through a component are linked by resistance.
If you plot them against each other, you can see how the resistance changes.

There's a **Formula** Linking **V** and **I**

You need to know this formula and be able to use and rearrange it:

Voltage = Current × Resistance

$$\frac{V}{I \times R}$$

Example

> A 4 Ω resistor in a circuit has a voltage of 6 V across it.
> What is the current through the resistor?
>
> ANSWER: Use the formula V = I × R. We need to find I,
> so the version we need is I = V/R.
> The answer is then: 6/4, which is 1.5 A.

1) You can use the formula R = V/I to work out the resistance for a pair of values (V, I) from an I-V graph.

2) The gradient (slope) of an I-V graph is equal to 1/R, so you can use it to calculate resistance. The steeper the graph the lower the resistance.

A straight-line graph has a constant gradient and shows a constant resistance.

If the graph curves, it means the resistance is changing.

Revise this page — without any resistance

Make sure you know how current, voltage and resistance are linked. You might need to draw an I-V graph in the exam, or interpret one to find the resistance — make sure you know what they show.

SECTION 2 — ELECTRICITY

Resistance and V = I × R

Current-voltage graphs can look different for different circuit components. Make sure you learn each one.

Four Hideously Important Voltage-Current Graphs

Current-voltage (I-V) graphs show how the current varies as you change the voltage. The gradient of each I-V graph is 1/R. Learn these four real well:

Metal Filament Lamp

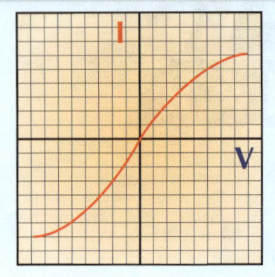

As the temperature of the metal filament increases, the resistance increases, hence the curve.

Wire

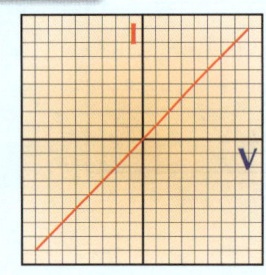

The current through a wire (at constant temperature) is proportional to voltage.

Different Resistors

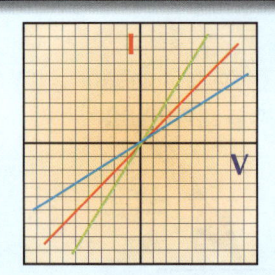

The current through a resistor (at constant temperature) is proportional to voltage. Different resistors have different resistances, hence the different slopes.

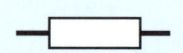

Diode

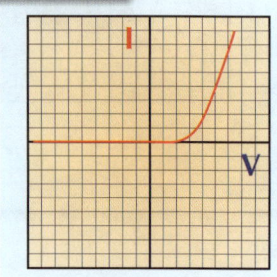

Current will only flow through a diode in one direction, as shown.

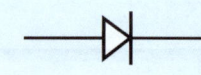

LDRs, Thermistors and LEDs

There are some really useful components that can be used in circuits to make all sorts of things work...

Light-Emitting Diodes are *Really Useful*

1) Light-emitting diodes (LEDs) emit light when a current flows through them in the forward direction. They have lots of practical applications.

2) They are used for the numbers on digital clocks, in traffic lights and in remote controls.

3) Unlike a light bulb, they don't have a filament that can burn out.

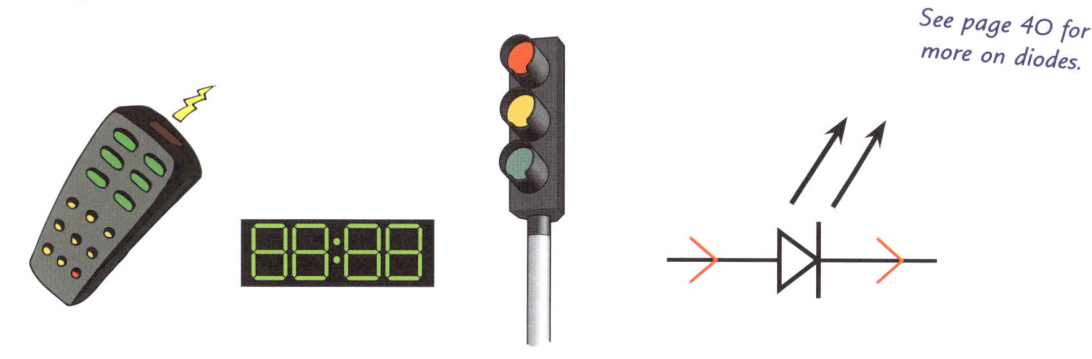

See page 40 for more on diodes.

LEDs, like lamps, indicate the presence of current in a circuit. They are often used in appliances to show that they are switched on.

Some *Components* Can Change *Resistance*

1) A light-dependent resistor (LDR) is a special type of resistor that changes its resistance depending on how much light falls on it.

2) In bright light, the resistance falls and in darkness, the resistance is highest.

3) This makes it a useful device for various electronic circuits, e.g. burglar detectors.

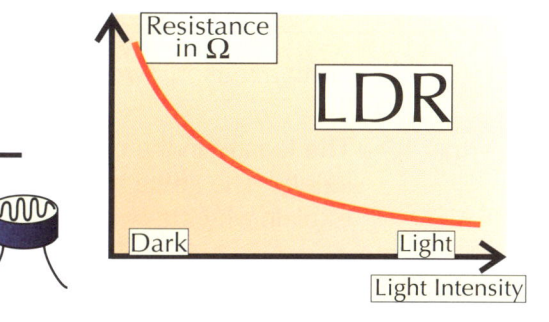

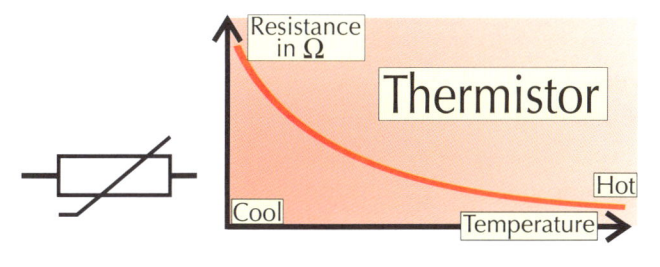

1) A thermistor is a temperature-dependent resistor.

2) In hot conditions, the resistance drops and in cool conditions, the resistance goes up.

3) Thermistors make useful temperature detectors, e.g. car engine temperature sensors.

Make sure you know your LEDs from your LDRs...

LDRs and thermistors are useful little things. LDRs can be used for automatic light switches and in digital cameras. Thermistors can be used in thermostats and fire alarms.

Section 2 — Electricity

Warm-Up and Exam Questions

Lots and lots about electricity on these last few pages. Let's see what you know...

Warm-Up Questions

1) What happens to a resistor when an electric current passes through it?
   How is the useful in toasters?
2) How does the current in a circuit change if you increase the voltage?
3) Is mains electricity usually a.c. or d.c.? What about the current supplied by a battery?

Exam Questions

1   The diagram shows some plug sockets and appliances in a kitchen.

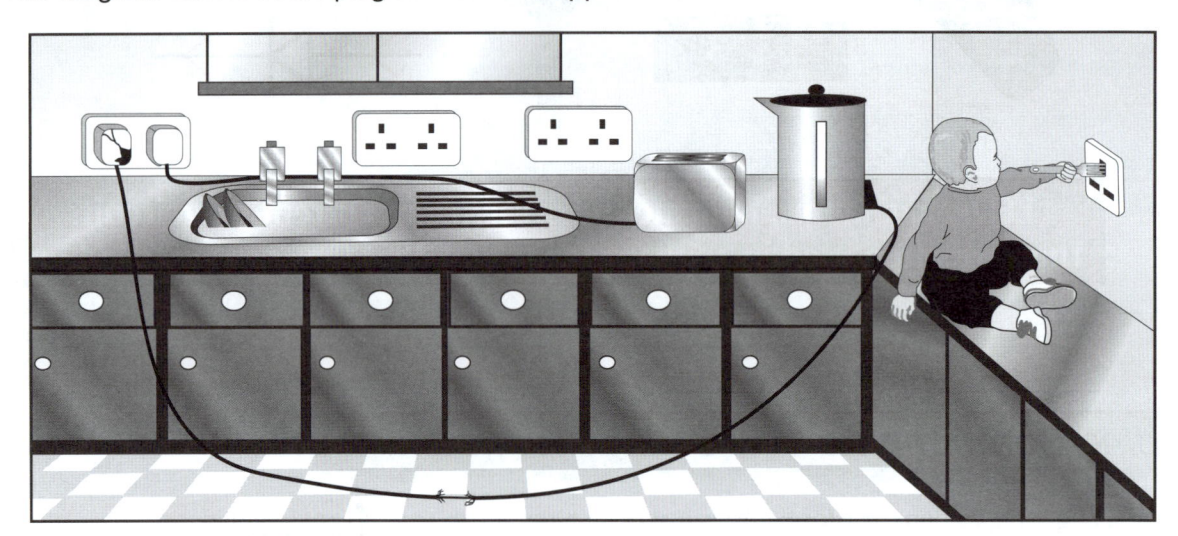

   a) Give, with a reason, **two** ways that plugs are being used dangerously in this kitchen.
   (4 marks)

   b) i) The toaster in the diagram has a metal case and is wired with an earth wire for safety. The kettle has a plastic case, and is not wired with an earth wire.
   Explain why the kettle is still safe to use.
   (2 marks)

   ii) A student says "If no current is flowing in the toaster's earth wire, there must be a fault in the toaster." Do you agree or disagree? Explain your answer.
   (1 mark)

2   A student is drilling holes to put up some shelves.
    His electric drill is attached to a 12 V battery and uses a current of 2.3 A.

   a) Drilling one hole transfers 828 J of electrical energy.
   Calculate the time taken to drill one hole.
   (3 marks)

   b) An electrical fault causes the fuse in the electric drill to blow. The student has the choice of replacing the blown fuse with a 1 A fuse or a 5 A fuse. The student says "I should use the 1 A fuse because it is closest to the operating current of the drill." Do you agree or disagree? Explain your answer.
   (2 marks)

SECTION 2 — ELECTRICITY

Exam Questions

3   The diagram below shows a circuit that contains an LED, a light-dependent resistor and a cell.

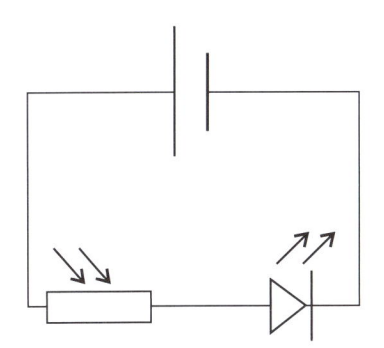

   a)   Describe how you could tell that a current is flowing in the circuit.
   (1 mark)

   b)   Thermistors are another type of resistor.
      i)   Give **one** similarity of thermistors and light-dependent resistors.
      (1 mark)

      ii) Give **one** difference between thermistors and light-dependent resistors.
      (1 mark)

4   The table below shows the power and voltage ratings for two kettles.

	Power (kW)	Voltage (V)
Kettle A	2.8	230
Kettle B	3.0	230

   a)   State the equation linking power, voltage and current.
   power = voltage × current
   (1 mark)

   b)   Calculate the current drawn from the mains supply by kettle A. State the correct unit.
   $I = \frac{P}{V} = \frac{2800}{230} = 12.2 A$
   (3 marks)

   c)   Which of the following current ratings should the fuse in kettle A have?

   1A   3A   5A   **(13A)**
   (1 mark)

   d)   A student is deciding whether to buy kettle A or kettle B.
   She wants to buy the kettle that boils water faster.
   Both kettles transfer 90% of the electrical energy supplied to the water.
   Suggest which kettle she should choose. Give a reason for your answer.
   (2 marks)

5   The diagram shows current-voltage (*I-V*) graphs for four components at a constant temperature.

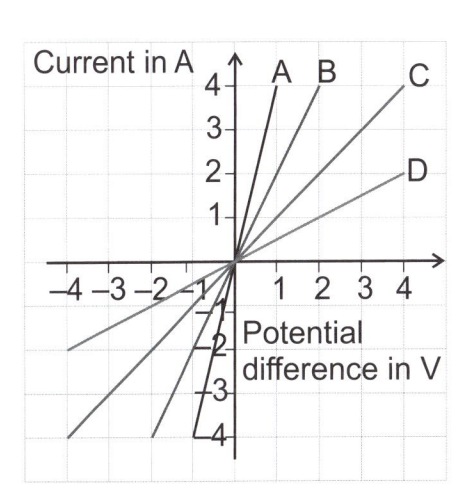

   a)   Are all four components types of **(resistor)**, **filament lamp** or **diode**?
   (1 mark)

   b)   State which component has the highest resistance. D
   (1 mark)

   c)   The resistance of component B is tested at different temperatures. At 30 °C, it has a resistance of 0.75 Ω when the voltage across it is 15 V. Calculate the current through the component.
   $I = \frac{V}{R} = \frac{15}{0.75} = 20 A$
   (2 marks)

Series Circuits

You can connect up circuits in two different ways — in series or in parallel. You need to know the differences between them, and be able to work out what circuits should be used in real-life applications.

Series Circuits — All or Nothing

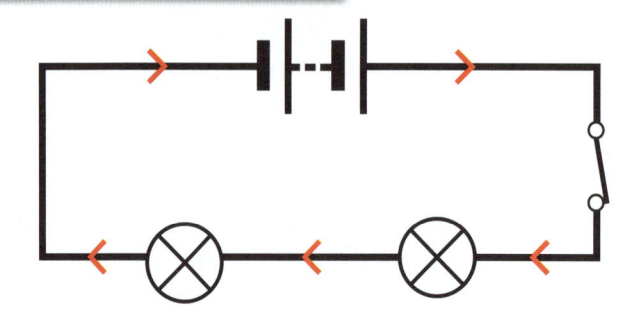

1) In series circuits, the different components are connected in a line, end to end, between the +ve and –ve of the power supply.

2) You can't control which components current flows through — it either flows through all the components, or none of them.

3) When drawing a circuit diagram, all the components will be one after the other along the wire.

4) If you remove or disconnect one component, the circuit is broken and they all stop.

5) This isn't very handy, and in practice only a few things are connected in series, e.g. fairy lights.

Current is the Same Everywhere

1) In series circuits the same current flows through all parts of the circuit, i.e: $A_1 = A_2$

2) The size of the current is determined by the total voltage of the cell(s) and the total resistance of the circuit: i.e. I = V/R (p. 39).

3) The total resistance of the circuit depends on the number of components and the type of components used. More components = more resistance.

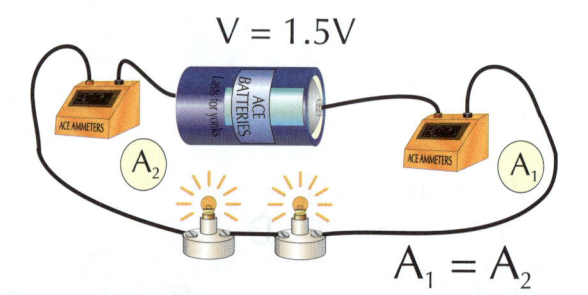

V = 1.5V

$A_1 = A_2$

Series circuits — same current everywhere

If you connect a lamp to a battery, it lights up with a certain brightness. If you then add more identical lamps in series with the first one, they'll all light up less brightly than before. That's because in a series circuit the resistance increases with more components. That doesn't happen in parallel circuits...

SECTION 2 — ELECTRICITY

Parallel Circuits

Parallel circuits are really useful, so keep an eye out for them.
You'll notice them popping up everywhere now...

Parallel Circuits — Independence and Isolation

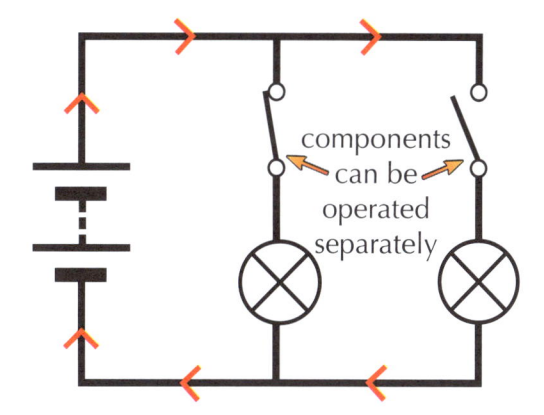

components can be operated separately

1) In parallel circuits, each component is separately connected to the +ve and −ve of the supply.

2) If you remove or disconnect one of them, it will hardly affect the others.

3) In a circuit diagram, each component is on its own loop in the circuit. To add a component in parallel, just add another loop to the diagram.

4) This is obviously how most things must be connected so that you're able to switch everything on and off separately.

> For example, household electrics...
> Each light switch in your house is part of a loop of a parallel circuit — it just turns one light (or set of lights) on and off.

Voltmeters and Ammeters are Exceptions to the Rule:

Ammeters and voltmeters are exceptions to the series and parallel rules.

Ammeters — are always connected in series even in a parallel circuit.

Voltmeters — are always connected in parallel with a component even in a series circuit.

Parallel circuits — separate components

Parallel circuits are useful in real-life applications. Imagine if your home was wired up in series like those pesky fairy lights — if one bulb went, the whole lot would go. Nightmare.

SECTION 2 — ELECTRICITY

Charge, Voltage and Energy Change

Charge Through a Circuit Depends on Current and Time

1) Current is the rate of flow of electrical charge (in amperes, A) around a circuit (see page 37).
2) In solid metal conductors (e.g. copper wire) charge is carried by negatively charged electrons.
3) When current (I) flows past a point in a circuit for a length of time (t) then the charge (Q) that has passed is given by this formula:

Charge = Current × Time

$$\frac{Q}{I \times t}$$

4) More charge passes around a circuit when a bigger current flows.

> EXAMPLE: A battery charger passes a current of 2.5 A through a cell over a period of 4 hours. How much charge does the charger transfer to the cell altogether?
> ANSWER: Q = I × t = 2.5 × (4 × 60 × 60) = 36 000 C (36 kC).

The time needs to be in seconds.

Charge is measured in coulombs, C.

When a Charge Drops Through a Voltage it Transfers Energy

1) When an electrical charge (Q) goes through a change in voltage (V), then energy (E) is transferred.
2) Energy is supplied to the charge at the power source to 'raise' it through a voltage.
3) The charge gives up this energy when it 'falls' through any voltage drop in components elsewhere in the circuit.
4) The bigger the change in voltage, the more energy is transferred for a given amount of charge passing through the circuit.

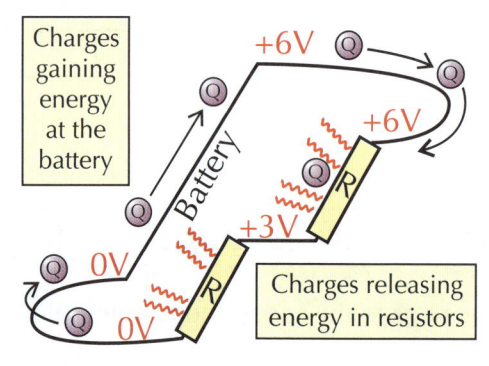

- Charges gaining energy at the battery
- Charges releasing energy in resistors

5) That means that a battery with a bigger voltage will supply more energy to the circuit for every coulomb of charge which flows round it, because the charge is raised up "higher" at the start (see above diagram) — and as the diagram shows, more energy will be dissipated in the circuit too.

Voltage is the energy transferred per unit charge passed

6) The unit for voltage, the volt, is defined as:

One volt is one joule per coulomb

SECTION 2 — ELECTRICITY

Static Electricity

Static electricity is all about charges which are not free to move. This causes them to build up in one place and it often ends with a spark or a shock when they do finally move.

Conductors Conduct Charge — Insulators Don't

1) Materials that are electrical conductors conduct charge easily — a current can flow through them. They're usually metals, e.g. copper and silver.
2) Electrical insulators don't conduct charge very well — so a current can't flow. Examples include plastic and rubber.

Build-up of Static is Caused by Friction

1) When two insulating materials are rubbed together, electrons will be scraped off one and dumped on the other.
2) This'll leave a positive electrostatic charge on one and a negative electrostatic charge on the other.
3) Which way the electrons are transferred depends on the two materials involved.
4) The classic examples are polythene and acetate rods being rubbed with a cloth duster, as shown in the diagrams.

With the polythene rod, electrons move from the duster to the rod.

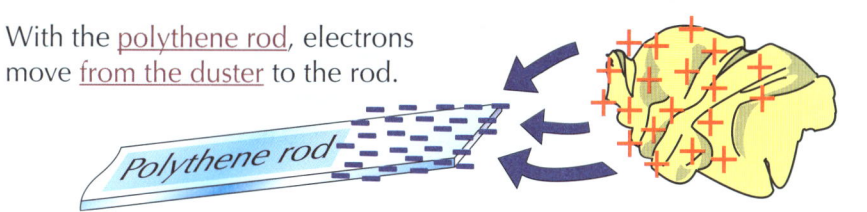

The rod becomes negatively charged and the duster is left with an equal positive charge.

With the acetate rod, electrons move from the rod to the duster.

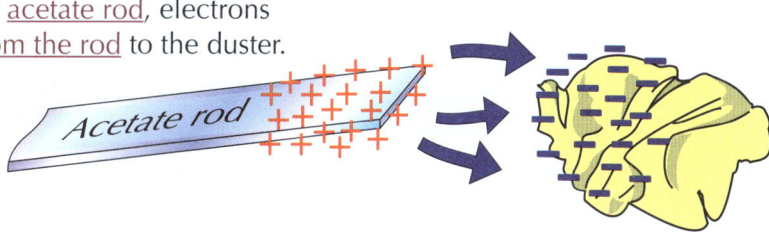

The duster becomes negatively charged and the rod is left with an equal positive charge.

5) Electrically charged objects attract small objects placed near them. (Try this: rub a balloon on a woolly pullover — then put it near tiddly bits of paper and watch them jump.)

Static electricity is caused by electrons being transferred

Static is a bit tricky. You've got to remember which way the electrons are moving. I find it helps to remember that electrons are negatively charged — so if something transfers electrons, it will become positive, but if something has electrons transferred to it, it will become negatively charged.

SECTION 2 — ELECTRICITY

Static Electricity

You can test whether an object is charged, and whether the charge is positive or negative, by looking for attraction and repulsion.

Only Electrons Move — Never the Positive Charges

1) Watch out for this in exams. Both +ve and –ve electrostatic charges are only ever produced by the movement of electrons. The positive charges definitely do not move!
2) A positive static charge is always caused by electrons moving away elsewhere (see previous page).

1) A charged conductor can be discharged safely by connecting it to earth with a metal strap.
2) The electrons flow down the strap to the ground if the charge is negative. They flow up the strap from the ground if the charge is positive.

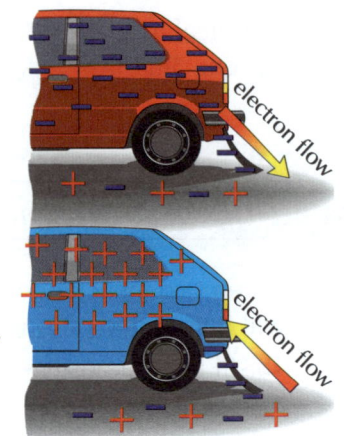

The rate of flow of electrical charge is called electric current (see p. 37).

As Charge Builds Up, So Does the Voltage — Causing Sparks

The greater the charge on an isolated object, the greater the voltage between it and the Earth. If the voltage gets big enough there's a spark which jumps across the gap (see page 50).

Like Charges Repel, Opposite Charges Attract

1) Two things with opposite electric charges are attracted to each other.
2) Two things with the same electric charge will repel each other.
3) These forces get weaker the further apart the two things are.

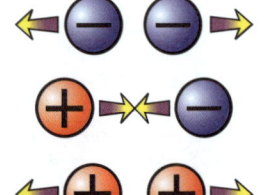

Static electricity — friend or foe?

Static electricity's great fun. You must have tried it — rubbing a balloon against your jumper and trying to get it to stick to the ceiling. It really works... well, sometimes. Bad hair days are caused by static too — it builds up on your hair, so your strands of hair repel each other. Which is nice...

SECTION 2 — ELECTRICITY

Static Electricity

Experiments Can Demonstrate Electrostatic Charge

Gold-Leaf Electroscope

1) You can see whether a material is charged by using something called a gold-leaf electroscope.
2) A gold-leaf electroscope has a metal disc connected to a metal rod, at the bottom of which are attached two thin pieces of gold leaf.
3) When a rod with a known charge is brought near to the disc of the electroscope, electrons will either be attracted to, or repelled from, the metal disc — depending on the charge of the rod.
4) This induces a charge in the metal disc, which in turn induces a charge in the gold leaves.
5) Both gold leaves will have the same charge, so they will repel each other, causing them to rise.
6) When the rod is taken away, the gold leaves will discharge and fall again.

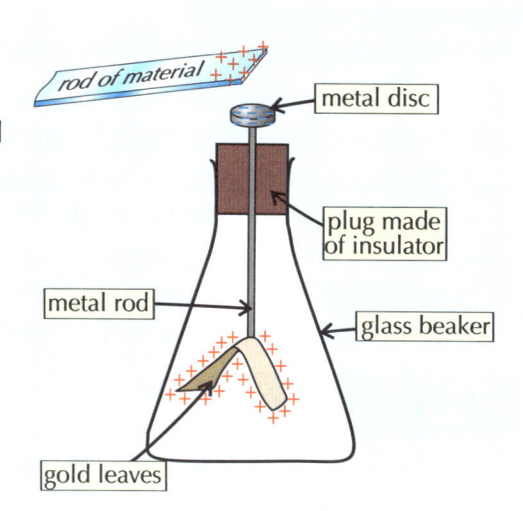

Suspending a Charged Rod

1) Another way of testing whether a rod of material is charged is to suspend a rod with a known charge on a thread and see if there is repulsion or attraction when the rod you're testing is brought close to it.
2) If there is an attraction, then the test rod has the opposite charge to the suspended rod.
3) If there is a repulsion, then the test rod has the same charge as the suspended rod.

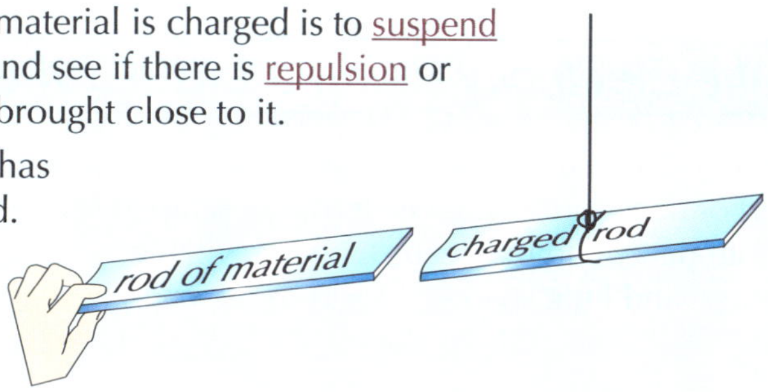

Van de Graaff Generators Make Your Hair Stand on End

1) A Van de Graaff generator is used to demonstrate electrostatic charges.
2) It's made up of a rubber belt moving round plastic rollers underneath a metal dome.
3) An electrostatic charge is built up on the metal dome as the belt goes round.
4) If you stand on an insulated chair and place your hands on the dome, electrons will move between your body and the dome, giving your body a charge.
5) The human body conducts charge, and like charges repel, so the charges will spread out as much as possible throughout your body.
6) The charge is strong enough to make your hairs repel each other and stand on end.

Static Electricity — Examples

They like asking you to give quite detailed examples in exams. Make sure you learn all these details.

Static Electricity Being **Helpful**:

1) Inkjet Printer

1) Tiny droplets of ink are forced out of a fine nozzle, making them electrically charged.
2) The droplets are deflected as they pass between two metal plates. A voltage is applied to the plates — one is negative and the other is positive.
3) The droplets are attracted to the plate of the opposite charge and repelled from the plate with the same charge.
4) The size and direction of the voltage across each plate changes so each droplet is deflected to hit a different place on the paper.
5) Loads of tiny dots make up your printout. Clever.

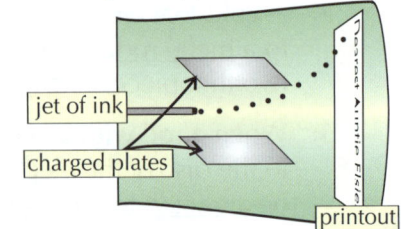

2) Photocopier

1) The image plate is positively charged. An image of what you're copying is projected onto it.
2) Whiter bits of what you're copying make light fall on the plate and the charge leaks away in those places.
3) The charged bits attract negatively charged black powder, which is transferred onto positively charged paper.
4) The paper is heated so the powder sticks.
5) Voilà, a photocopy of your piece of paper (or whatever else you've shoved in there).

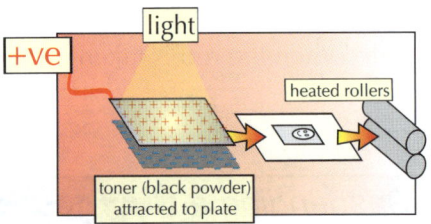

Static Electricity Being a **Little Joker**: Clothing Crackles

When synthetic clothes are dragged over each other (like in a tumble dryer) or over your head, electrons get scraped off, leaving static charges on both parts, and that leads to the inevitable — attraction (they stick together) and little sparks / shocks as the charges rearrange themselves.

Static Electricity Being a **Serious Problem**:

1) Lightning

Rain drops and ice bump together inside storm clouds, knocking off electrons and leaving the top of the cloud positively charged and the bottom of the cloud negative. This creates a huge voltage and a big spark.

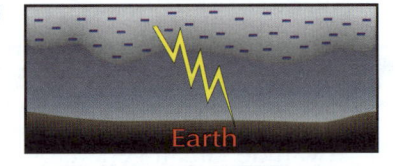

2) The Fuel-Filling Nightmare

1) As fuel flows out of a filler pipe, static can build up.
2) This can easily lead to a spark and in dusty or fumy places — BOOM!
3) The solution: make the nozzles out of metal so that the charge is conducted away, instead of building up.
4) It's also good to have earthing straps between the fuel tank and the fuel pipe.

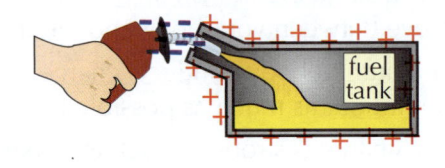

Warm-Up and Exam Questions

Right, enough reading. Try your hand at these questions and see what you've taken in...

Warm-Up Questions

1) What is an electrical conductor? Give an example.
2) What is an electrical insulator? Give an example.

Exam Questions

1. 14 fairy light bulbs are wired in series with a 12 V battery.
   a) i) Give **one** advantage of wiring the fairy lights in parallel instead.
      (1 mark)

      ii) The current through one of the bulbs is 0.5 A.
      Calculate the total resistance in the circuit.
      (3 marks)

      iii) Describe how the current in the circuit would change if there were only 9 bulbs in series connected to the same battery.
      (1 mark)

   b) A student makes the following observation.

      > The windscreen wipers, headlights and air conditioning can all be turned on and off separately in my parents' car.

      Explain her observation.
      (1 mark)

2. A 3 volt battery can supply a current of 5 amps for 20 minutes before it needs recharging.

   a) i) State what is meant by **current**.
      (1 mark)

      ii) How does current flow through metal wires in a circuit?
      (1 mark)

   b) i) State the equation that links charge, current and time.
      (1 mark)

      ii) Calculate how much charge will pass through the circuit before the battery needs recharging. State the correct unit.
      (4 marks)

      iii) A student recharges the battery and uses it again.
      This time it discharges in half the original time, but the same amount of charge passes through the circuit in that time.
      State how this will affect the current that the battery supplies over this time.
      (1 mark)

   [PAPER 2]

   c) State, with a reason, how much energy is transferred by the battery per coulomb of charge passed through the circuit. State the correct unit.
      (3 marks)

SECTION 2 — ELECTRICITY

Exam Questions

PAPER 2

3   A student does some experiments to study static electricity. He uses a cloth duster to rub a rubber balloon. The balloon gains an electrostatic charge.

   a)   Explain, in terms of charge movement, how the balloon becomes positively charged.
   (2 marks)

   b)   Describe an experiment that could be used to show that the balloon has an electrostatic charge.
   (2 marks)

   c)   The balloon has a charge of 1.5 μC. What charge does the cloth used to rub it have? Give a reason for your answer.
   (2 marks)

PAPER 2

4   A student prints a document from a computer using an inkjet printer.

   a)   An inkjet printer works by firing charged droplets of ink towards a piece of paper. Explain how the printer can control and alter the direction of the droplets of ink.
   (3 marks)

   b)   The student then photocopies the document. The diagram below shows the main steps that a photocopier uses to make a paper copy of a document.

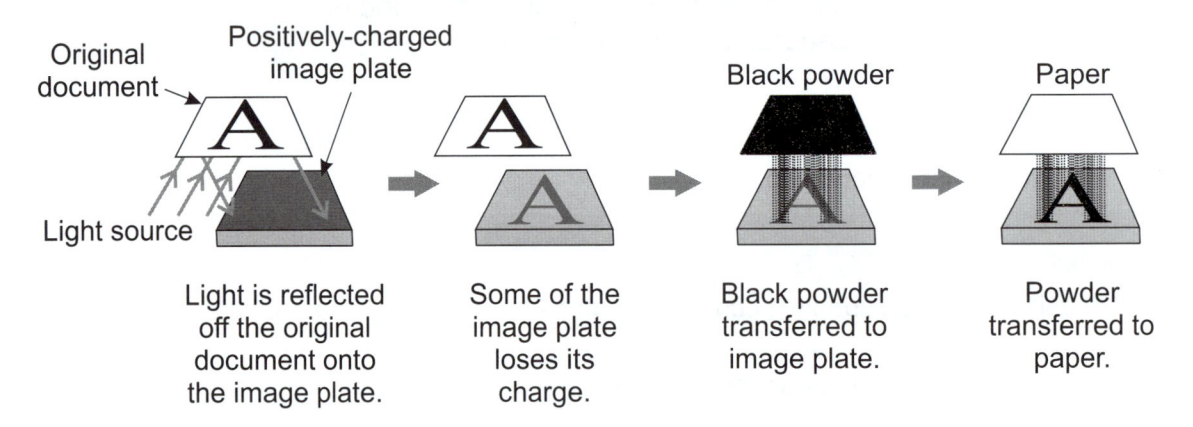

Original document / Positively-charged image plate		Black powder	Paper
Light is reflected off the original document onto the image plate.	Some of the image plate loses its charge.	Black powder transferred to image plate.	Powder transferred to paper.

   i)   Before the process starts, the image plate is positively charged. Describe what causes some parts of the image plate to lose their charge.
   (1 mark)

   ii) Describe how the original image is transferred to the paper after the light source has been reflected off it.
   (5 marks)

PAPER 2

5   When refuelling a vehicle, fuel flows out of a fuel nozzle and into the vehicle's fuel tank.

   a)   Explain why it is dangerous if static charge is allowed to build up during this process.
   (2 marks)

   b)   Give **two** safety features that can be taken to reduce the build-up of static charge when fuelling.
   (2 marks)

Revision Summary for Section 2

Well, wasn't that section just electrifying? Now let's switch that brain on to recap everything that you've gone through in this last section. These revision questions will let you know what's gone in...

1) Sketch a properly wired three-pin plug.
2) What does it mean if an appliance is 'double insulated'?
3) Give three safety precautions you should take when using plugs.
4) Explain how a fuse and earth wire work together in a plug.
5) Explain how a Residual Current Circuit Breaker (RCCB) works.
6) Give two advantages of using an RCCB instead of a fuse and an earthing wire.
7) Why does the wire in a fuse melt when the current gets too high?
8)* Find the appropriate fuse (3 A, 5 A or 13 A) for these appliances:
    a) a toaster rated at 230 V, 1100 W   b) an electric heater rated at 230 V, 2000 W
9)* A light bulb has a voltage of 20 V across it and transfers 7.2 kJ of electrical energy over a 2 minute period. What current flows through the bulb?
10) Explain what current, voltage and resistance are in an electric circuit.
11) In a standard test circuit, where must the ammeter be placed? Where must the voltmeter be placed?
12) What is the difference between a.c. and d.c.?
13)* Calculate the resistance of a wire if the voltage across it is 12 V and the current through it is 2.5 A.
14) Sketch typical current-voltage graphs for:
    a) a wire (at constant temperature),
    b) a resistor (at constant temperature),
    c) a filament lamp,
    d) a diode.
    Explain the shape of each graph.
15) What can LEDs be used to indicate the presence of?
16) Describe how the resistance of an LDR varies with light intensity. Give an application of an LDR.
17) Describe how the resistance of a thermistor varies with temperature. Give an application of a thermistor.
18) What does the current in a series circuit depend on?
19) Why are parallel circuits often more useful than series ones?
20)* If 80 C of charge is carried past a certain point in a wire in 2 s, how much current is flowing?
21) Give the definition of a volt.
22) Give an example of an electrical conductor and an electrical insulator.
23) What causes the build-up of static electricity? Which particles move when static builds up?
24) Give an example of an experiment that would show you if a material was charged.
25) Give two examples of how static electricity can be helpful.
26) Give one example of static electricity being a nuisance.
27) Give two examples of static electricity being dangerous.

*Answers on page 185.

Waves — The Basics

We're constantly bombarded by waves (light, sound, heat)... and they've all got stuff in common.

All Waves Have Wavelength, Frequency, Amplitude and Speed

1) WAVELENGTH (λ) is the distance from one peak to the next.
2) FREQUENCY (f) is how many complete waves there are per second (passing a certain point). It's measured in hertz (Hz). 1 Hz is 1 wave per second.
3) AMPLITUDE is the height of the wave (from rest to crest).
4) The SPEED (v, for velocity) is, well, how fast it goes.
5) The PERIOD (T) is the time it takes (in s) for one complete wave to pass a point. E.g. a wave with period 0.002 s has a frequency of 1 ÷ 0.002 = 500 Hz.

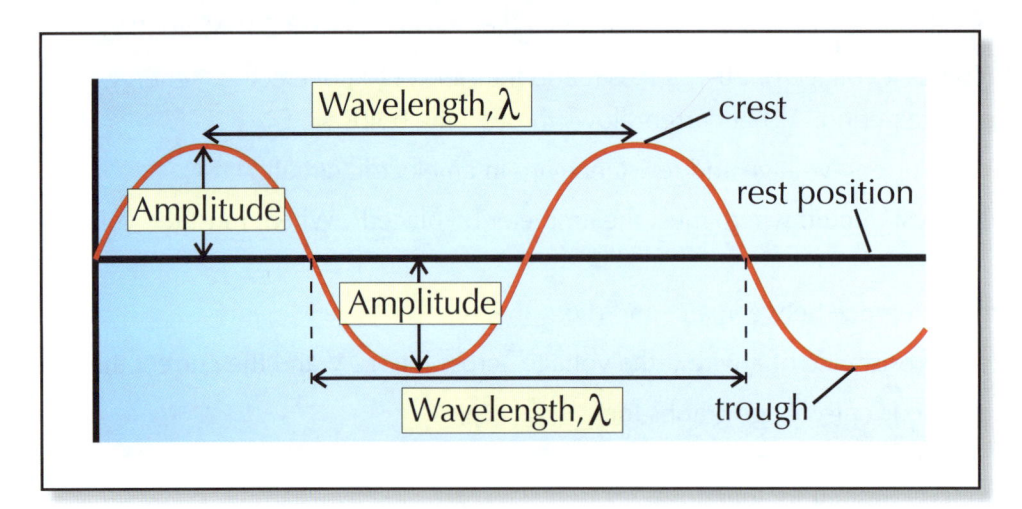

$$f = \frac{1}{T}$$

Wave Speed = Frequency × Wavelength

1) You need to learn this equation — and practise using it.

$$\text{Speed} \ (\text{m/s}) = \text{Frequency} \ (\text{Hz}) \times \text{Wavelength} \ (\text{m}) \quad \text{OR} \quad v = f \times \lambda$$

2) You won't always be asked for the speed though, so you might need this triangle too...

$$\frac{v}{f \times \lambda}$$

> **EXAMPLE:** Find the frequency of a wave with wavelength 1×10^{-7} m. (Speed of light = 3×10^8 m/s.)
> **ANSWER:** Using the triangle, frequency = speed ÷ wavelength
> $= (3 \times 10^8) \div (1 \times 10^{-7}) = \underline{3 \times 10^{15} \text{ Hz}}$.

3) Waves often have high frequencies which are given in awkward units like kHz or MHz: 1 kHz (kilohertz) = 1000 Hz, and 1 MHz (megahertz) = 1 000 000 Hz. For example, 900 MHz = 900 000 000 Hz.

Waves — The Basics

Waves Can Be Transverse...

Most waves are TRANSVERSE: 1) Light and all other EM waves (see p. 56).
2) A slinky spring wiggled up and down.
3) Waves on strings.
4) Ripples on water.

In TRANSVERSE waves the vibrations are at 90° to the DIRECTION ENERGY IS TRANSFERRED by the wave.

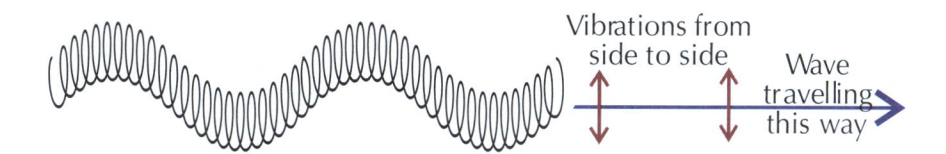

Vibrations from side to side

Wave travelling this way

...or Longitudinal

Some LONGITUDINAL waves are: 1) Sound and ultrasound.
2) Shock waves, e.g. some seismic waves.
3) A slinky spring when you push the end.

In LONGITUDINAL waves the vibrations are along the SAME DIRECTION as the wave transfers energy.

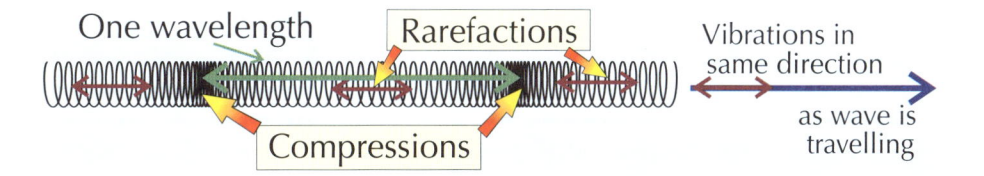

One wavelength

Rarefactions

Compressions

Vibrations in same direction as wave is travelling

Waves Transfer Energy and Information Without Transferring Matter

1) All waves carry and transfer energy in the direction they're travelling in. E.g. microwaves in an oven make things warm up — their energy is transferred to the food you're cooking. Sound waves can make things vibrate or move, e.g. loud bangs can start avalanches.

2) Waves can also be used as signals to transfer information from one place to another — e.g. light in optical fibres, or radio waves travelling through the air. There's more on this on pages 57-58.

Wiggling from side to side — must be transverse

Compressions and rarefactions — must be longitudinal. Remember, light and all other EM waves are transverse. Sound waves are longitudinal. Now get those diagrams and definitions learnt.

Wave Behaviour and EM Waves

The properties you saw on the last page can affect how waves behave. There's one type of wave which has very different properties at different wavelengths — we call these waves electromagnetic...

All Waves Can be Reflected, Refracted and Diffracted

When waves arrive at an obstacle (or meet a new material), their direction of travel can be changed...

1) The waves might be reflected — so the waves 'rebound off' the material (see p. 63).
2) They could be refracted — which means they go through the new material but change direction (p. 65).
3) Or they could be diffracted — this means the waves 'bend round' edges and through gaps, causing the waves to spread out. This allows waves to 'travel round corners'. Here's how diffraction works.

All waves diffract (spread out) when they pass through a gap or past the edge of an object. The amount of diffraction depends on the size of the gap relative to the wavelength of the wave. The narrower the gap, or the longer the wavelength, the more the wave spreads out:

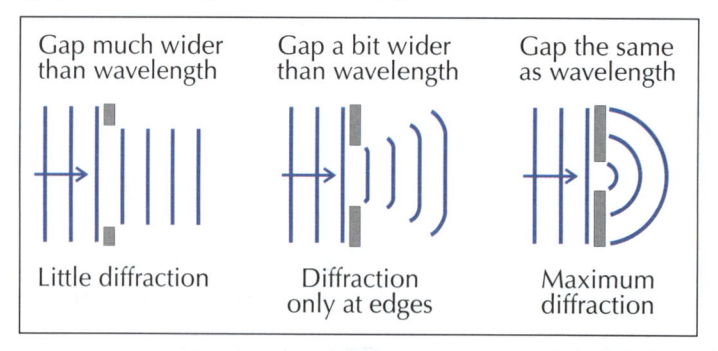

Gap much wider than wavelength	Gap a bit wider than wavelength	Gap the same as wavelength
Little diffraction	Diffraction only at edges	Maximum diffraction

When waves encounter obstacles (e.g. radio waves passing hills and tall buildings), diffraction is what causes them to bend around the obstacle.

The longer the wavelength of the wave, the more they diffract and bend around.

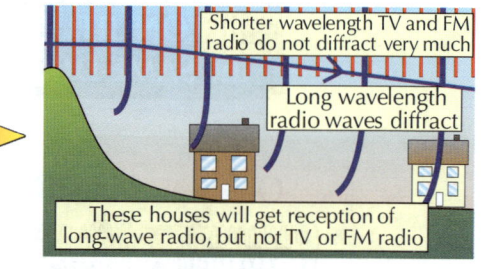

Shorter wavelength TV and FM radio do not diffract very much
Long wavelength radio waves diffract
These houses will get reception of long-wave radio, but not TV or FM radio

There are Seven Types of Electromagnetic (EM) Waves

1) Electromagnetic (EM) waves with different wavelengths have different properties. They're grouped into seven types depending on their wavelength. But the types actually merge to form a continuous spectrum.

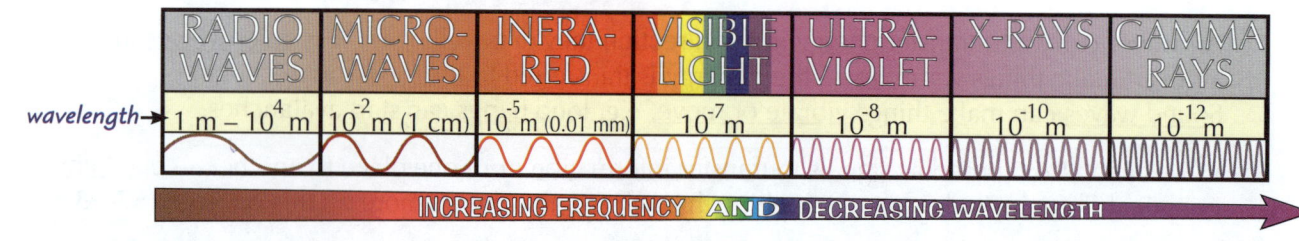

RADIO WAVES	MICRO- WAVES	INFRA- RED	VISIBLE LIGHT	ULTRA- VIOLET	X-RAYS	GAMMA RAYS
$1\,m - 10^4\,m$	$10^{-2}\,m$ (1 cm)	$10^{-5}\,m$ (0.01 mm)	$10^{-7}\,m$	$10^{-8}\,m$	$10^{-10}\,m$	$10^{-12}\,m$

INCREASING FREQUENCY AND DECREASING WAVELENGTH →

2) All types of EM radiation are transverse waves and travel at the same speed through free space (a vacuum).
3) The different colours of visible light depend on the wavelength — red has the longest wavelength (and lowest frequency) and violet has the shortest wavelength (and highest frequency).

Uses of Electromagnetic Waves

First, let's look at the uses of radio waves and microwaves — the longest types of EM waves.

Radio Waves are Used Mainly for Communications

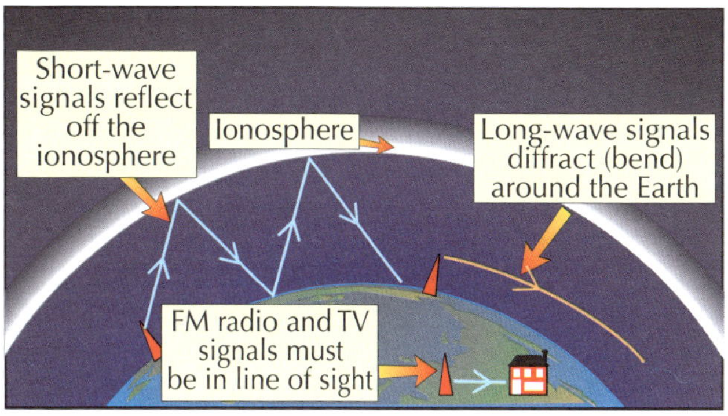

1) Radio waves are EM radiation with wavelengths longer than about 10 cm.

2) Long-wave radio (wavelengths of 1 – 10 km) can be transmitted from London, say, and received halfway round the world. That's because long wavelengths diffract (bend) around the curved surface of the Earth. They also get around hills, into tunnels and all sorts (see page 56).

3) The radio waves used for TV and FM radio broadcasting have very short wavelengths (10 cm – 10 m). To get reception, you must be in direct sight of the transmitter — the signal doesn't bend around hills or travel far through buildings.

4) Short-wave radio signals (wavelengths of about 10 m – 100 m) can, like long-wave, be received at long distances from the transmitter. That's because they are reflected from the ionosphere — an electrically charged layer in the Earth's upper atmosphere. Medium-wave signals (well, the shorter ones) can also reflect from the ionosphere, depending on atmospheric conditions and the time of day.

Microwaves are Used for Satellite Communication

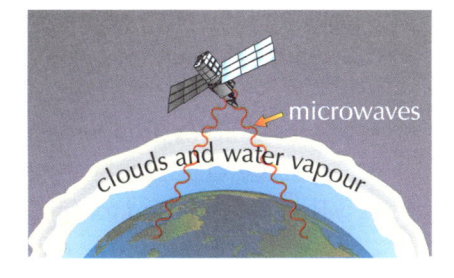

1) Microwaves have shorter wavelengths than radio waves (around 1 – 10 cm) but can still be used for communication.

2) Satellite communication (including satellite TV signals and satellite phones) uses microwaves. But you need to use wavelengths of microwaves which can pass easily through the Earth's watery atmosphere without being absorbed.

3) For satellite TV, the signal from a transmitter is transmitted into space...

4) ...where it's picked up by the satellite receiver dish orbiting thousands of kilometres above the Earth. The satellite transmits the signal back to Earth in a different direction...

5) ...where it's received by a satellite dish on the ground.

6) Mobile phone calls also travel as microwaves from your phone to the nearest transmitter.

7) And microwaves are used by remote-sensing satellites — to 'see' through the clouds and monitor oil spills, track the movement of icebergs, see how much rainforest has been chopped down and so on.

Microwaves in Ovens are Absorbed by Water Molecules

1) Microwaves are also used for cooking, but the microwaves used in microwave ovens have a different wavelength to those used in communication.

2) These microwaves are actually absorbed by the water molecules in the food. They penetrate a few centimetres into the food before being absorbed. The energy is then conducted or convected (see pages 84-86) to other parts of the food.

SECTION 3 — WAVES

Uses of Electromagnetic Waves

Infrared (a.k.a. heat) and visible light are from the middle of the EM spectrum and are both really useful.

Infrared is Used for Heating and to Monitor Temperature

1) Infrared radiation (or IR) is also known as heat radiation. Electrical heaters radiate IR to keep us warm, and things like grills use IR to cook food.

2) IR is given out by all objects — the hotter the object, the more IR radiation it gives out.

3) The infrared radiation given out by objects can be detected in the dark of night by night-vision equipment.

4) The equipment turns it into an electrical signal, which is displayed on a screen as a picture, allowing things which would otherwise be hidden in the dark (e.g. criminals on the run) to be seen.

Light Signals Can Travel Through Optical Fibres

1) As well as using it to look at things around us, visible light can be used for communication using optical fibres — which carry data over long distances as pulses of light.

2) Optical fibres work by bouncing waves off the sides of a very narrow core.

3) The pulse of light enters the fibre at a certain angle at one end and is reflected again and again until it emerges at the other end.

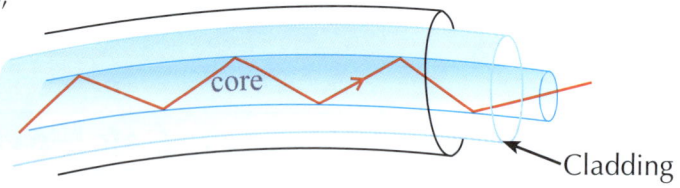

This is known as total internal reflection — see p. 67-68.

- Optical fibres are increasingly being used for telephone and broadband internet cables, replacing the old electrical ones.
- They're also used for medical purposes to 'see inside' the body without having to operate.
- You'll probably know them best though as the things that give us twinkly lights at the ends of the branches of artificial Christmas trees...

Visible Light is Also Useful for Photography

It sounds pretty obvious, but photography would be kinda tricky without visible light.

1) Cameras use a lens to focus visible light onto a light-sensitive film or electronic sensor.

2) The lens aperture controls how much light enters the camera (like the pupil in an eye).

3) The shutter speed determines how long the film or sensor is exposed to the light.

4) By varying the aperture and shutter speed (and also the sensitivity of the film or the sensor), a photographer can capture as much or as little light as they want in their photograph.

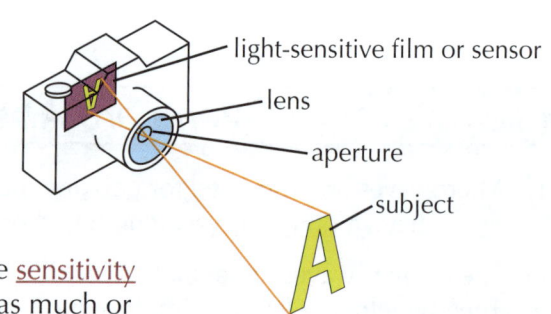

Uses of Electromagnetic Waves

Ultraviolet, X-rays and gamma rays are the shortest waves in the spectrum, and we use them for all sorts.

Ultraviolet is Used in *Fluorescent Lamps*

The Sun also emits a lot of UV radiation — it can cause damage to skin cells (see p.60).

1) Fluorescence is a property of certain chemicals, where ultraviolet radiation (UV) is absorbed and then visible light is emitted. That's why fluorescent colours look so bright — they actually emit light.

2) Fluorescent lights (like the ones you might have in your classroom) use UV radiation to emit visible light. They're safe to use as nearly all the UV radiation is absorbed by a phosphor coating on the inside of the glass which emits visible light instead.

3) Fluorescent lights are more energy-efficient (see page 78) than filament light bulbs, which is why they're often used in places (like classrooms and offices) where they'll be needed for long periods.

X-Rays Let Us See *Inside* Things

1) X-rays are used to view the internal structure of objects and materials, including our bodies — which is why they're so useful in medicine.

2) To produce an X-ray image, X-ray radiation is directed through the object or body onto a detector plate. The brighter bits are where fewer X-rays get through. This is a negative image. The plate starts off all white.

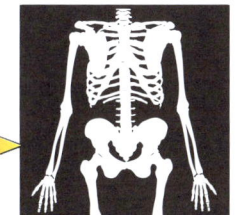

3) Radiographers in hospitals take X-ray photographs to help doctors diagnose broken bones — X-rays pass easily through flesh but not through denser material like bones or metal.

4) Because exposure to X-rays can cause mutations which lead to cancer, radiographers and patients are protected as much as possible by lead aprons and shields, and exposure to the radiation is kept to a minimum.

Gamma Radiation Can be *Very Useful* For...

...*Sterilising* Medical Equipment

1) Gamma rays are used to sterilise medical instruments by killing all the microbes.

2) This is better than trying to boil plastic instruments, which might be damaged by high temperatures.

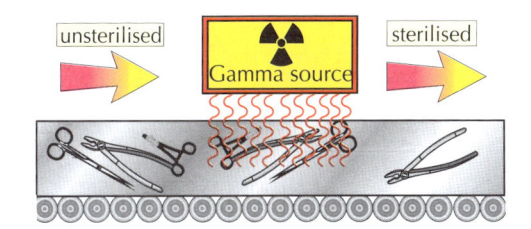

...*Sterilising* Food

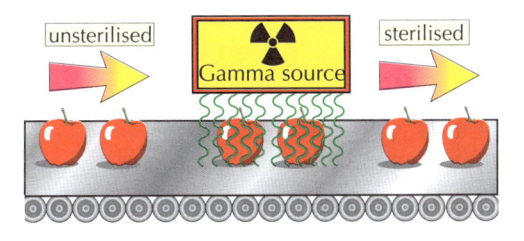

1) Food can be sterilised in the same way as medical instruments — again killing all the microbes.

2) This keeps the food fresh for longer, without having to freeze it or cook it or preserve it some other way.

3) The food is not radioactive afterwards, so it's perfectly safe to eat.

Dangers of Electromagnetic Waves

Okay, so you know how useful electromagnetic radiation can be — well, it can also be pretty dangerous.

Some EM Radiation Can be Harmful to People

When EM radiation enters living tissue — like you — it's often harmless, but sometimes it creates havoc.

1) Some EM radiation mostly passes through soft tissue without being absorbed — e.g. radio waves.
2) Other types of radiation are absorbed and cause heating of the cells — e.g. microwaves.
3) Some radiations can cause cancerous changes in living cells — e.g. gamma rays can cause cancer.

Higher Frequency EM Radiation is Usually More Dangerous

1) The effects of EM radiation depend on its frequency. The higher the frequency of EM radiation, the more energy it has and generally the more harmful it can be.
2) In general, waves with lower frequencies (like radio waves — which are harmless as far as we know) are less harmful than high frequency waves like X-rays and gamma rays.
3) From a safety point of view, it's how radiation affects human tissue that's most vital. You need to know how the body can be affected if exposed to too much of the following radiation:

INCREASING FREQUENCY

Microwaves
Microwaves have a similar frequency to the vibrations of many molecules, and so they can increase these vibrations. The result is internal heating — the heating of molecules inside things (as in microwave ovens). Microwaves HEAT HUMAN BODY TISSUE internally in this way.
Microwave ovens need to have shielding to prevent microwaves from reaching the user.

Infrared
The infrared (IR) range of frequencies can make the surface molecules of any substance vibrate — and like microwaves, this has a heating effect. But infrared has a higher frequency, so it carries more energy than microwave radiation. If the human body is exposed to too much infrared radiation, it can cause some nasty SKIN BURNS. You can protect yourself using insulating materials to reduce the amount of IR reaching your skin.

Ultraviolet
UV radiation can DAMAGE SURFACE CELLS and cause BLINDNESS. It's 'ionising' — it carries enough energy to knock electrons off atoms. This can cause cell mutation or destruction, and cancer.
You should wear sunscreen with UV filters whenever you're out in the sun, and stay out of strong sunlight to protect your skin from UV radiation.

Gamma
Very high-frequency waves, such as gamma rays, are also ionising, and carry much more energy than UV rays. This means they can be much more damaging and they can penetrate further into the body. Like all ionising radiation, they can cause CELL MUTATION or destruction, leading to TISSUE DAMAGE or CANCER.
Radioactive sources of gamma rays should be kept in lead-lined boxes when not in use. When people need to be exposed to them, e.g. in medical treatment, the exposure time should be as short as possible.

Section 3 — Waves

Warm-Up and Exam Questions

Practice, practice and more practice is the only real way to succeed in life.
So practice you shall have...

Warm-Up Questions

1) Define the following: a) wavelength b) amplitude c) period (of a wave).
2) Describe how transverse and longitudinal waves are different in terms of the direction of their vibrations.
3) True or false? Radio waves travel more slowly than visible light through free space.
4) What type of EM radiation is used in grills and electric heaters?
5) Describe how an X-ray image is produced.
6) Explain how gamma rays can be dangerous for the human body and describe one way of reducing the risk when using them.

Exam Questions

1   A wave in a pond, travelling at 0.5 m/s, makes a floating ball move up and down twice every second.

← wave speed 0.5 m/s

     a)   What is the frequency of the wave? State the correct unit.

(2 marks)

     b)   i)   State the equation linking wave speed, frequency and wavelength.

(1 mark)

           ii)   The ball is on a crest of the wave.
                Calculate how far away the next crest is from the ball.

(2 marks)

           iii)   Calculate the time period of the wave.

(2 marks)

PAPER 2

2   All types of waves can undergo diffraction.

     a)   Describe what is meant by **diffraction**.

(1 mark)

     b)   i)   The range of wavelengths of visible light is around 400-700 nm. Explain why visible light does not appear to diffract when it passes through doorways.

(2 marks)

           ii)   A student claims: "Radio waves are a type of electromagnetic wave, just like visible light. This means you won't be able to detect radio waves diffracting as they pass through doorways either."
                Do you agree or disagree? Explain your answer.

(2 marks)

Exam Questions

3   The radio transmitter shown transmits long-wave radio signals as well as short-wave TV signals. A mountain blocks the line of sight between the transmitter and a house, as shown.

   a)   Explain why the mountain does not stop long-wave
        radio signals from reaching the house.
        (2 marks)

   b)   Describe how short-wave TV signals from the transmitter reach the house.
        (1 mark)

   c)   The home owner decides to get satellite TV installed.
        i)   State what type of electromagnetic radiation is used to send signals to satellites.
             (1 mark)

        ii) Describe how satellite TV signals are transmitted
             from a transmitter on the ground to the house.
             (2 marks)

4   The diagram shows electromagnetic radiation
    being used to sterilise a surgical instrument.

   a)   State what type of electromagnetic
        radiation is being used.
        (1 mark)

   b)   A similar process can be used to treat fruit
        before it is exported to other countries.
        Suggest why this process is used.
        (2 marks)

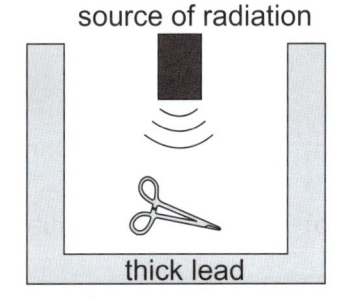

5   Mobile phones use microwaves to transmit signals.

   a)   Suggest why people might be worried that excessive
        mobile phone use could be harmful.
        (1 mark)

   b)   Explain why it would be more dangerous to use infrared radiation
        instead of microwaves for mobile phone signals.
        (2 marks)

6   Ultraviolet radiation can damage skin cells and cause cancer in humans.

   a)   A student claims, "Fluorescent lamps are always harmful to humans because they
        emit ultraviolet radiation." Do you agree or disagree? Explain your answer.
        (2 marks)

   b)   Photographers sometimes use ultraviolet filters to prevent ultraviolet radiation from
        reaching the camera's sensor or film. Describe how a camera creates a photograph
        using visible light, and how the camera and the photographer can control the
        amount of visible light entering it.
        (3 marks)

Reflection of Waves

It's time to shed some more light on... er... light. First up — a chance for reflection on... reflection.

Reflection of Light Lets Us See Things

1) Visible light is a transverse wave (see page 55), like all EM waves.

2) Reflection of visible light is what allows us to see most objects. Light bounces off them into our eyes.

3) When light reflects from an uneven surface such as a piece of paper, the light reflects off at all different angles and you get a diffuse reflection.

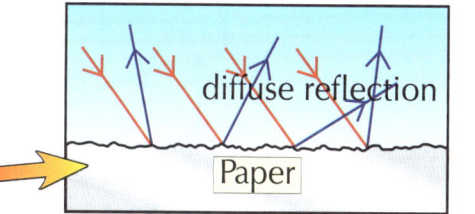

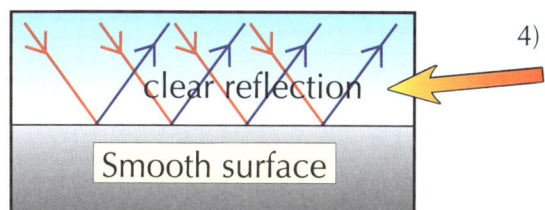

4) When light reflects from an even surface (smooth and shiny like a mirror) then it's all reflected at the same angle and you get a clear reflection.

You Need to Learn the Law of Reflection

Don't forget, the LAW OF REFLECTION applies to every reflected ray:

Angle of INCIDENCE = Angle of REFLECTION

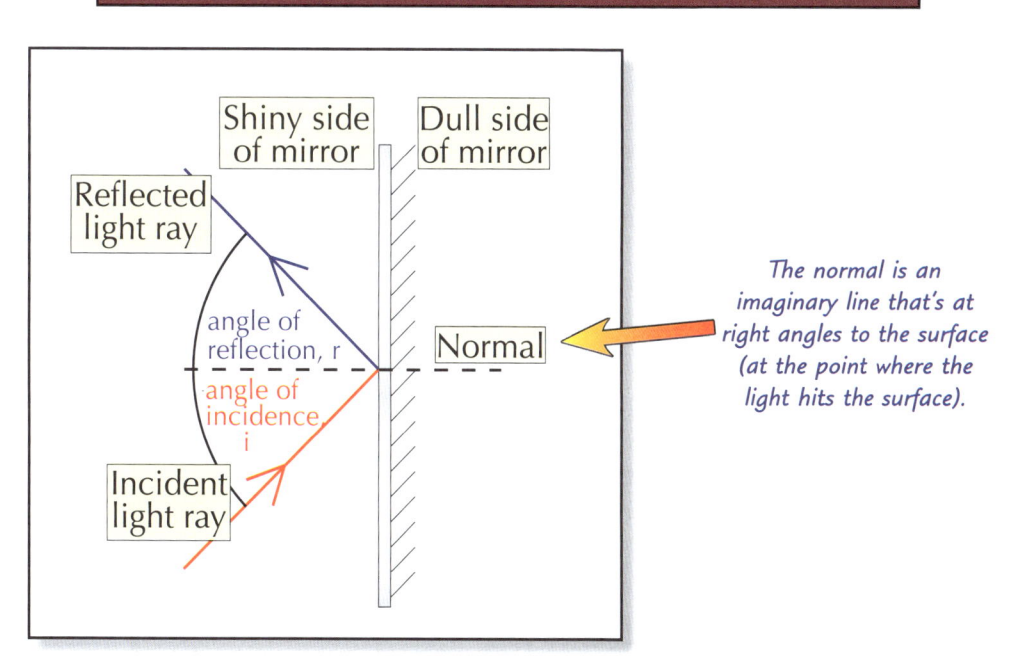

The normal is an imaginary line that's at right angles to the surface (at the point where the light hits the surface).

Note that the angle of incidence and the angle of reflection are ALWAYS defined between the ray itself and the dotted NORMAL. Don't ever label them as the angle between the ray and the surface.

Reflection of Waves

Draw a *Ray Diagram* for an *Image* in a *Plane Mirror*

A virtual image is formed when the light rays bouncing off an object onto a mirror are diverging, so the light from the object appears to be coming from a completely different place. You need to be able to reproduce this entire diagram of how an image is formed in a PLANE MIRROR.

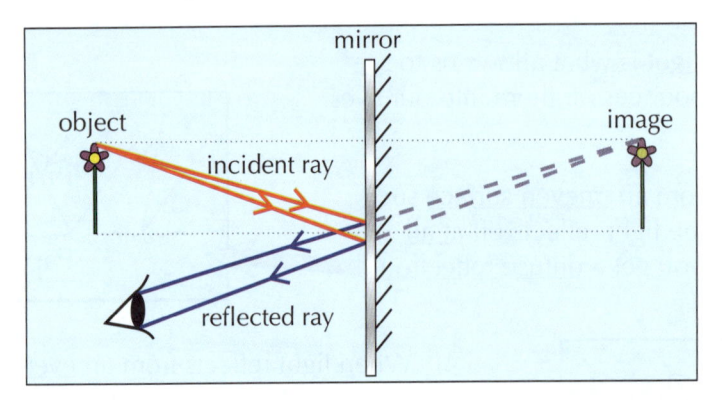

Learn these three important points:

1) The image is the same size as the object.
2) It is AS FAR BEHIND the mirror as the object is in front.
3) It's formed from diverging rays, which means it's a virtual image.

1) First off, draw the virtual image. Don't try to draw the rays first. Follow the rules in the above box — the image is the same size, and it's as far behind the mirror as the object is in front.

2) Next, draw a reflected ray going from the top of the virtual image to the top of the eye. Draw a bold line for the part of the ray between the mirror and eye, and a dotted line for the part of the ray between the mirror and the virtual image.

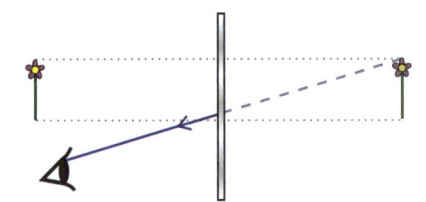

3) Now draw the incident ray going from the top of the object to the mirror. The incident and reflected rays follow the law of reflection — but you don't actually have to measure any angles. Just draw the ray from the object to the point where the reflected ray meets the mirror.

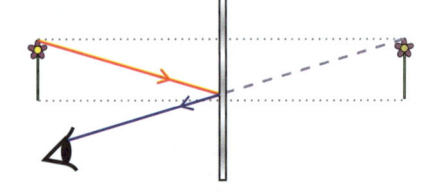

4) Now you have an incident ray and reflected ray for the top of the image. Do steps 2 and 3 again for the bottom of the eye — a reflected ray going from the image to the bottom of the eye, then an incident ray from the object to the mirror.

Section 3 — Waves

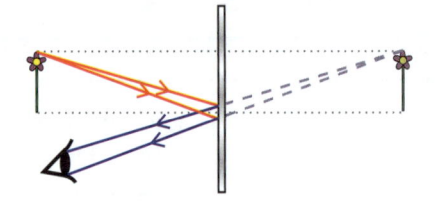

Refraction of Waves

All waves can be refracted — it's a fancy way of saying 'change direction'.

Waves Can be Refracted

1) Waves travel at different speeds in substances which have different densities. EM waves travel more slowly in denser media (usually). Sound waves travel faster in denser substances.
2) So when a wave crosses a boundary between two substances, from glass to air, say, it changes speed.

If the wave hits the boundary 'face on', it slows down but carries on in the same direction.

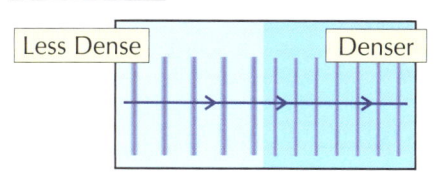

But if a wave meets a different medium at an angle, this part of the wave hits the denser layer first and slows down...

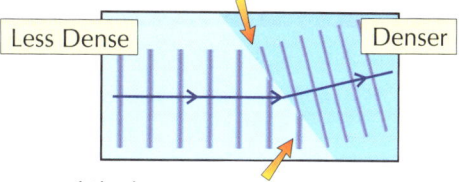

... while this part carries on at the first, faster speed. So the wave changes direction — it's been REFRACTED.

3) You can experiment with refraction using a light source and a rectangular block of a particular material (e.g. glass) resting on top of a piece of paper...

4) Shine a light ray at an angle into the block, as shown. Some of the light is reflected, but a lot of it passes through the glass and gets refracted as it does so.

5) Trace the incident and emergent rays onto the piece of paper and remove the block. You can draw in the refracted ray through the block by joining the ends of the other two rays with a straight line.

6) You should see that as the light passes from the air into the block (a denser medium), it bends towards the normal. This is because it slows down.

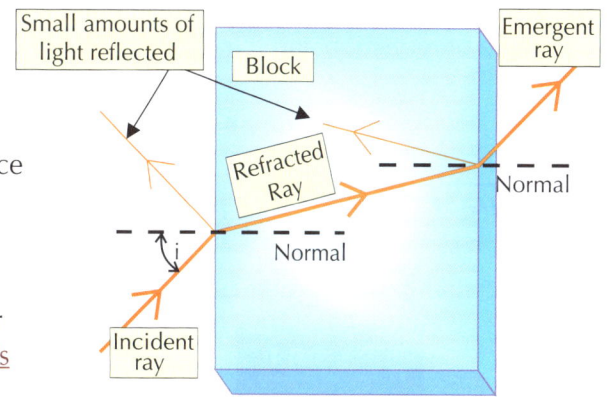

7) When the light reaches the boundary on the other side of the block, it's passing into a less dense medium. So it speeds up and bends away from the normal. (Some of the light is also reflected at this boundary.)

8) The light ray that emerges on the other side of the block is now travelling in the same direction it was to begin with — it's been refracted towards the normal and then back again by the same amount.

9) You can measure the angles between the rays and the normal to work out the refractive index of the material in the block (see pages 66-67).

Triangular Prisms Disperse White Light

1) Different wavelengths of light refract by different amounts, so white light disperses into different colours as it enters a prism.
2) A rectangular block has parallel boundaries, so the rays bend by the same amount when they leave the block as when they entered — so the rays emerge parallel.
3) But with a triangular prism, the boundaries aren't parallel, which means the different wavelengths don't emerge parallel, and you get a nice rainbow effect.

Refractive Index and Snell's Law

So you're totally happy with the last two pages. And you're sure about that. Good. Gets a bit hairy here.

Every Transparent Material Has a Refractive Index

1) The refractive index of a transparent material tells you how fast light travels in that material. The refractive index of a material is defined as:

$$\text{refractive index, } n = \frac{\text{speed of light in a vacuum, c}}{\text{speed of light in that material, v}} \qquad n = \frac{c}{v}$$

(Remember — the speed of light in a vacuum, $c = 3 \times 10^8$ m/s)

You don't need to remember this equation for the exam.

2) Light slows down a lot in glass, so the refractive index of glass is high (around 1.5).

3) The refractive index of water is a bit lower (around 1.33) — so light doesn't slow down as much in water as in glass.

4) The speed of light in air is about the same as in a vacuum, so the refractive index of air is 1 (to 2 d.p.).

5) According to Snell's law, the angle of incidence, angle of refraction and refractive index are all linked...

Snell's Law Says...

When an incident ray passes into a material:

$$n = \frac{\sin i}{\sin r}$$

Thankfully you don't have to know why Snell's law works. Just that it does.

So if you know any two of n, i or r, you can work out the missing one.

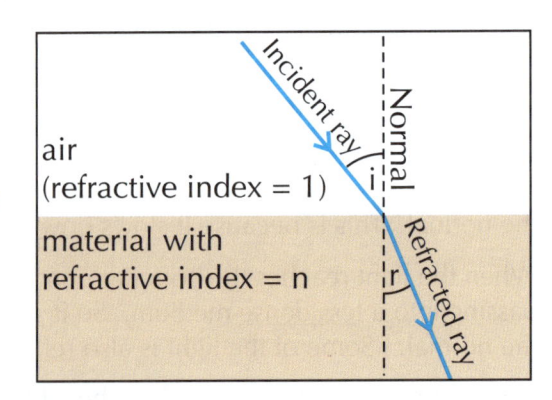

Example:

A beam of light travels from air into water.
The angle of incidence is 23°. Refractive index of water = 1.33.
Calculate the angle of refraction to the nearest degree.

ANSWER: Using Snell's law, $\sin r = \frac{\sin i}{n} = \frac{\sin 23°}{1.33} = 0.29...$

$r = \sin^{-1}(0.29...) = \underline{17°}$

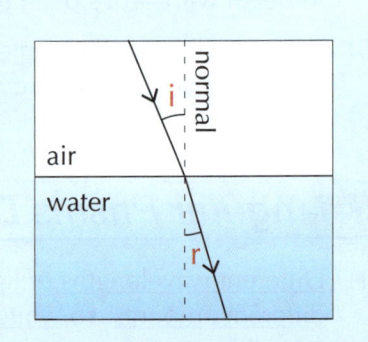

Revise refraction — but don't let it slow you down

Learn all the facts about refractive index and Snell's law — you need to be able to use them too.

Refractive Index and Snell's Law

Yep, more Snell's law I'm afraid. Best get stuck in...

Find the Refractive Index of Glass Using a Glass Block

You need to be able to describe an experiment to find the refractive index of a glass block — it's pretty much the same as the rectangular block experiment on page 65.

1) Draw around a rectangular glass block on a piece of paper and direct a ray of light through it at an angle. Trace the incident and emergent rays, remove the block, then draw in the refracted ray between them.
2) You then need to draw in the normal at 90° to the edge of the block, at the point where the ray enters the block.
3) Use a protractor to measure the angle of incidence (i) and the angle of refraction (r), as shown. Remember — these are the angles made with the normal.
4) Calculate the refractive index (n) using Snell's law: $n = \frac{\sin i}{\sin r}$.
5) The refractive index of glass should be around 1.5, so if you get a ridiculous answer then you've gone wrong somewhere.

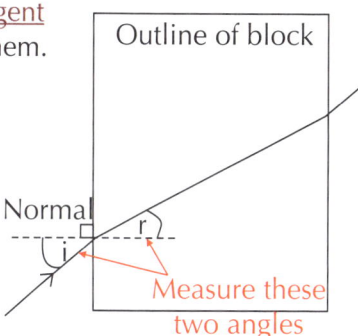

Use Semicircular Blocks to Show Total Internal Reflection

1) As you've just seen, light going from a material with a higher refractive index to a material with a lower refractive index speeds up and so bends away from the normal — e.g. when travelling from glass into air.
2) If you keep increasing the angle of incidence, the angle of refraction gets closer and closer to 90°.
3) Eventually i reaches a critical angle C for which r = 90°. The light is refracted right along the boundary.
4) Above this critical angle, you get total internal reflection — no light leaves the medium.
5) An experiment to demonstrate this uses a semicircular block instead of a rectangular one. The incident light ray is aimed at the curved edge of the block so that it always enters at right angles to the edge. This means it doesn't bend as it enters the block, only when it leaves from the straight edge.
6) To investigate the critical angle, C, mark the positions of the rays and the block on paper and use a protractor to measure i and r for different angles of incidence. Record your results in a table.

IF THE ANGLE OF INCIDENCE (i) IS...

Remember — the angle of incidence and the angle of reflection are equal, and always measured from the normal.

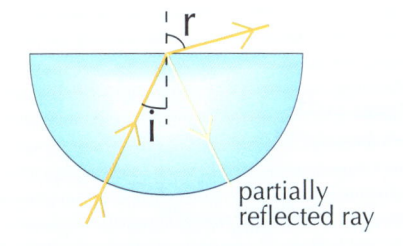

...LESS than Critical Angle:-
Most of the light passes out but a little bit of it is internally reflected.

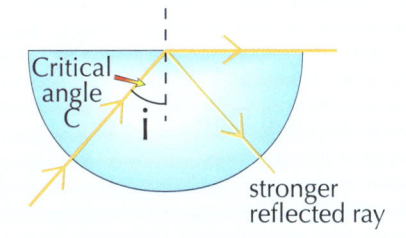

...EQUAL to Critical Angle:-
The emerging ray comes out along the surface. There's quite a bit of internal reflection.

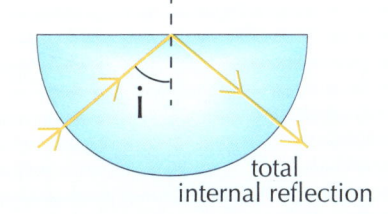

...GREATER than Critical Angle:-
No light comes out. It's all internally reflected, i.e. total internal reflection.

Snell's Law and Critical Angles

You'll be pleased to know that this page covers all the final bits and bobs you need to learn about Snell.

You Can Use Snell's Law to find Critical Angles

You can find the critical angle, C, of a material using this equation:

$$\sin C = \frac{1}{n}$$

n is the refractive index of the material.

This equation comes from Snell's law that you saw on page 66 — you don't need to know how, but you do need to learn both equations.

The higher the refractive index, the lower the critical angle. For water, C is 49°.

Example:

Jacob does an experiment to find out the refractive index of his strawberry flavour jelly. He finds that the critical angle for a light beam travelling from his jelly into air is 42°. Calculate the refractive index of Jacob's jelly.

ANSWER: $\sin C = \frac{1}{n}$, so $n = \frac{1}{\sin C}$

$\sin C = \sin 42° = 0.66...$,

so $n_{jelly} = \frac{1}{0.66...} = 1.49$ (2 d.p.)

Jelly n = ? 42°
air n = 1

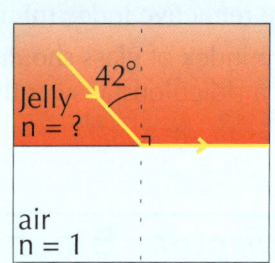

Optical Fibres Use Total Internal Reflection

1) Optical fibres made of plastic or glass (see p. 58) consist of a central core surrounded by cladding that has a lower refractive index.

2) The core of the fibre is so narrow that light signals passing through it always hit the core-cladding boundary at angles higher than C — so the light is always totally internally reflected.

3) It only stops working if the fibre is bent too sharply.

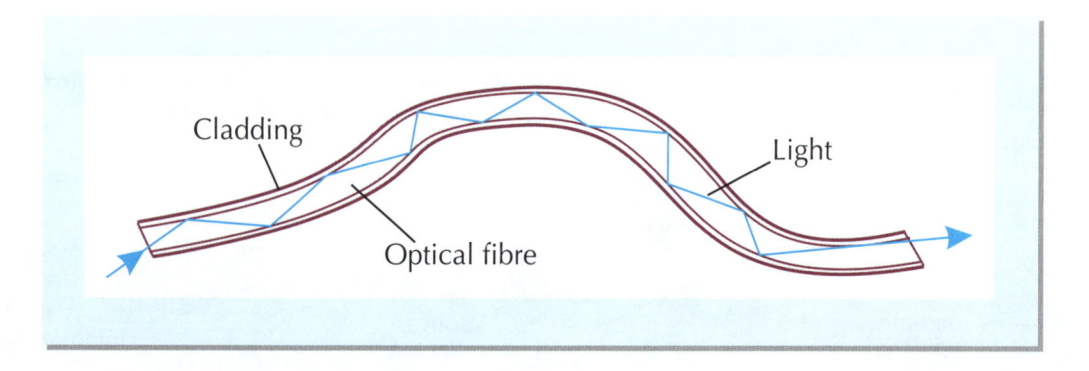

Remember — the critical angle is measured from the normal

Remember... total internal reflection only works when the light's going into something with a lower refractive index. Got it? Good. Well, at least that's Snell's law over and done with anyway.

Warm-Up and Exam Questions

Another load of pages learnt, another load of practice questions to do.
Will the monotony ever end? Well, no — it's the best way to learn, so tough.

Warm-Up Questions

1) Is visible light a transverse or longitudinal wave?
2) What is Snell's law?
3) Describe an experiment you could do to find the refractive index of a glass block.

Exam Questions

1   A student looks in the mirror at himself and sees an image formed from reflected light.
   a) i)   State what is meant by the normal of a ray of light hitting a surface.
   (1 mark)

       ii) State the law of reflection.
   (1 mark)

   b) On the diagram, draw the paths of **two** rays of light to show how the student sees an image in the plane mirror of point A.
   (2 marks)

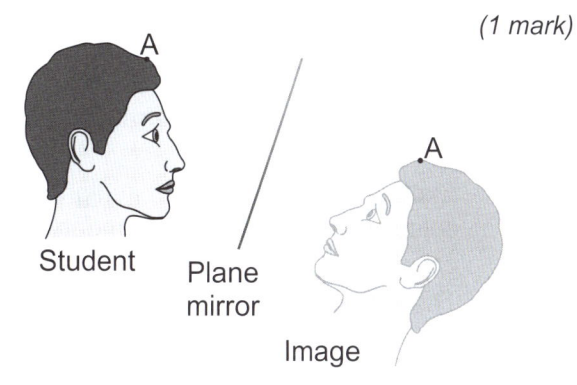

2   The diagram shows a ray of red light entering a glass prism.
   a) Complete the diagram to show the ray passing through the prism and emerging from the other side. Label the angles of incidence, i, and refraction, r, for both boundaries.
   (3 marks)

   b) Describe an experiment that you could do to measure i and r at both boundaries.
   (4 marks)

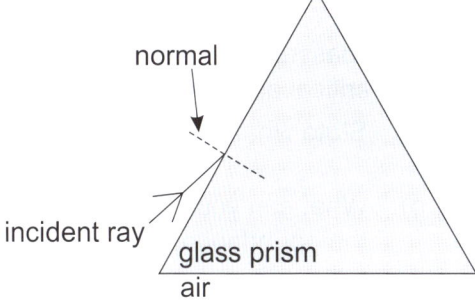

   c) When a ray of white light enters the prism, several rays of light, each of a separate colour, emerge from the prism. Each ray of light travels in a slightly different direction.
       i)   Explain why this happens.
   (2 marks)

       ii) When white light shines through a rectangular block of glass instead of through a triangular prism, all the light that emerges travels in the same direction. Explain why.
   (2 marks)

Exam Questions

3 Endoscopes use optical fibres to look inside a patient's body. When light meets the boundary between the optical fibre core and the outer cladding, there is total internal reflection.

   a) State what is meant by **total internal reflection**.
   (1 mark)

   b) Explain why bending the endoscope too sharply may result in reduced image quality.
   (2 marks)

4 The diagram shows white light refracting at an air-glass boundary and separating into colours.

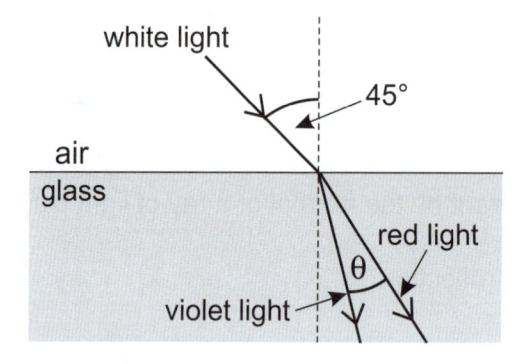

   a) The refractive index of glass for red light is 1.514.
   Calculate the angle of refraction for red light.
   (4 marks)

   b) Explain why the ray of white light would not separate into colours if it crossed the boundary along the normal.
   (2 marks)

   c) The refractive index of glass for violet light is 1.528.
   Calculate the angle θ shown in the diagram.
   (4 marks)

5 Light passes through the acrylic bottom of a boat into the water below it.
   The critical angle (C) of the acrylic-water boundary for the light is 63.2°.

   a) State what is meant by the **critical angle** for a boundary.
   (1 mark)

   b) What can you say about the angle of incidence of a ray of light that passes through the boundary between the acrylic and the water?
   (1 mark)

   c) Another ray of light meets the acrylic-water boundary at an angle of incidence of 70°. Describe what will happen to the ray of light at the boundary.
   (1 mark)

   d) The diagram shows a ray of light hitting the boundary between the same acrylic and air. Calculate the refractive index of the acrylic.
   (3 marks)

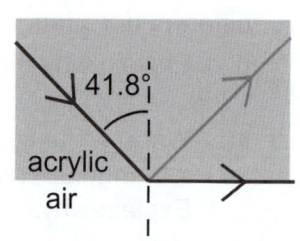

SECTION 3 — WAVES

Analogue and Digital Signals

Digital technology is taking over from analogue — it's got loads of advantages.

Information is Converted into Signals

1) To communicate any kind of information (e.g. sounds, pictures) over a long distance, it needs to be converted into electrical signals before it's transmitted.
2) These signals can then be sent down telephone wires or carried on EM waves.
3) The signals can either be analogue or digital.

Analogue Signals Vary but Digital's Just On or Off

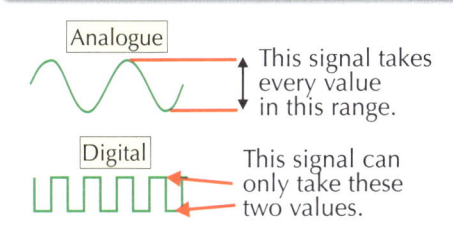

1) An analogue signal can take any value within a certain range. (Remember: analogue — any.) The amplitude and frequency of an analogue wave can vary continuously.
2) A digital signal can only take two values. These values tend to be called on/off, or 1/0. For example, you can send data along optical fibres as short pulses of light.

Digital Signals Have Advantages Over Analogue

1) Both digital and analogue signals weaken as they travel, so they need to be amplified along their route.
2) They also pick up interference or noise from electrical disturbances or other signals.
3) When you amplify an analogue signal, the noise is amplified too — so every time it's amplified, the signal loses quality. With a digital signal, the noise is just ignored, so the signal remains high quality.

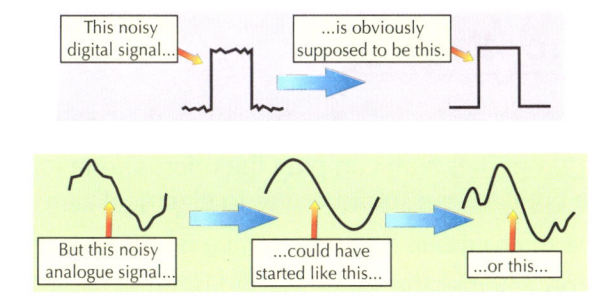

> When two or more waves of a similar frequency meet, they can create one combined signal with a new amplitude. This is called interference. You get it when two radio stations transmit on similar frequencies.

4) Because of this, it's easier to transmit multiple signals at the same time with just one cable or EM wave (a process called multiplexing) if the signal is digital. If analogue waves are of a similar frequency, it can cause interference when the signal loses quality. With digital signals, it's much easier to tell them apart, so you can transmit more information along the same channel.
5) Quantisation is the process of 'rounding' multiple values to a smaller set. By doing this, you can pack more information into the same amount of space. Because digital signals can only have two values (on or off), quantisation doesn't lose much information — with analogue, however, a lot of information is lost when a continuous range is rounded off (see right).

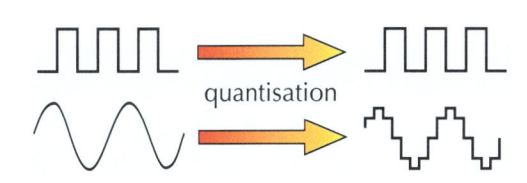

SECTION 3 — WAVES

Sound Waves

You hear sounds when vibrations reach your eardrums...

Sound Travels as a Wave

1) Sound waves are longitudinal waves caused by vibrating objects. The vibrations are passed through the surrounding medium as a series of compressions.

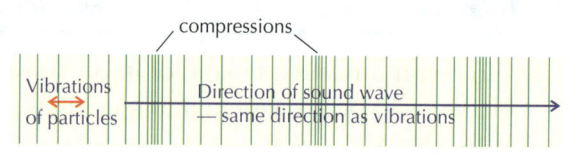

2) The sound may eventually reach someone's eardrum, at which point the person might hear it — the human ear is capable of hearing sounds with frequencies between 20 Hz and 20 000 Hz. (Although in practice some people can't hear some of the higher frequency sounds.)

3) Because sound waves are caused by vibrating particles, in general the denser the medium, the faster sound travels through it. This also means it can't travel through a vacuum where there aren't any particles.

4) Sound generally travels faster in solids than in liquids, and faster in liquids than in gases.

Sound Waves Can Reflect, Refract and Diffract

1) Sound waves will be reflected by hard flat surfaces. Things like carpets and curtains act as absorbing surfaces which will absorb sounds rather than reflect them.

2) Sound waves will also refract (change direction) as they enter different media. As they enter denser material, they speed up. (However, since sound waves are always spreading out so much, the change in direction is hard to spot under normal circumstances.)

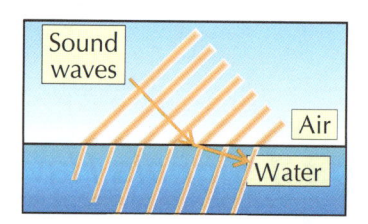

3) Sound waves can also be diffracted through gaps and around obstacles (see page 56). This is why you can hear someone talking from around a corner or outside a room — the sound waves will bend and spread out.

An Oscilloscope Can Display Sound Waves

1) A sound wave receiver, such as a microphone, can pick up sound waves travelling through the air.

2) To display these sound waves, and measure their properties, you can plug the microphone into an oscilloscope (see pages 73-74). The microphone converts the sound waves to electrical signals.

3) An oscilloscope is a device which can display the microphone signal as a trace on a screen.

4) The appearance of the wave on the screen tells you whether the sound is loud or quiet, and high- or low-pitched. You can even take detailed measurements to calculate the frequency of the sound (see next page) by adjusting the settings of the display.

Loudness Increases with Amplitude

1) The greater the amplitude of a wave or vibration, the more energy it carries.

2) In sound this means it'll be louder.

3) Louder sound waves will also have a trace with a larger amplitude on an oscilloscope.

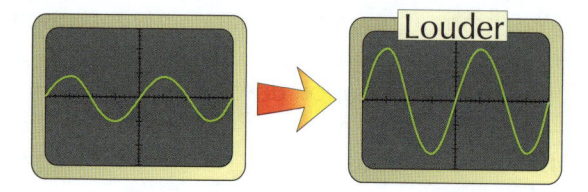

Sound Waves

You can measure the pitch of sounds using an oscilloscope. Here's how...

The **Higher** the **Frequency**, the Higher the **Pitch**

1) Frequency is the number of complete vibrations each second, and it's measured in hertz (Hz) — 1 Hz is equal to 1 vibration per second. Other common units are kHz (1000 Hz) and MHz (1 000 000 Hz).

2) You can compare the frequency of waves on an oscilloscope — the more complete cycles displayed on the screen, the higher the frequency (if the waves are being compared on the same scale — see below).

3) If the source of sound vibrates with a high frequency the sound is high-pitched, e.g. a squeaking mouse.

4) If the source of sound vibrates with a low frequency the sound is low-pitched, e.g. a mooing cow.

5) These traces are very important, so make sure you know all about them:

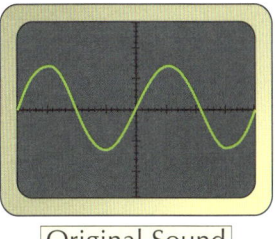

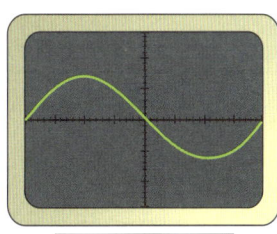

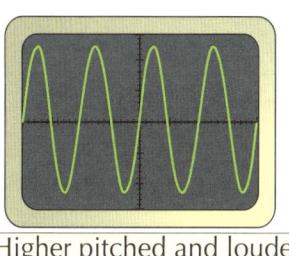

| Original Sound | Higher pitched | Lower pitched | Higher pitched and louder |

How to **Measure Frequency** Using an **Oscilloscope**

1) The horizontal axis on the display is time. The time between each division on the scale can be adjusted to get a clear, readable trace.

2) Adjust the time division setting until the display shows at least 1 complete cycle, like this.

3) Read off the period — the time taken for one complete cycle.

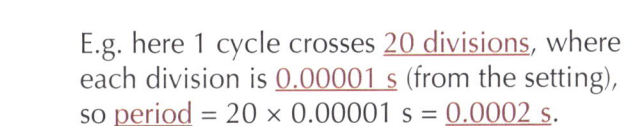

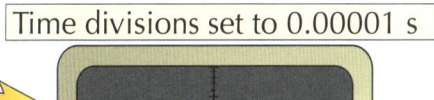

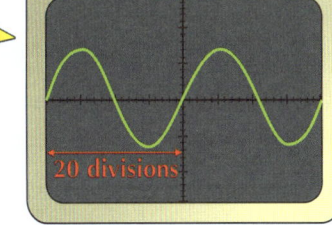

   E.g. here 1 cycle crosses 20 divisions, where each division is 0.00001 s (from the setting), so period = 20 × 0.00001 s = 0.0002 s.

   Time divisions set to 0.00001 s
   20 divisions

4) Frequency = 1 ÷ period (see p. 54) = 1 ÷ 0.0002 s = 5000 Hz = 5 kHz.

Frequency is measured in hertz (Hz)

Remember: if the waves on the oscilloscope get closer together, the frequency has increased and the sound will be high-pitched. If they get taller, the amplitude has increased and the sound will be louder.

Sound Waves

This page is all about how to measure the speed of sound. Exciting stuff.

You Can Use an Oscilloscope to Measure the Speed of Sound

1) By attaching a signal generator to a speaker you can generate sounds with a specific frequency. You can use two microphones and an oscilloscope to find the wavelength of the sound waves generated:

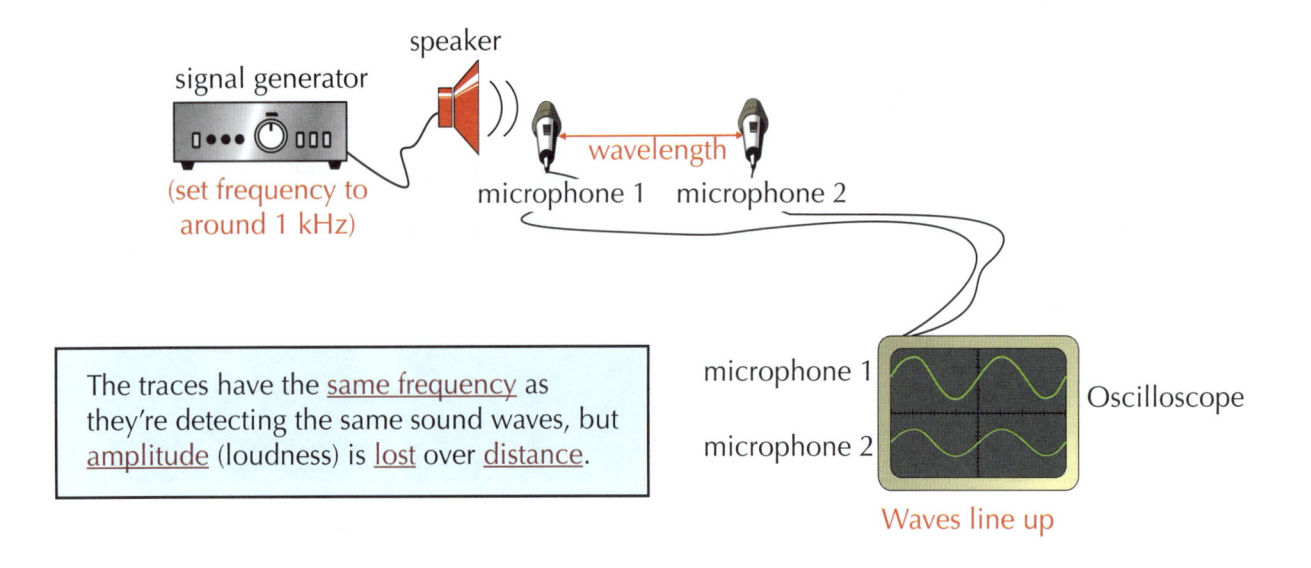

signal generator (set frequency to around 1 kHz) — speaker — microphone 1 — wavelength — microphone 2 — Oscilloscope — Waves line up

The traces have the same frequency as they're detecting the same sound waves, but amplitude (loudness) is lost over distance.

2) The detected waves at each microphone can be seen as a separate wave on the oscilloscope.

3) Start with both microphones next to the speaker, then slowly move one away until the two waves are aligned on the display, but exactly one wavelength apart.

4) Measure the distance between the microphones to find the wavelength (λ).

5) You can then use the formula $v = f \times \lambda$ (see p. 54) to find the speed (v) of the sound waves passing through the air — the frequency (f) is whatever you set the signal generator to in the first place.

6) The speed of sound in air is around 340 m/s, so check your results roughly agree with this.

You can measure the speed of sound in other ways...

For example, you can ask a friend to stand a long distance away (e.g. 100 m) and bang a drum (or do something that makes a loud bang). You can use a stopwatch to measure the time taken between you seeing the person make the noise, and when you hear it. Then use the s = d/t equation (p.1) to work out the speed. Phew. Don't worry, only a few more question pages to go...

Warm-Up and Exam Questions

Here's the final page of warm-up and exam questions of this section. There's still the revision summary to go after these though, but that'll be a doddle after all the hard work you've put in so far.

Warm-Up Questions

1) Describe the difference between an analogue signal and a digital signal.
2) Which type of signal can carry more information, analogue or digital?
3) Is sound a transverse or longitudinal wave?
4) What is the frequency range for human hearing?
5) What happens to sound waves when they hit a soft surface such as carpet?
6) What is the relationship between the loudness of a sound and its amplitude?

Exam Question

1   The diagram shows how an oscilloscope can be used to display sound waves by connecting microphones to it. Trace 1 shows the sound waves detected by microphone 1 and trace 2 shows the sound waves detected by microphone 2.

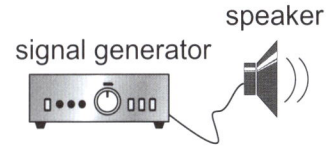

   a) i)   A student uses the equipment. He begins with both microphones at equal distances from the speaker and the signal generator set at a fixed frequency. He gradually moves microphone 2 away from the speaker, which causes the trace shown for microphone 2 to move. He stops moving microphone 2 when the traces for both microphones line up again as shown in the diagram. He measures the distance the microphone has moved.

   Explain how his measurement could be used to work out the speed of sound.
   (2 marks)

   ii) With the signal generator set to 50 Hz, the distance between the microphones was measured to be 6.8 m. Calculate the speed of sound in air. State the correct unit.
   (4 marks)

PAPER 2

   b) One microphone is removed and the signal generator is adjusted. The diagram shows the trace produced on the oscilloscope.

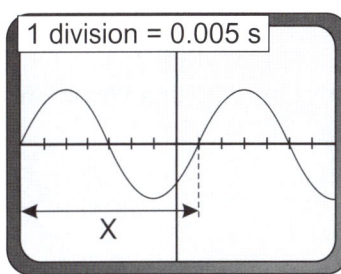

   i)   Which of the following does the quantity marked X represent?

   wavelength   amplitude   frequency   time period
   (1 mark)

   1 division = 0.005 s

   ii) Calculate the frequency of the wave.
   (2 marks)

SECTION 3 — WAVES

Revision Summary for Section 3

Phew, hurrah, yay — made it to the end of this section. A lot of tricky ideas to remember — especially all that stuff on drawing ray diagrams for mirrors and blocks. So get stuck into these revision questions and make sure you've learnt it all...

1) Draw a diagram to illustrate frequency, wavelength and amplitude.
2) What is the formula to calculate the frequency of a wave from the period?
3)* Find the speed of a wave with frequency 50 kHz and wavelength 0.3 cm.
4) What affects the amount a wave diffracts as it passes through a gap?
5) Write down all seven types of EM radiation in order of increasing frequency and decreasing wavelength.
6) Write down all the colours of visible light in order of increasing frequency and decreasing wavelength.
7) Describe one common use of each of the seven types of EM waves.
8) Which is generally more hazardous — low frequency or high frequency EM radiation?
9) Describe the harmful effects on the human body that can be caused by microwaves, infrared, UV and gamma rays.
10) A ray of light hits the surface of a mirror at an incident angle of 10° to the normal. What is the angle of reflection for the ray of light?
11) Copy and complete this diagram, showing:
    a) the reflected rays,
    b) the position of the virtual image. 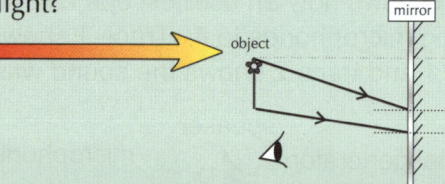
12) Draw a diagram to show the path of a ray of light that travels from air, enters a rectangular block of glass, then exits the block back into air on the other side (use an angle of incidence larger than 0°).
13)* A beam of light travelling through air enters a material with i = 30°. It refracts so that r = 20°. What is the refractive index of the material?
14)* In which of the cases A to D below would the ray of light be totally internally reflected? (The critical angle for glass is approximately 42°.)

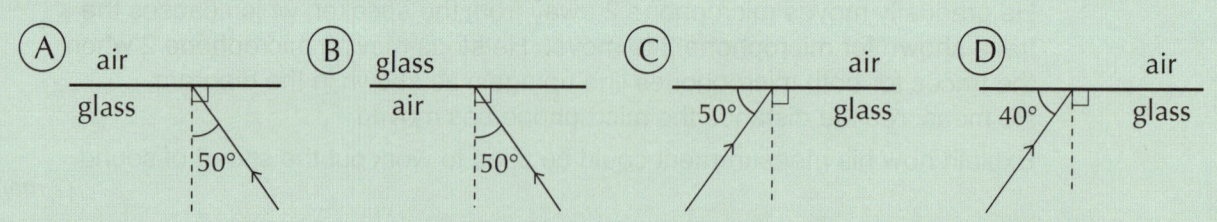

15)* Find the critical angle of a liquid-air boundary if the refractive index of the liquid is 1.35.
16) Draw diagrams illustrating analogue and digital signals. What advantages are there to using digital signals instead of analogue?
17) This is a diagram of a sound wave displayed on an oscilloscope.
    a) What is happening to the loudness of the sound?
    b) What is happening to the pitch of the sound?
18) Explain how you would use an oscilloscope to find the frequency of a sound wave. 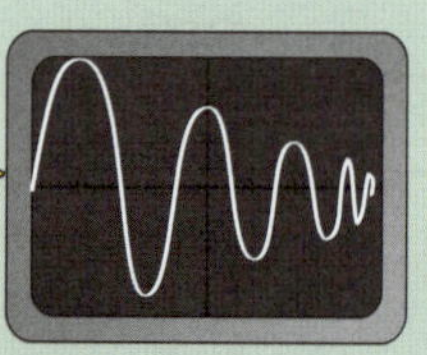
19) Describe an experiment to measure the speed of sound in air.

*Answers on page 187.

SECTION 4 — ENERGY RESOURCES AND ENERGY TRANSFER

Conservation of Energy

I hope you're feeling lively — this module is all about <u>energy</u>. The main thing to always remember about energy is that you can never make it or lose it — you just <u>change it</u> from one form to another.

Learn These *Nine Types* of Energy

You should know all of these <u>well enough</u> by now to list them <u>from memory</u>, including the examples:

1) <u>ELECTRICAL</u> Energy............................. — whenever a <u>current</u> flows.
2) <u>LIGHT</u> Energy..................................... — from the <u>Sun</u>, <u>light bulbs</u>, etc.
3) <u>SOUND</u> Energy.................................. — from <u>loudspeakers</u> or anything <u>noisy</u>.
4) <u>KINETIC</u> Energy or <u>MOVEMENT</u> Energy...... — anything that's <u>moving</u> has it.
5) <u>NUCLEAR</u> Energy............................... — released only from <u>nuclear reactions</u>.
6) <u>THERMAL</u> Energy or <u>HEAT</u> Energy............ — <u>flows</u> from <u>hot objects</u> to colder ones.
7) <u>GRAVITATIONAL POTENTIAL</u> Energy......... — possessed by anything which can <u>fall</u>.
8) <u>ELASTIC POTENTIAL</u> Energy..................... — possessed by <u>springs</u>, <u>elastic</u>, <u>rubber bands</u>, etc.
9) <u>CHEMICAL</u> Energy............................... — possessed by <u>foods</u>, <u>fuels</u>, <u>batteries</u> etc.

Potential and *Chemical* are Forms of *Stored Energy*

The <u>last three</u> above are forms of <u>stored energy</u> because the energy is not obviously <u>doing</u> anything. It's kind of <u>waiting to happen</u>, i.e. waiting to be turned into one of the <u>other</u> forms.

There are Two Types of "Energy Conservation"

Try and get your head round the difference between these two:

1) "<u>ENERGY CONSERVATION</u>" is all about <u>using fewer resources</u> because of the damage they do and because they might <u>run out</u>. That's all <u>environmental stuff</u> — which is important to us, but fairly trivial on a <u>cosmic scale</u>.

2) The "<u>PRINCIPLE OF THE CONSERVATION OF ENERGY</u>", on the other hand, is one of the <u>major cornerstones</u> of modern physics. It's an <u>all-pervading principle</u> which governs the workings of the <u>entire physical Universe</u>. If this principle were not so, then life as we know it would simply cease to be. Got it now? Good. <u>Well don't forget</u>.

The *Principle of the Conservation of Energy* is:

ENERGY CAN NEVER BE <u>CREATED NOR DESTROYED</u> — IT'S ONLY EVER <u>TRANSFERRED</u> FROM ONE FORM TO ANOTHER.

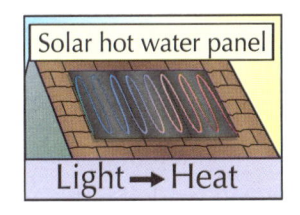

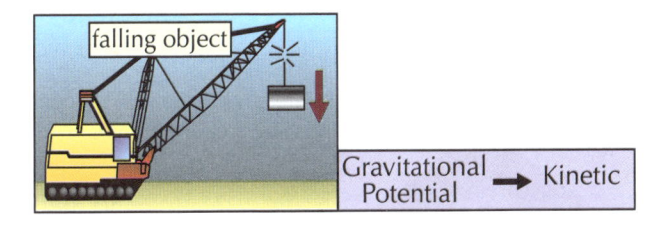

Solar hot water panel: Light → Heat

Falling object: Gravitational Potential → Kinetic

Another <u>important principle</u> which you need to <u>learn</u> is this one:

Energy is <u>only useful</u> when it can be <u>transferred</u> from one form to another.

Efficiency

More! More! Tell me more about energy transfers please! OK, since you insist:

Most Energy Transfers Involve Some Losses, Often as Heat

1) Useful devices are only useful because they can convert energy from one form to another.
2) In doing so, some of the useful input energy is always lost or wasted, often as heat.
3) The less energy that is wasted, the more efficient the device is said to be.
4) The energy flow diagram is pretty much the same for all devices:

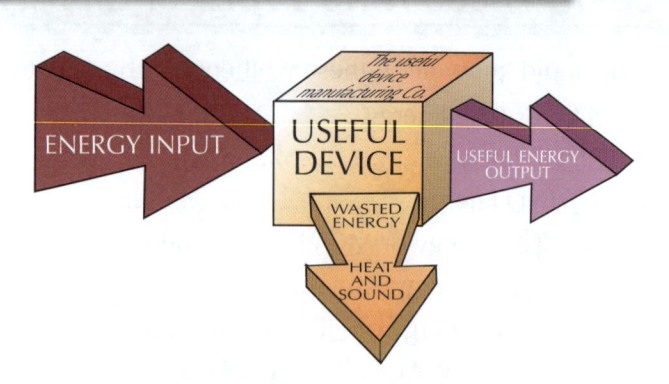

It's Really Simple to Calculate the Efficiency...

A machine is a device which turns one type of energy into another.
The efficiency of any device is defined as:

$$\text{Efficiency} = \frac{\text{Useful Energy OUTPUT}}{\text{Total Energy INPUT}}$$

You can give efficiency as a decimal or percentage, e.g. 0.75 or 75%.

How to Use the Formula — Nothing to it

1) You find how much energy is supplied to a machine. (The Total Energy INPUT.)
2) You find how much useful energy the machine delivers. (The Useful Energy OUTPUT.) An exam question either tells you this directly or tells you how much it wastes as heat/sound.
3) Either way, you get those two important numbers and then just divide the smaller one by the bigger one to get a value for efficiency somewhere between 0 and 1 (or 0 and 100%). Easy.
4) The other way they might ask it is to tell you the efficiency and the input energy and ask for the energy output — so you need to be able to swap the formula round. In comes the formula triangle...

The Efficiency Formula Triangle:

Formula triangles are well useful — they're worth getting used to. (Especially if you're doing any science beyond this level.) Here's a reminder of how to use them...

Write the bits of the formula in the triangle like this:

$$\frac{\text{Useful Output}}{\text{Efficiency} \times \text{Total Input}}$$

1) Put your finger over the thing you're trying to find.
2) Read off what's left — that's how you work out your answer.
3) E.g. cover up Total Input and you're left with $\frac{\text{Useful Output}}{\text{Efficiency}}$.

So that's how you work it out:

$$\text{Total Input} = \frac{\text{Useful Output}}{\text{Efficiency}}$$

4) Magic. You just need to learn that triangle.

Energy Transfers

An open fire looks cosy, but a lot of its heat energy goes straight up the chimney, instead of heating up your living room. All this energy is 'wasted', so open fires aren't very efficient.

Almost All Devices Waste Energy

For any specific example you can give more detail about the types of energy being input and output, but remember this:

> **No device is 100% efficient and the wasted energy is always dissipated as heat.**

Dissipated means spread out and lost.

Ultimately, all energy ends up as heat energy. If you use an electric drill, it gives out various types of energy but they all quickly end up as heat. That's an important thing to realise.

We Call It Wasted Energy Because We Can't Do Anything Useful with It

1) Useful energy is concentrated energy. As you know, the entire energy output by a machine, both useful and wasted, eventually ends up as heat.

2) This heat is transferred to cooler surroundings, which then become warmer.

3) As the heat is transferred to cooler surroundings, the energy becomes less concentrated — it dissipates.

4) According to the Principle of Conservation of Energy, the total amount of energy stays the same. So the energy is still there, but it can't be easily used or collected back in again.

Revise this — it won't be wasted energy

So I think the take-home message here is: all the energy given out by a machine ultimately ends up as heat. Got that? Good. Because there's more on energy transfers coming up. You lucky thing.

Energy Transfers

In the exam, they can ask you about any device or energy transfer system they feel like. So it's no good just learning the examples on this page — you need to understand the patterns.

They Like Giving Exam Questions on Energy Transfers

ELECTRICAL DEVICES convert **ELECTRICAL ENERGY** into sound, light, heat, etc.

(and, of course, a bit of wasted heat)

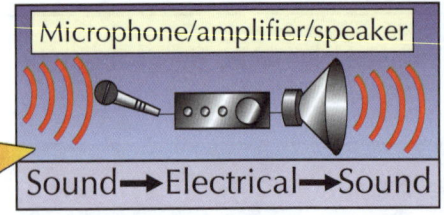

Microphone/amplifier/speaker: Sound → Electrical → Sound

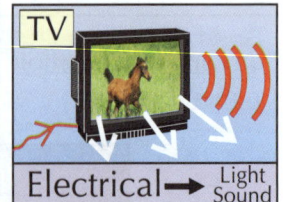

TV: Electrical → Light, Sound

BATTERIES convert **CHEMICAL ENERGY** to **ELECTRICAL** to run electric devices.

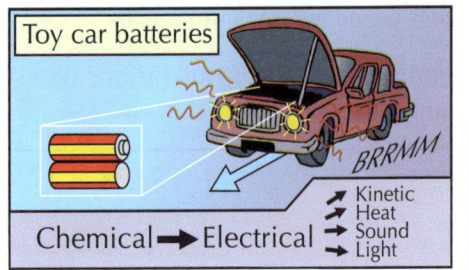

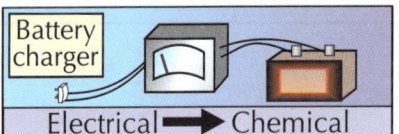

(and, of course, there's a bit of wasted heat)

Toy car batteries: Chemical → Electrical → Kinetic, Heat, Sound, Light

Battery charger: Electrical → Chemical

GRAVITATIONAL POTENTIAL ENERGY always gets converted into **KINETIC ENERGY FIRST**...

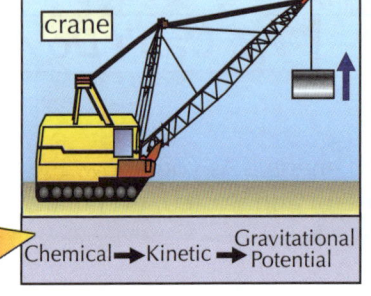

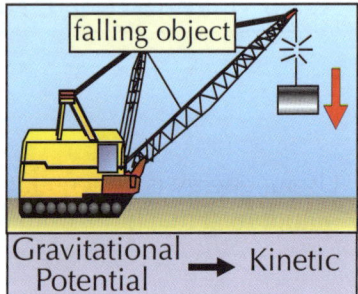

crane: Chemical → Kinetic → Gravitational Potential

falling object: Gravitational Potential → Kinetic

...and so does **ELASTIC POTENTIAL ENERGY**.

(Now, repeat after me — and there's a bit of wasted heat)

Archer/bow: Chemical → Elastic potential

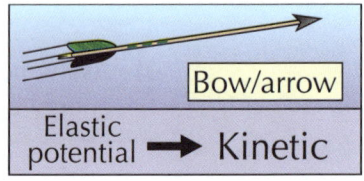

Bow/arrow: Elastic potential → Kinetic

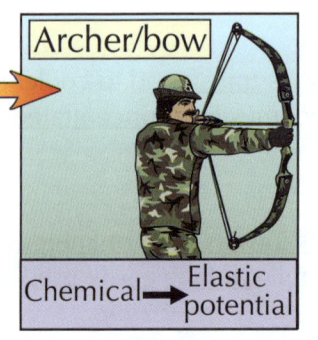

And don't forget — all types of energy are measured in joules.

ELECTRICITY GENERATION always involves converting other forms of energy into **ELECTRICAL ENERGY** (see pages 93-97).

(and guess what — there's a bit of wasted heat)

SECTION 4 — ENERGY RESOURCES AND ENERGY TRANSFER

Sankey Diagrams

Another opportunity for a MATHS question. Fantastic. Here's what Sankey diagrams are all about...

The Thickness of the Arrow Represents the Amount of Energy

The idea of Sankey (energy transformation) diagrams is to make it easy to see at a glance how much of the input energy is being usefully employed compared with how much is being wasted.

The thicker the arrow, the more energy it represents — so you see a big thick arrow going in, then several smaller arrows going off it to show the different energy transformations taking place.

You can have either a little sketch or a properly detailed diagram where the width of each arrow is proportional to the number of joules it represents.

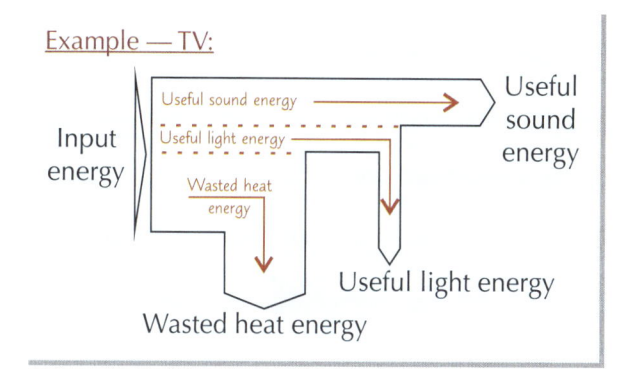

Example — TV:

Example — Sankey Diagram for a Simple Motor:

HERE'S THE SKETCH VERSION:

You don't know the actual amounts, but you can see that most of the energy is being wasted, and that it's mostly wasted as heat.

EXAM QUESTIONS:
With sketches, you might be asked to compare two different devices and say which is more efficient. You generally want to be looking for the one with the thickest useful energy arrow(s).

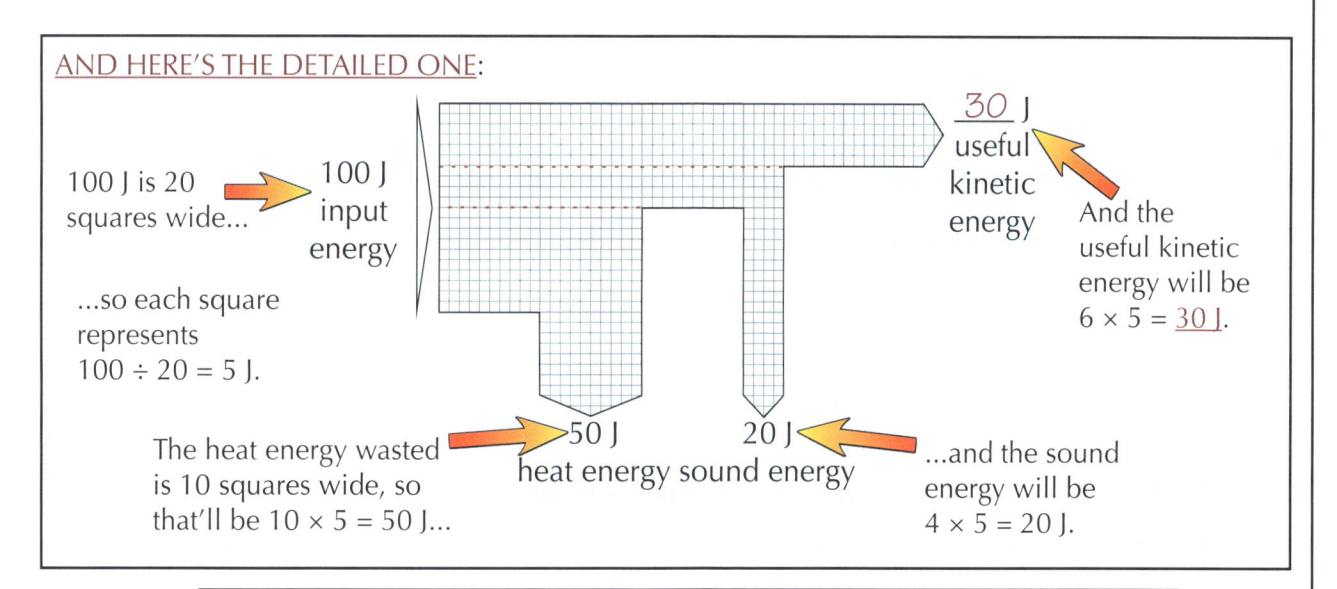

AND HERE'S THE DETAILED ONE:

100 J is 20 squares wide...

...so each square represents 100 ÷ 20 = 5 J.

The heat energy wasted is 10 squares wide, so that'll be 10 × 5 = 50 J...

And the useful kinetic energy will be 6 × 5 = 30 J.

...and the sound energy will be 4 × 5 = 20 J.

EXAM QUESTIONS:
In an exam, the most likely question you'll get about detailed Sankey diagrams is filling in one of the numbers or calculating the efficiency. The efficiency is straightforward enough if you can work out the numbers (see p. 78).

SECTION 4 — ENERGY RESOURCES AND ENERGY TRANSFER

Warm-Up and Exam Questions

You must be getting used to the routine by now — the warm-up questions get you, well, warmed up, and the exam questions give you some idea of what you'll have to cope with on the day.

Warm-Up Questions

1) What type of energy is stored in food?
2) State the principle of the conservation of energy.
3) What is wasted energy always dissipated as?
4) List the energy transfers that take place when an archer fires an arrow from a bow.

Exam Questions

1   This question is about energy transfers.

Copy and complete the table below showing the energy input and useful energy output for various devices.

Device	Energy input	Useful energy output
A spring-loaded catapult		kinetic energy
A portable radio	chemical energy	
	electrical energy	heat energy

(3 marks)

2   Torch A transfers 20 J of chemical energy per second. It emits 8 J of light energy, 11.5 J of heat energy and 0.5 J of sound energy every second.

a) Name the useful output energy of torch A.

(1 mark)

b) i) State the equation linking efficiency, useful energy output and total energy input.

(1 mark)

   ii) Calculate the efficiency of torch A.

(2 marks)

c) Torch B has an efficiency of 0.55 and emits 10 J of useful light energy each second. Calculate how much energy is supplied to the torch per second.

(2 marks)

d) Each torch is powered by an identical battery. A student claims that the battery in torch B will go 'flat' quicker than in torch A because it emits more light energy. Do you agree or disagree? Explain your answer.

(1 mark)

Exam Questions

3   The manufacturer of a toy crane creates a Sankey diagram to show the energy transfers involved when the crane is in operation.

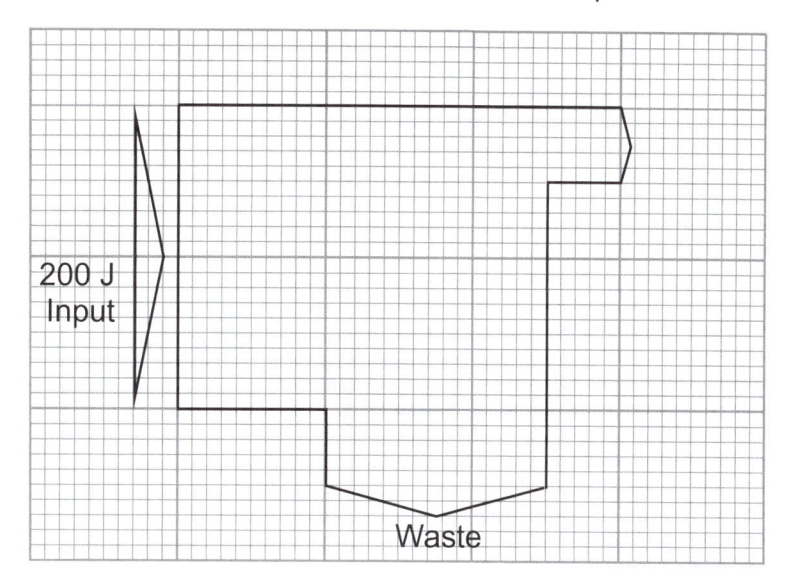

200 J Input

Waste

a) Calculate the value represented by each small square.

(1 mark)

b) Calculate how much energy is transferred usefully by the toy crane for every 200 J of energy supplied.

(1 mark)

4   A winch uses a cable and a hook to lift a weight by winding the cable around a drum. On the right is a Sankey diagram for the winch lifting a weight.

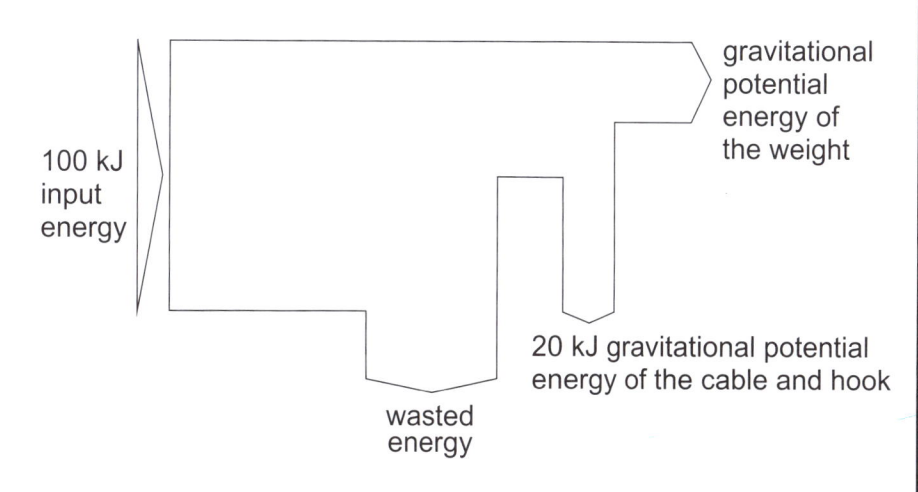

100 kJ input energy → gravitational potential energy of the weight
20 kJ gravitational potential energy of the cable and hook
wasted energy

a) Suggest **one** type of energy that contributes to the energy wasted by the winch.

(1 mark)

b) The winch wastes a total of 50 kJ.
Calculate the gravitational potential energy transferred to the weight by the winch.

(1 mark)

c) The weight is released and falls to the ground. 1.5 kJ of energy is transferred into heat and sound energy during the fall due to the air resistance on the weight. Sketch and label a Sankey diagram to show the energy transfers that take place during the weight's fall.

(3 marks)

Heat Transfer

Heat energy tends to flow away from a hotter object to its cooler surroundings. But then you knew that already. I would hope.

Heat is Transferred in Three Different Ways

1) Heat energy can be transferred by radiation, conduction or convection.
2) Thermal (infrared) radiation is the transfer of heat energy by electromagnetic waves (see below).
3) Conduction and convection involve the transfer of energy by particles.
4) Conduction is the main form of heat transfer in solids (see next page).
5) Convection is the main form of heat transfer in liquids and gases. See next page for more on convection.
6) Emission of thermal radiation occurs in solids, liquids and gases. Any object can both absorb and emit heat radiation, whether or not conduction or convection are also taking place.
7) The bigger the temperature difference, the faster heat is transferred between a body and its surroundings. Kinda makes sense.

Thermal Radiation Involves Emission of Electromagnetic Waves

Heat radiation can also be called infrared radiation, and it consists purely of electromagnetic waves of a certain range of frequencies. It's next to visible light in the electromagnetic spectrum (see p. 56).

1) All objects are continually emitting and absorbing heat radiation.
2) An object that's hotter than its surroundings emits more radiation than it absorbs (as it cools down). And an object that's cooler than its surroundings absorbs more radiation than it emits (as it warms up).
3) You can feel this heat radiation if you stand near something hot like a fire or if you put your hand just above the bonnet of a recently parked car.

(recently parked car)   (after an hour or so)

Heat radiation and infrared radiation are the same thing

Of the three heat transfer methods, radiation is the only one that works through a vacuum — since it doesn't rely on there being any particles about. And that's how we can get heat from the Sun across the great vacuum of space, of course. If it wasn't for infrared radiation, we'd all be jolly cold.

Heat Conduction and Convection

Two more methods of heat transfer here: conduction (which happens mainly in solids) and convection (which only happens in liquids and gases).

Conduction of Heat — Occurs Mainly in Solids

In a solid, the particles are held tightly together. So when one particle vibrates, it collides with other particles nearby and the vibrations quickly pass from particle to particle.

HOT → HEAT FLOW → **COLD**

CONDUCTION OF HEAT is the process where VIBRATING PARTICLES pass on their EXTRA KINETIC ENERGY (see p. 91) to NEIGHBOURING PARTICLES.

This process continues throughout the solid and gradually some of the extra kinetic energy (or heat) is passed all the way through the solid, causing a rise in temperature at the other side of the solid. And hence an increase in the heat radiating from its surface.

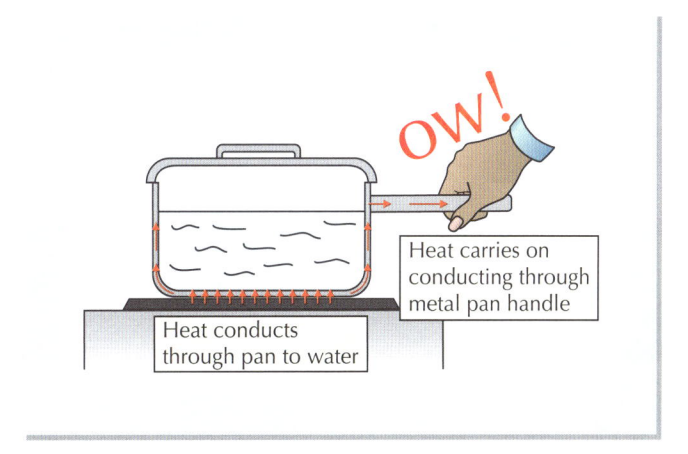

ow!

Heat carries on conducting through metal pan handle

Heat conducts through pan to water

Convection of Heat — Liquids and Gases Only

CONVECTION occurs when the more energetic particles MOVE from the HOTTER REGION to the COOLER REGION — AND TAKE THEIR HEAT ENERGY WITH THEM.

1) This is how immersion heaters in kettles and hot water tanks and (unsurprisingly) convector heaters work. Immersion heaters are explained in more detail on the next page.
2) Convection simply can't happen in solids because the particles can't move (apart from vibrating, see page 104).

SECTION 4 — ENERGY RESOURCES AND ENERGY TRANSFER

Examples of Heat Convection

Here are some everyday examples of convection in action...

The *Immersion Heater* Example

1) Heat energy is transferred from the heater coils to the water by conduction (particle collisions).

2) The particles near the coils get more energy, so they start moving around faster.

3) This means there's more distance between them, i.e. the water expands and becomes less dense.

4) This reduction in density means that hotter water tends to rise above the denser, cooler water.

5) As the hot water rises it displaces (moves) the colder water out of the way, making it sink towards the heater coils.

6) This cold water is then heated by the coils and rises — and so it goes on. You end up with convection currents going up, round and down, circulating the heat energy through the water.

Fast-moving particles collide with slow-moving particles & transfer heat

Less dense water rises → Water cools and becomes more dense
Hot water less dense → Denser water sinks again
Water heats

Water (and heat) circulates by convection
Heater coils
Almost no conduction
Water stays cold below the heater

Note that convection is most efficient in roundish or squarish containers, because they allow the convection currents to work best. Shallow, wide containers or tall, thin ones just don't work quite so well.

Also note that because the hot water rises (because of the lower density) you only get convection currents in the water above the heater. The water below it stays cold because there's almost no conduction.

CONVECTION CURRENTS are all about CHANGES IN DENSITY. Remember that.

The *Radiator* Example

1) Heating a room with a radiator relies on convection currents too.

2) Hot, less dense air by the radiator rises and denser, cooler air flows to replace it.

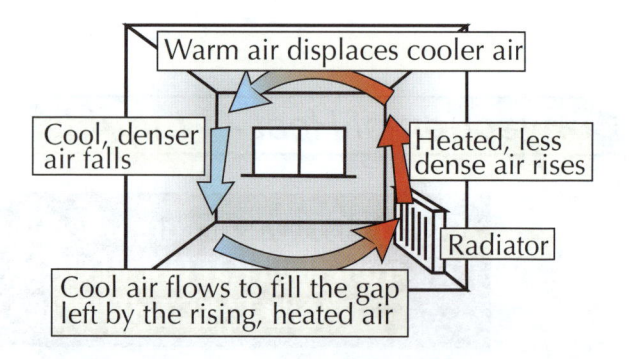

Warm air displaces cooler air
Cool, denser air falls
Heated, less dense air rises
Radiator
Cool air flows to fill the gap left by the rising, heated air

There's a great experiment with purple crystals to show this

You stick some potassium permanganate crystals in the bottom of a beaker of cold water, then heat it gently over a Bunsen flame. The potassium permanganate starts to dissolve and make a gorgeous bright purple solution that gets moved around the beaker by the convection currents as the water heats.

Reducing Energy Transfers

Heat transfer's great... but not if you're feeling a bit chilly. There are loads of things you can do to reduce heat escaping from buildings by radiation, convection and conduction. Your body's got a few tricks up its sleeve to help keep you warm (and cool you down) too.

Insulating Your House Reduces Heat Transfer

Loft Insulation
A thick layer of fibreglass wool laid out across the loft floor and ceiling reduces heat loss from the house by conduction and radiation.

Hot Water Tank Jacket
Lagging such as fibreglass wool reduces conduction and radiation.

Draught-proofing
Strips of foam and plastic around doors and windows stop draughts of cold air blowing in, i.e. they reduce heat loss due to convection.

Double Glazing
Two layers of glass with a narrow air gap between reduce conduction and convection.

Cavity Wall Insulation
Foam squirted into the gap between the bricks stops convection currents being set up in the gap and radiation across the gap. The insulating foam and the air pockets trapped in it (air is an insulator) also helps reduce heat loss by conduction.

Thick Curtains
Big bits of cloth over the window to reduce heat loss by conduction and radiation.

Humans Have Ways of Reducing Heat Transfer Too

1) In the cold, the hairs on your skin 'stand up' to trap a thicker layer of insulating air around the body. This limits the amount of heat loss by convection.

2) Humans wear layers of clothes to reduce heat transfer (that's right — they're not just there to look good). The pockets of air trapped in the clothes and between layers mainly reduce heat transfer by conduction and convection (remember... air is an insulator).

3) Clothes also reduce heat loss by radiation from the body, as the material absorbs some heat radiated out by our bodies.

Section 4 — Energy Resources and Energy Transfer

Warm-Up and Exam Questions

Hopefully the last few pages have stuck, but there's only one way to check — and that's with some questions. Warm-up questions to get you started, and exam questions to really get your teeth into.

Warm-Up Questions

1) What is thermal (infrared) radiation?
2) How does heat conduction work?
3) Why does heat convection only take place in liquids and gases?
4) Explain how an immersion heater works.
5) Explain how clothes reduce heat loss from the human body.

Exam Questions

1   Three flasks, each containing 100 ml of water, are placed in closed boxes filled with a clear gel at an initial temperature of 50 °C. The water in each flask is at a different temperature, as shown.

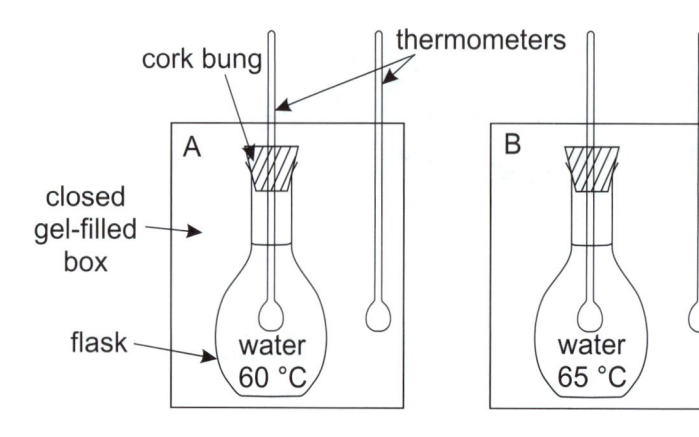

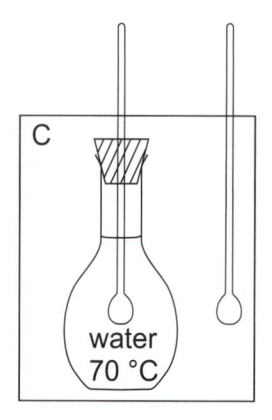

(Diagram: Three gel-filled boxes A, B, C, each with a cork bung, thermometers, and a flask of water. A: water at 60 °C, B: water at 65 °C, C: water at 70 °C.)

   a) Name **two** ways in which the flasks will transfer heat to the gel surrounding them.
   (2 marks)

   b) State which flask will transfer heat to the gel the fastest. Explain your answer.
   (2 marks)

2   A homeowner is worried that her house is losing a lot of heat energy through its walls and windows.

   a) The outer walls of the house are made up of two layers of bricks separated by an air cavity.
      i) Which type of energy transfer does having an air gap in the wall help to reduce?
      (1 mark)

      ii) The homeowner is considering having cavity wall insulation installed. State **one** type of energy transfer this will help to reduce. Explain your answer.
      (1 mark)

   b) Suggest **two** ways in which heat loss through or around windows can be reduced. Explain how each of your suggestions will help reduce heat loss.
   (4 marks)

SECTION 4 — ENERGY RESOURCES AND ENERGY TRANSFER

Work

Work (like a lot of things) means something slightly different in Physics than it does in everyday life.

"Work Done" is Just "Energy Transferred"

When a force moves an object, energy is transferred and work is done.

That statement sounds far more complicated than it needs to. Try this:

1) Whenever something moves, something else is providing some sort of "effort" to move it.
2) The thing putting the effort in needs a supply of energy (like fuel or food or electricity etc.).
3) It then does "work" by moving the object — and one way or another it transfers the energy it receives (as fuel) into other forms.
4) Whether this energy is transferred "usefully" (e.g. by lifting a load) or is "wasted" (e.g. lost as heat), you can still say that "work is done". Just like Batman and Bruce Wayne, "work done" and "energy transferred" are indeed "one and the same". (And they're both in joules.)
5) When you do work against friction (see page 9), most of the energy gets transformed into heat, and usually some into sound. This is generally "wasted" energy.

And Another Formula to Learn...

Work Done = Force × Distance moved

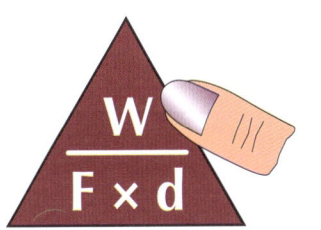

This formula only works if the force is in exactly the same direction as the movement.

Whether the force is friction or weight or tension in a rope, it's always the same. To find how much work has been done (in joules), you just multiply the force in newtons by the distance moved in metres. Easy as that. I'll show you...

Example:

Some hooligan kids drag an old tractor tyre 5 m over flat ground. They pull with a total force of 340 N. Find the work done.

Answer: W = F × d = 340 × 5 = 1700 J. Phew — easy peasy isn't it?

Section 4 — Energy Resources and Energy Transfer

Power

Power is about the rate of energy transfer — and energy is transferred wherever you look.

Power is the 'Rate of Doing Work' — i.e. How Much **per Second**

1) POWER is not the same thing as force, nor energy. A powerful machine is not necessarily one which can exert a strong force (though it usually ends up that way).

2) A POWERFUL machine is one which transfers A LOT OF ENERGY IN A SHORT SPACE OF TIME.

3) We say power is the rate of energy transfer, or the rate of doing work.

4) This is the very easy formula for power:

$$\text{Power} = \frac{\text{Work done}}{\text{Time taken}}$$

$$\frac{W}{P \times t}$$

Example:

A motor transfers 4.8 kJ of useful energy in 2 minutes. Find its power output.

1 kJ = 1000 J

ANSWER: P = W / t = 4800/120 = 40 W (or 40 J/s)

(Note that the kJ had to be turned into J, and the minutes into seconds.)

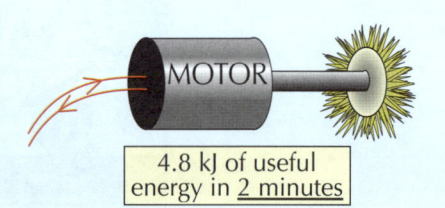

Power is **Measured in Watts** *(or J/s)*

1) The proper unit of power is the watt.

One watt = 1 joule of energy transferred per second.

2) Power means 'how much energy per second', so watts are the same as 'joules per second' (J/s).

3) Don't ever say 'watts per second' — it's nonsense.

You've got the power

The power of a car is often measured in a funny unit called brake horsepower. 1 horsepower is the rate of work when a horse raises a mass of 550 lb through a height of 1 ft in 1 second... Hmm. I'd stick to watts if I were you. Make sure you've learnt the formula for power anyway.

Kinetic and Gravitational Potential Energy

Kinetic Energy is Energy of Movement

1) Anything which is moving has kinetic energy.
2) The kinetic energy of something depends both on its mass and speed. The greater its mass and the faster it's going, the bigger its kinetic energy will be.
3) There's a slightly tricky formula for it, so you have to concentrate a little bit harder for this one. But hey, that's life — it can be real tough sometimes:

$$\text{Kinetic Energy} = \tfrac{1}{2} \times \text{mass} \times \text{speed}^2$$

$$\frac{KE}{\tfrac{1}{2} \times m \times v^2}$$

Example: A car of mass 2450 kg is travelling at 38 m/s. Calculate its kinetic energy.

Answer: It's pretty easy. You just plug the numbers into the formula — but watch the "v^2" !
KE = $\tfrac{1}{2}mv^2$ = $\tfrac{1}{2} \times 2450 \times 38^2$ = 1 768 900 J (joules because it's energy)
(When the car stops suddenly, all this energy is dissipated as heat at the brakes — it's a lot of heat.)

- small mass, not fast — low kinetic energy
- big fast lorries Ltd
- big mass, real fast — high kinetic energy

Gravitational Potential Energy is Energy Due to Height

Gravitational potential energy (GPE) is the energy stored in an object of mass m (in kg) when you raise it to a height h (in m) against gravity g (about 10 m/s²):

$$\text{Gravitational Potential Energy} = m \times g \times h$$

$$\frac{GPE}{m \times g \times h}$$

You can think of GPE as a way of storing kinetic energy. You have to put work in to move something to increase its gravitational potential energy, and that energy is only released when the object falls (movement again).

Falling Objects Convert GPE into KE

When something falls, its gravitational potential energy is converted into kinetic energy. So the further it falls, the faster it goes. In practice, some of the GPE will be dissipated as heat due to air resistance, but in exam questions they'll likely say you can ignore air resistance, in which case you'll just need to remember this simple and really quite obvious formula:

Kinetic Energy gained = Gravitational Potential Energy lost

It's all to do with the Principle of the Conservation of Energy — see page 77.

SECTION 4 — ENERGY RESOURCES AND ENERGY TRANSFER

Warm-Up and Exam Questions

There were lots of definitions and equations to get to grips with on the last few pages.
Try these questions to see what you can remember.

Warm-Up Questions

1) What is meant by the work done by a force?
2) Define power. What's the formula linking power and work done?
3) State the equation linking kinetic energy, mass and speed.

Exam Questions

1   A student kicks a football, transferring 50 J of energy to the ball.
    a) How much work does the student do when she kicks the ball?
        State the correct unit.
        (1 mark)

    b) The student kicks the ball along the ground with a force of 250 N.
        Calculate the distance over which her foot is in contact with the ball.
        (3 marks)

2   A student builds a model boat with a 1 litre petrol tank and a 150 W petrol motor.
    a) Calculate the energy that the model boat transfers in 10 minutes.
        (2 marks)

    b) The motor provides a driving force of 155 N.
        Calculate work done by the motor to move the boat 1.2 m.
        (2 marks)

    c) The boat's motor is replaced with a motor that has a higher power, but has the same
        fuel efficiency. State and explain how you would expect this change to affect the
        maximum speed and how often the boat will need refuelling.
        (4 marks)

3   A roller coaster cart with a mass of 105 kg is rolling along a horizontal track at 2.39 m/s.

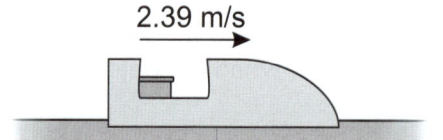

    a) Calculate the kinetic energy of the cart.
        (3 marks)

    b) The cart reaches a downhill slope in the track with a vertical height of 20.2 m.
        It rolls down the slope with no driving force other than gravity.
        i) Calculate the gravitational potential energy lost
            by the cart as it rolls down the slope.
            (3 marks)

        ii) Assuming no friction acts against the cart, explain what happens to the
            gravitational potential energy that is lost.
            (1 mark)

SECTION 4 — ENERGY RESOURCES AND ENERGY TRANSFER

Non-Renewable Energy and Power Stations

There are different types of energy resource.
They fit into two broad types: renewable and non-renewable.

Non-Renewable Energy Resources Will Run Out One Day

The non-renewables are the three FOSSIL FUELS and NUCLEAR:

1) Coal
2) Oil
3) Natural gas
4) Nuclear fuels (uranium and plutonium) (see p.94)

a) They will all 'run out' one day.
b) They all do damage to the environment.
c) But they provide most of our energy.

Most Power Stations Use Steam to Drive a Turbine

Most of the electricity we use is generated from the four NON-RENEWABLE sources of energy (coal, oil, natural gas and nuclear) in big power stations, which are all pretty much the same apart from the boiler. Learn the basic features of the typical power station shown here and the energy transfers involved.

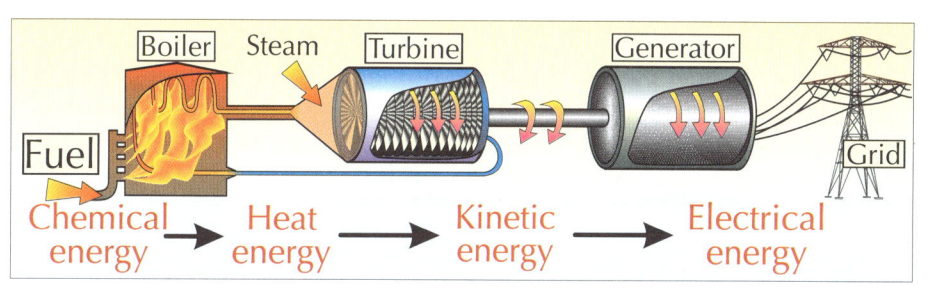

Chemical energy → Heat energy → Kinetic energy → Electrical energy

The heat energy released from the fuel is used to heat water to create steam which turns a turbine.

Fossil Fuels are Linked to Environmental Problems

Burning fossil fuels (oil, natural gas and coal) causes a lot of problems, mainly environmental. But at the moment we still rely on them the most to provide the energy needed to generate electricity.

ADVANTAGES:

1) Burning fossil fuels releases a lot of energy, relatively cheaply.
2) Energy from fossil fuels doesn't rely on the weather, like a lot of renewable energy (see pages 94-97), so it's a reliable energy source.
3) We have lots of fossil fuel power stations already, so we don't need to spend money on new technology to use them.

DISADVANTAGES:

1) All three fossil fuels release carbon dioxide (CO_2) into the atmosphere when burned in power stations. All this CO_2 contributes to global warming and climate change.
2) Burning coal and oil also releases sulfur dioxide (SO_2), which causes acid rain. Acid rain can harm trees and soils and can have a huge impact on wildlife.
3) And a massive disadvantage of using fossil fuels is that THEY'RE EVENTUALLY GOING TO RUN OUT.

SECTION 4 — ENERGY RESOURCES AND ENERGY TRANSFER

Nuclear and Geothermal Energy

Well, who'd have thought... there's energy lurking about inside atoms and deep underground.

Nuclear Reactors are Just Fancy Boilers

1) A nuclear power station is mostly the same as the one on p. 93. The difference is that nuclear fission (p. 135), e.g. of uranium, produces the heat to make steam to drive turbines etc., rather than burning. So the boiler is a bit different:

2) During the process, energy is converted from nuclear energy to heat energy, to kinetic energy, and finally to electrical energy.

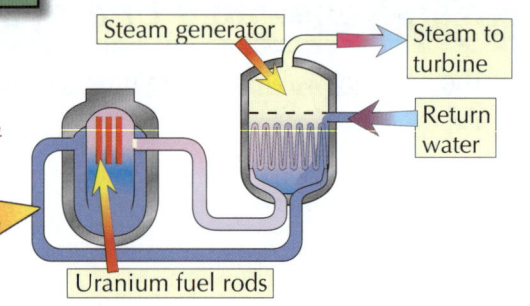

3) Nuclear reactors are expensive to build and maintain, and take longer to start up than fossil fuel ones.

4) Processing the uranium before you use it causes pollution, and there's always a risk of leaks of radioactive material, or even a major catastrophe like at Chernobyl.

5) A big problem with nuclear power is the radioactive waste that you always get.

6) When they're too old and inefficient, nuclear power stations have to be decommissioned (shut down and made safe) — that's expensive too.

7) But there are many advantages to nuclear power. It doesn't produce any of the greenhouse gases which contribute to global warming. Also, there's still plenty of uranium left in the ground (although it can take a lot of money and energy to make it suitable for use in a reactor).

Geothermal Energy — Heat from Underground

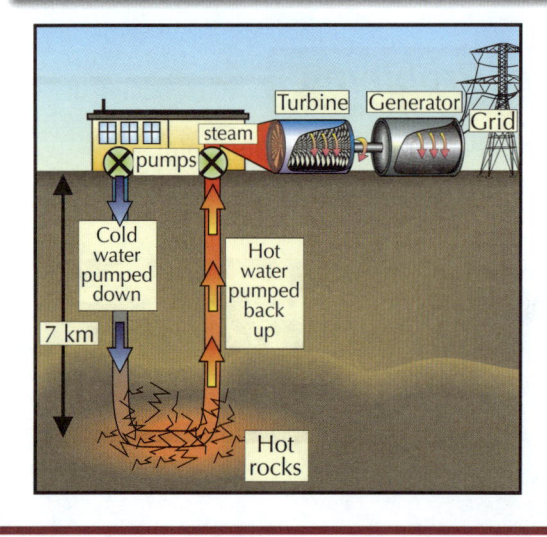

1) This is only possible in certain places where hot rocks lie quite near to the surface. The source of much of the heat is the slow decay of various radioactive elements including uranium deep inside the Earth.

2) Water is pumped in pipes down to the hot rocks and forced back up due to pressure to turn a turbine which drives a generator. So the energy is transferred from heat to kinetic to electrical.

3) In some places, geothermal heat is used to heat buildings directly.

4) This is actually brilliant, free, renewable energy with no real environmental problems.

5) The main drawback is the cost of drilling down several km.

6) The cost of building a power plant is often high compared to the amount of energy we can get out of it.

7) So there are very few places where this seems to be an economic option (for now).

Section 4 — Energy Resources and Energy Transfer

Wind and Wave Energy

A nice, cool breeze and waves lapping against the shore... two more ways of generating electricity.

Wind Farms — Lots of Wind Turbines

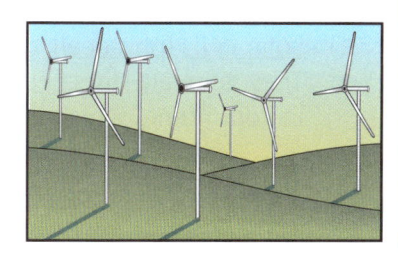

1) Wind power involves putting lots of wind turbines up in exposed places — like on moors, around the coast or out at sea.
2) Wind turbines convert the kinetic energy of moving air into electrical energy. Wind turns the blades, which turn a generator inside it.
3) Wind turbines are quite cheap to run — they're very tough and reliable, and the wind is free.
4) Even better, wind power doesn't produce any polluting waste and it's renewable — the wind's never going to run out.
5) But there are disadvantages. They spoil the view. You need about 1500 wind turbines to replace one coal-fired power station and 1500 of them cover a lot of ground — which would have a big effect on the scenery. And they can be very noisy, which can be annoying for people living nearby.
6) Another problem is that sometimes the wind isn't strong enough to generate any power. It's also impossible to increase supply when there's extra demand (e.g. when Coronation Street starts).
7) And although the wind is free, it's expensive to set up a wind farm, especially out at sea.

Wave Power — Lots of Little Wave Converters

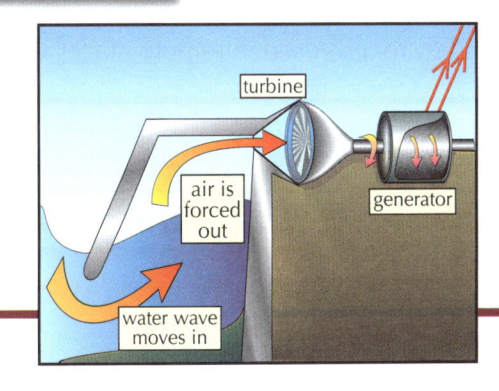

1) One way of harvesting wave power is with lots of small wave converters located around the coast. As waves come in to the shore they provide an up and down motion which can be used to drive a generator.
2) The kinetic energy of the waves is converted into electrical energy.
3) There's no pollution and it's renewable.
4) The main problems are spoiling the view and being a hazard to boats.
5) It's fairly unreliable, since waves tend to die out when the wind drops.
6) Initial costs are high but there are no fuel costs and minimal running costs. Wave power is unlikely to provide energy on a large scale but it can be very useful on small islands.

More renewable energy resources to learn

You need to be able to describe the energy transfers involved in all these methods of generating electricity, as well as the ones described over the next few pages. If you're sitting Paper 2, you also need to be able to write about the advantages and disadvantages of each method.

Section 4 — Energy Resources and Energy Transfer

Solar Energy

You Can **Capture** the Sun's Energy Using **Solar Cells**

1) Solar cells (photocells) transform light energy from the Sun directly into electrical energy. They generate direct current (d.c.) — the same as a battery (not like the mains electricity in your home, which is a.c. (alternating current) — see p. 38).

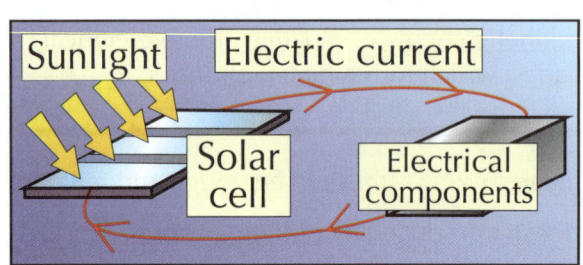

2) The Sun provides a renewable energy resource — it won't run out (not for 5 billion years anyway).

3) Solar cells are very expensive initially, but after that the energy is free and running costs are almost nil. And there's no pollution (although they use a fair bit of energy to manufacture in the first place).

4) They're usually used to generate electricity on a relatively small scale, e.g. powering individual homes.

5) It's often not practical or too expensive to connect them to the National Grid — the cost of connecting them to the National Grid can be enormous compared with the value of the electricity generated. Solar cells can only generate enough electricity to be useful if they have enough sunlight — which can be a problem at night (and in winter in some places). But the cells can be linked to rechargeable batteries to create a system that can store energy during the day for use at night.

6) Solar cells are often the best way to power calculators or watches that don't use much energy. They're also used in remote places where there's not much choice (e.g. deserts) and in satellites.

Solar Heating Systems — No Complex Mechanical Stuff

Solar Panels

1) Solar panels are more simple than solar cells — they're basically just black water pipes inside a glass box.

2) The glass lets heat and light from the Sun in, which is then absorbed by the black pipes and heats up the water.

3) Like solar cells, they cost money to set up, but are renewable and free after that. They're only used for small-scale energy production.

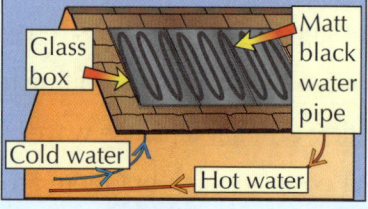

Cooking with Solar Power

If you get a curved mirror, then you can focus the Sun's light and heat. This is what happens in a solar oven. They provide a renewable energy resource for outdoor cooking. But they're slow, bulky and unreliable — they need strong sunlight to work.

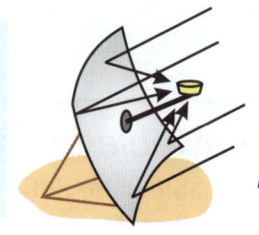

All the radiation that lands on the curved mirror is focused right on your pan.

SECTION 4 — ENERGY RESOURCES AND ENERGY TRANSFER

Generating Electricity Using Water

Water, water, everywhere. Perfect for generating electricity.

Tidal Barrages Generate Energy When the Tide Goes In and Out

1) Tidal barrages are big dams built across river estuaries, with turbines in them. As the tide comes in it fills up the estuary to a height of several metres. This water can then be allowed out through turbines at a controlled speed. It also drives the turbines on the way in.

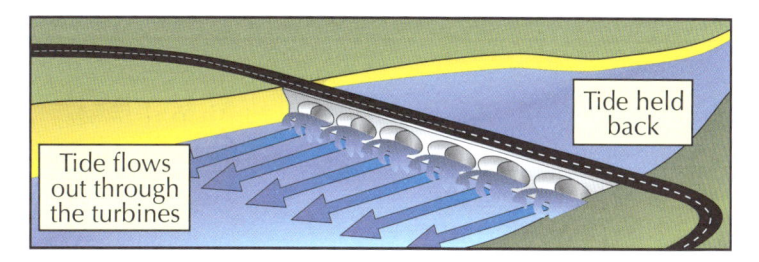

2) The kinetic energy of the water is converted into electrical energy by the turbines and a generator.

3) There's no pollution and it's renewable. The main problems are preventing free access by boats, spoiling the view and altering the habitat of the wildlife.

4) Tides are pretty reliable, but the height of the tide is variable so lower tides will provide less energy than higher ones.

5) Initial costs are moderately high, but there's no fuel costs and minimal running costs.

Hydroelectricity — Catching Rainwater

1) Hydroelectric power often requires the flooding of a valley by building a big dam. Rainwater is caught and allowed out through turbines, converting the gravitational potential energy of the water to kinetic energy as it falls, which is then converted to electrical energy by the generator.

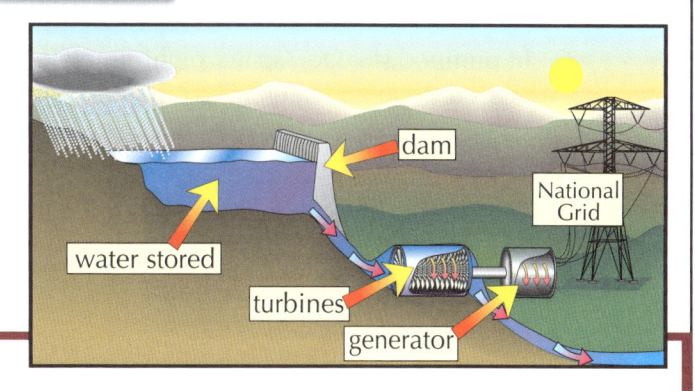

2) It's a renewable energy resource.

3) There is no pollution (as such), but there's a big impact on the environment due to flooding the valley (rotting vegetation releases methane and CO_2) and possible loss of habitat for some species. The reservoirs can also look very unsightly when they dry up. Location in remote valleys can avoid some of these problems.

4) A big advantage is immediate response to increased demand. If more energy is needed than the National Grid can supply, the water's released. There's no problem with reliability except in times of drought.

5) Initial costs are high, but there's no fuel and low running costs.

Section 4 — Energy Resources and Energy Transfer

Pumped Storage

Phew. Nearly at the end of all this energy supply stuff now. Just one more page.

Pumped Storage Gives Extra Supply Just When it's Needed

Most large power stations have huge boilers which have to be kept running all night even though demand is very low. This means there's a surplus of electricity at night — and it's surprisingly difficult to find a way of storing this spare energy for later use. Pumped storage is one of the best solutions.

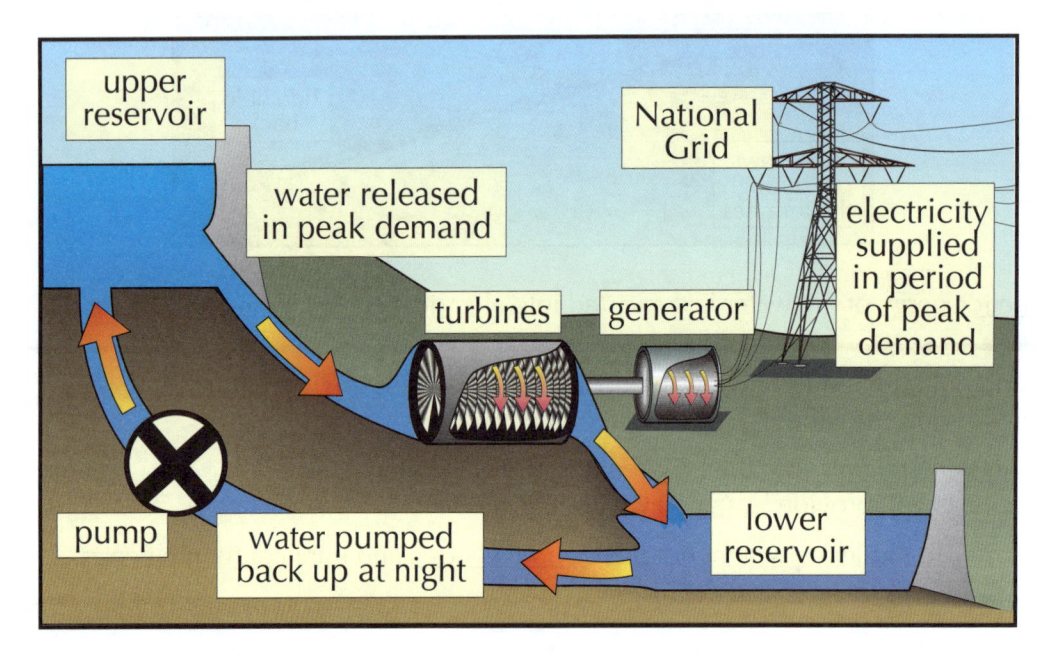

Here's How it Works...

1) In pumped storage, 'spare' night-time electricity is used to pump water up to a higher reservoir.

2) This can then be released quickly during periods of peak demand such as at teatime each evening, to supplement the steady delivery from the big power stations.

3) Remember, pumped storage uses the same idea as hydroelectric power but it isn't a way of generating power — but simply a way of storing energy which has already been generated.

Pumped storage doesn't generate power — it stores it

Did you know that there's a surge in demand for electricity just as EastEnders finishes? It's all those people switching their kettles on. The same thing happens at half-time in a World Cup football match. Clever people at the National Grid have to try to predict what electricity we'll need and when. They can then employ pumped storage facilities, like the one at Dinorwig in Wales, to try to meet demand.

SECTION 4 — ENERGY RESOURCES AND ENERGY TRANSFER

Warm-Up and Exam Questions

It's very nearly the end of this section. But don't shed a tear — try these questions instead.

Warm-Up Questions

1) How does burning coal contribute to acid rain? Give one problem caused by acid rain.
2) Describe the energy transfer(s) that occur in a nuclear power station to produce the steam.
3) Give two advantages of using nuclear power to generate electricity instead of fossil fuels.

Exam Questions

1 Non-renewable energy sources can be used to generate electricity.

   a) Which of the following energy sources is **not** a non-renewable energy source?

   coal   **nuclear**   **wind**   **oil**

   (1 mark)

   PAPER 2

   b) Natural gas is a non-renewable energy source. Natural gas is burned in power stations to transfer the chemical energy of the gas into heat energy.
   Describe the process and the energy transfers that occur in a natural gas power station to transfer this heat energy into electrical energy.

   (3 marks)

   c) Describe **two** advantages of generating electricity using natural gas.

   (2 marks)

2 In some coastal regions, electricity is generated from waves using wave converters.

   a) Name the type of energy that is converted into electrical energy in wave converters.

   (1 mark)

   PAPER 2

   b) A student claims:

   > Using waves is a reliable method of generating electricity that has low set-up costs and running costs.

   Do you agree or disagree? Explain your answer.

   (2 marks)

3 Energy from the Sun is used in different ways.

   a) Name **one** device used to transfer energy from the Sun directly into electrical energy.

   (1 mark)

   PAPER 2

   b) Give **two** reasons why electricity generated from the Sun is rarely supplied to the National Grid.

   (2 marks)

SECTION 4 — ENERGY RESOURCES AND ENERGY TRANSFER

Exam Questions

4   Electricity can be generated using wind and geothermal energy.

   a)   i)   Copy and complete the chart to show the energy transfers when generating electricity using a wind turbine.

   .... → .... → ....

   energy of the turbine   energy of the generator   energy in wires

   (3 marks)

   PAPER 2

   ii)   Give **one** advantage and **one** disadvantage of generating electricity using wind.

   (2 marks)

   PAPER 2

   b)   Give **one** advantage and **one** disadvantage of generating electricity using geothermal resources.

   (2 marks)

5   Water can be used in many ways to generate electricity. In some countries, electricity is generated using hydroelectric dams. Water is held back behind the dam before being allowed to flow out through turbines to produce electricity.

   a)   Describe the energy transfers involved when water flowing through the turbines is used to produce electricity.

   (2 marks)

   PAPER 2

   b)   Hydroelectric power stations don't produce any carbon dioxide when generating electricity. Give **two** ways that using hydroelectric power stations to generate electricity damages the environment.

   (2 marks)

   c)   In some hydroelectric power stations, electrical energy is used to pump water back into the reservoir during times of low electricity demand. Give the name of this type of system.

   (1 mark)

   PAPER 2

   d)   Sea tides can also be used to generate electricity using tidal barrages. Give **two** advantages of generating electricity using tidal barrages.

   (2 marks)

SECTION 4 — ENERGY RESOURCES AND ENERGY TRANSFER

Revision Summary for Section 4

Phew... what a relief — you've made it to the end of yet another nice long section. This one's been fairly straightforward though — it's mainly about energy being converted from one form to another. But don't kid yourself — there are definitely a shedload of facts to remember here and you need to know the lot of them. The best way to check that you know it all is to work your way through these revision questions — and make sure you go back and revise anything you get wrong.

1) Name nine types of energy and give an example of each.
2)* What is the efficiency of a motor that converts 100 J of electrical energy into 70 J of useful kinetic energy?
3) List the energy transfers that occur in a battery-powered toy car.
4)* The following Sankey diagram shows how energy is converted in a catapult.
   a) How much energy is converted into kinetic energy?
   b) How much energy is wasted?
   c) What is the efficiency of the catapult?
5) Describe the three ways that heat energy can be transferred.
6) Describe how the heat from a heating element is transferred throughout the water in a kettle. What is this process called?
7) What types of heat transfer are reduced by double glazing?
8) Describe three other ways of insulating your home.
9) Describe two ways that humans can reduce heat energy escaping from their body.
10)* What's the formula for work done? A crazy dog drags a big branch 12 m over the next-door neighbour's front lawn, pulling with a force of 535 N. How much work was done?
11)* An electric motor uses 540 kJ of electrical energy in 4.5 minutes. What is its power consumption?
12)* Write down the formula for kinetic energy. Find the KE of a 78 kg sheep moving at 23 m/s.
13) What is gravitational potential energy?
14)* Write down the formula for gravitational potential energy. Find the gravitational potential energy of a 78 kg sheep on top of a 2 m ladder (use g = 10 m/s^2).
15) a) Describe the energy transformations that take place when burning fossil fuels to generate electricity in a typical power station.
    b) How does this differ in a nuclear power station?
16) State two advantages and two disadvantages of using fossil fuels to generate electricity.
17) Outline two arguments against increasing the use, in the UK, of nuclear power.
18) Describe the energy transformations that take place when the following renewable resources and methods are used to generate electricity:
    a) wind   b) geothermal energy   c) solar cells   d) solar heating
    e) waves   f) the tide   g) hydroelectricity
19) State one advantage and one disadvantage for each resource or method above.

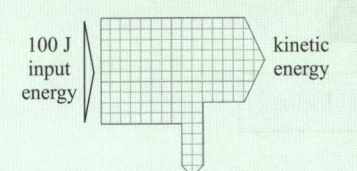

* Answers on page 188.

Density

Density's a pretty easy concept once you've got your head around it.
So, read this page and let's see if you sink or swim...

Density is Mass per Unit Volume

Density is a measure of the 'compactness' (for want of a better word) of a substance.
It relates the mass of a substance to how much space it takes up.

The symbol for density is a Greek letter rho (ρ) — it looks like a p but it isn't.

$$\text{Density} = \frac{\text{mass}}{\text{volume}}$$

$$\frac{m}{\rho \times V}$$

The units of density are g/cm³ or kg/m³. N.B. 1 g/cm³ = 1000 kg/m³.

1) The density of an object depends on what it's made of.
   Density doesn't vary with size or shape.

2) The average density of an object determines whether it floats or sinks.

3) A solid object will float on a fluid if it has a lower density than the fluid.

Pine ρ = 0.5 g/cm³
Oil ρ = 0.8 g/cm³
Water ρ = 1 g/cm³
Iron ρ = 7.9 g/cm³

4) To measure the density of a substance, take measurements
   of the mass and volume and use the formula.

- If the volume is difficult to measure (e.g. it's an oddly shaped solid),
  you can measure the volume by completely immersing the object in
  a measuring container (e.g. a measuring cylinder) of water.
- The amount the volume reading on the container increases by when
  you add the object to the water is the volume of the object.
- This only works for objects denser than water though (i.e. ones that sink).

A dense material has a lot of mass in a small volume

Dense materials will feel really heavy for their size. If you look at the equation for density, you'll see
that a dense material will have a big mass in comparison to its volume. Learn it.

Pressure

You might find this stuff a bit tricky — but just read it through carefully and take the pressure off.

Pressure is Force per Unit Area

Pressure is a measure of the force being applied to the surface of something. It relates how much force is being applied to an object (in N) to the area that it is applied over (in m²). Pressure is measured in pascals (Pa) or kilopascals (kPa). 1 pascal is defined as 1 N/m².

1 kPa = 1000 Pa

$$\text{Pressure} = \frac{\text{force}}{\text{area}}$$

The symbol for pressure is a p — don't confuse it with density (ρ).

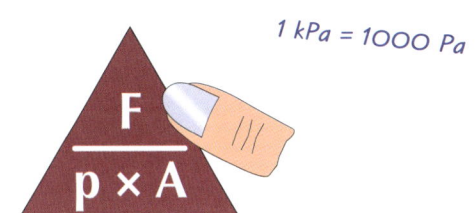

1) The same force applied over a larger area creates a lower pressure.

2) In gases and liquids at rest, the pressure at any point acts equally in all directions.

3) In gases and liquids, the pressure increases with depth.
   The pressure is higher at the bottom of the sea than at the surface, and it is lower high up in the atmosphere than close to the Earth.

Pressure Difference in Liquids and Gases Depends on Density

Pressure difference is the difference in pressure between two points in a liquid or gas. It depends on the height difference (in m), and the density (in kg/m³) of the substance. Gravity has an effect too — g is the acceleration due to gravity, which is around 10 m/s².

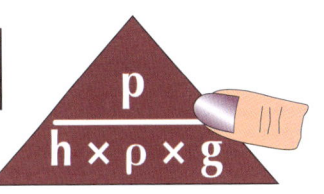

$$\text{Pressure difference} = \text{height} \times \text{density} \times g$$

EXAMPLE: The density of water is 1 g/cm³. Find the pressure difference between the top and bottom of a 3 m vertical column of water.

ANSWER: 1 kg = 1000 g and 1 m³ = 1 000 000 cm³,
so 1 g/cm³ = 1 ÷ 1000 × 1 000 000 = 1000 kg/m³
Pressure difference = h × ρ × g = 3 × 1000 × 10 = 30 000 Pa (or N/m²)

Pressure increases with depth in liquids and gases

The gases in the Earth's atmosphere apply a pressure of around 100 000 pascals onto our bodies all the time. Luckily we've evolved to be able to survive this pressure. If not we'd all be crushed...

Changes of State

solid ═melts═▶ liquid ═boils═▶ gas ═condenses═▶ liquid ═solidifies═▶ solid. Easy peasy.

Kinetic Theory Can Explain the Three States of Matter

1) The three states of matter are solid (e.g. ice), liquid (e.g. water) and gas (e.g. water vapour). The particles of a substance in each state are the same — only the arrangement and energy of the particles are different.

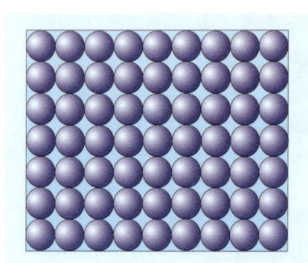

SOLIDS — strong forces of attraction hold the particles close together in a fixed, regular arrangement. The particles don't have much energy so they can only vibrate about their fixed positions.

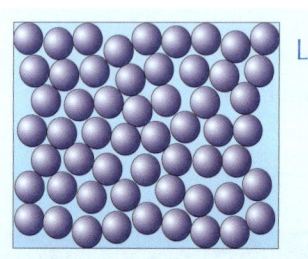

LIQUIDS — there are weaker forces of attraction between the particles. The particles are close together, but can move past each other, and form irregular arrangements. They have more energy than the particles in a solid — they move in random directions at low speeds.

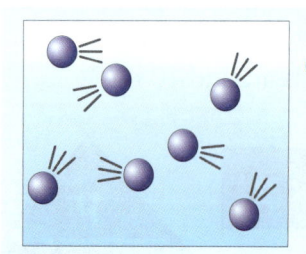

GASES — there are almost no forces of attraction between the particles. The particles have more energy than those in liquids and solids — they are free to move, and travel in random directions and at high speeds.

2) When you heat a liquid, the heat energy makes the particles move faster. Eventually, when enough of the particles have enough energy to overcome their attraction to each other, big bubbles of gas form in the liquid — this is boiling.

3) It's similar when you heat a solid. Heat energy makes the particles vibrate faster until eventually the forces between them are overcome and the particles start to move around — this is melting.

4) The melting point of a chemical is the temperature at which it turns from a solid to a liquid. Believe it or not, the boiling point is the temperature at which a liquid becomes a gas.

The arrangement and energy of particles is important

It's no good getting your solids and your gases mixed up. Make sure you learn the arrangement of particles in each state, and how this changes when substances change state.

Evaporation

This page is all about what happens when a liquid boils and turns into a gas.

Evaporation *is a Special Example of* Changing States

1) Evaporation is when particles escape from a liquid and become gas particles.

2) Particles can evaporate from a liquid at temperatures that are much lower than the liquid's boiling point.

3) Particles near the surface of a liquid can escape and become gas particles if:

- The particles are travelling in the right direction to escape the liquid.
- The particles are travelling fast enough (they have enough kinetic energy) to overcome the attractive forces of the other particles in the liquid.

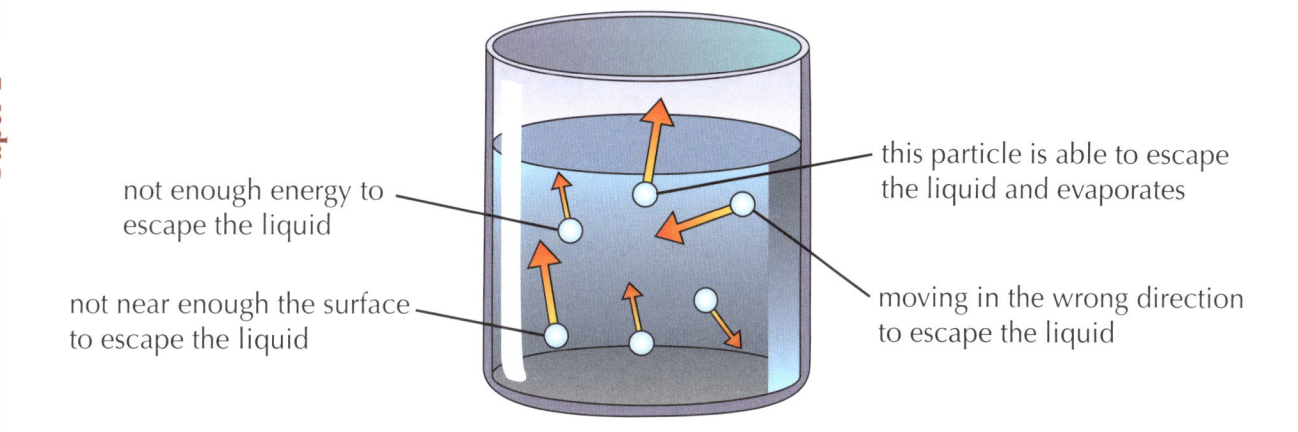

- not enough energy to escape the liquid
- not near enough the surface to escape the liquid
- this particle is able to escape the liquid and evaporates
- moving in the wrong direction to escape the liquid

4) The fastest particles (with the most kinetic energy) are most likely to evaporate from the liquid — so when they do, the average speed and kinetic energy of the remaining particles decreases.

5) This decrease in average particle energy means the temperature of the remaining liquid falls — the liquid cools.

6) This cooling effect can be really useful. For example, you sweat when you exercise or get hot. As the water from the sweat on your skin evaporates, it cools you down.

Evaporation depends on kinetic energy

Particles in a liquid need to have a high kinetic energy to evaporate. When a particle evaporates, it takes its kinetic energy with it — so the average kinetic energy of the particles in the liquid decreases.

Particle Theory and Temperature in Gases

Particles in gases, absolute zero and the Kelvin scale of temperature — ooh, sounds like fun...

Kinetic Energy is Proportional to Temperature

1) Particle theory says that gases consist of very small particles which are constantly moving in completely random directions. The particles hardly take up any space — most of the gas is empty space.

2) The particles constantly collide with each other and with the walls of their container, bouncing off each other, or off the walls.

3) If you increase the temperature of a gas, you give its particles more energy.

4) In fact, if you double the temperature (measured in kelvins — see below), you double the average kinetic energy of the particles.

> The temperature of a gas (in kelvins) is proportional to the average kinetic energy of its particles.

5) As you heat up a gas, the average speed of its particles increases. Anything that's moving (e.g. a bunch of particles) has kinetic energy. Kinetic energy is $\frac{1}{2}mv^2$, remember (see p. 91).

Brownian Motion Supports Particle Theory

1) In 1827, botanist Robert Brown noticed that pollen grains in water moved with a zigzag, random motion.

2) This type of movement of any particles in a suspension is known as Brownian motion. It supports the particle theory of the different states of matter.

3) Large, heavy particles (e.g. smoke) can be moved with Brownian motion by smaller, lighter particles (e.g. air) travelling at high speeds — which is why smoke particles in air appear to move around randomly when you observe them in the lab.

Absolute Zero is as Cold as Stuff Can Get — 0 Kelvins

1) If you increase the temperature of something, you give its particles more energy — they move about more quickly or vibrate more. In the same way, if you cool a substance down, you're reducing the kinetic energy of the particles.

2) The coldest that anything can ever get is -273 °C — this temperature is known as absolute zero. At absolute zero, atoms have as little kinetic energy as it's possible to get.

3) Absolute zero is the start of the Kelvin scale of temperature.

4) A temperature change of 1 °C is also a change of 1 kelvin. The two scales are pretty similar — the only difference is where the zero occurs.

5) To convert from degrees Celsius to kelvins, just add 273. And to convert from kelvins to degrees Celsius, just subtract 273.

	Absolute zero	Freezing point of water	Boiling point of water
Celsius scale	-273 °C	0 °C	100 °C
Kelvin scale	0 K	273 K	373 K

There's no degree symbol ° when you write a temperature in kelvins. Just write K, not °K. OK.

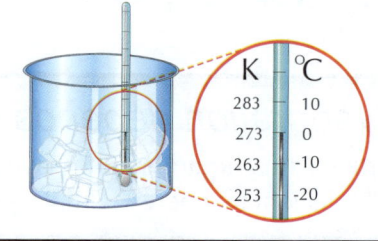

SECTION 5 — SOLIDS, LIQUIDS AND GASES

Particle Theory and Pressure in Gases

Particle Theory Says Colliding Gas Particles Create Pressure

1) As gas particles move about, they randomly bang into each other and whatever else gets in the way.
2) Gas particles are very light, but they sure ain't massless. When they collide with something, they exert a force on it and their momentum and direction change. In a sealed container, gas particles smash against the container's walls — creating an outward pressure.
3) This pressure depends on how fast the particles are going and how often they hit the walls.
4) If you heat a gas, the particles move faster and have more kinetic energy. This increase in kinetic energy means the particles hit the container walls harder and more often, creating more pressure. In fact, temperature (in K) and pressure are proportional — double the temp, and you double the pressure.
5) And if you put the same amount of gas in a bigger container, the pressure will decrease, cos there'll be fewer collisions between the gas particles and the container's walls. When the volume's reduced, the particles get more squashed up and so they hit the walls more often, hence the pressure increases.

At Constant Temperature "pV = Constant"

This all applies to so-called ideal gases. Ideal gases are gases that are 'well behaved', i.e. ones that this equation works for.

Learn this equation. For a fixed mass of gas at a constant temperature:

pressure × volume = constant ➡ pV = constant

You can also write the equation as: $p_1 V_1 = p_2 V_2$ (where p_1 and V_1 are your starting conditions and p_2 and V_2 are your final conditions).

Writing it like that is much more useful a lot of the time.

EXAMPLE: A gas at a pressure of 250 kilopascals is compressed from a volume of 300 cm³ down to a volume of 175 cm³. The temperature of the gas does not change. Find the new pressure of the gas, in kilopascals.

ANSWER: $p_1 V_1 = p_2 V_2$ gives: $250 \times 300 = p_2 \times 175$, so $p_2 = (250 \times 300) \div 175 = \underline{429 \text{ kPa}}$ (3 s.f.).

At Constant Volume "p/T = Constant"

Learn this equation too. In a sealed container (i.e. constant volume):

$$\frac{\text{pressure}}{\text{temperature (in K)}} = \text{constant} \Rightarrow \frac{p}{T} = \text{constant}$$

You can also write the equation as: $p_1 / T_1 = p_2 / T_2$ (where p_1 and T_1 are your starting conditions and p_2 and T_2 are your final conditions).

EXAMPLE: A container has a volume of 30 litres. It is filled with gas at a pressure of 100 kPa and a temperature of 290 K. Find the new pressure if the temperature is increased to 315 K.

ANSWER: $p_1 / T_1 = p_2 / T_2$ gives: $100 \div 290 = p_2 \div 315$ so $p_2 = 315 \times (100 \div 290) = \underline{109 \text{ kPa}}$ (3 s.f.).

NB: The temperatures in this formula must always be in kelvins, so if they give you the temperatures in °C, convert to kelvins FIRST (by adding 273). Always keep the pressure units the same as they are in the question (in this case, kPa).

Warm-Up and Exam Questions

It's time again to test what you've learnt from the last section. Have a go at these...

Warm-Up Questions

1) Smoke particles in the air appear to move with a random motion. What is the name of this type of motion?
2) The temperature in kelvins of the air increases by a factor of 3. How will the kinetic energy of the air particles change, and by what factor?
3) Use particle theory to explain how gas particles create pressure in a sealed container.

Exam Questions

1. Pressure is a measure of the force applied to the surface of a substance.

   a) Copy out the passage below, using the words from the box to fill in the gaps.

   | equal | smaller | different | greater |

   In gases and liquids at rest, the pressure at any point is .... in all directions.

   The pressure is .... the deeper the gas or liquid gets.

   (2 marks)

   b) i) State the equation linking pressure, force and area.

   (1 mark)

   ii) Calculate the pressure created by a force of 18 N acting over an area of 0.45 m².

   (2 marks)

2. A company tests a water-resistant watch under high pressure. The watch is designed to be used underwater if the pressure difference from the surface is 240 kPa or less.

   a) State the equation linking pressure difference, height, density and the acceleration due to gravity (g).

   (1 mark)

   b) i) The mass of a 0.5 m³ volume of water is 500 kg. Calculate the density of water.

   (4 marks)

   ii) Calculate the maximum depth from the surface of the water that the watch can be used at.

   (3 marks)

3. The Kelvin scale and the Celsius scale are two scales that can be used to measure temperature.

   a) i) A gas is cooled. Describe what effect this has on the average speed of its particles.

   (1 mark)

   ii) Explain why there is a minimum possible temperature that any substance can reach, known as the absolute zero of temperature.

   (2 marks)

   iii) Give the numerical value of the absolute zero of temperature in degrees Celsius.

   (1 mark)

   b) Temperature can be converted between the Kelvin and Celsius scales.

   i) Convert 10 K into °C.   ii) Convert 631 °C into K.

   (2 marks)

Exam Questions

4   A student has a collection of metal toy soldiers of different sizes made from the same metal.

    a)   Copy out the statement below that is true.

           The masses and densities of each of the toy soldiers are the same.

           The masses of each of the toy soldiers are the same, but their densities may vary.

           The densities of each of the toy soldiers are the same, but their masses may vary.

           The densities and masses of each toy soldier may vary.

(1 mark)

    b)   The student wants to measure the density of one of the toy soldiers.
He has a measuring cylinder, a mass balance and some water.

        i)   State the **two** quantities the student should measure.

(2 marks)

        ii)   Describe the steps the student could take to find the density of the toy soldier using the equipment he has.

(5 marks)

PAPER 2

5   Substances can exist in different states of matter.

    a)   Describe the arrangement and movement of the particles in a solid.

(2 marks)

    b)   If a substance is heated to a certain temperature it can change from a solid to a liquid.

        i)   Give the name of this process.

(1 mark)

        ii)   Explain why the temperature rising above a certain level causes this process to happen.

(2 marks)

    c)   If a liquid is heated to a certain temperature it starts to boil and become a gas.
Name the other process that causes a liquid to start to become a gas.
Explain how it is different to boiling.

(3 marks)

6   A sealed balloon contains 0.014 m³ of gas at a pressure of 98 kPa. The balloon is compressed to 0.013 m³. The temperature of the air inside it remains constant. Calculate the air pressure inside the balloon after the compression.

(3 marks)

PAPER 2

7   A sealed container with a fixed volume is fitted with internal temperature and pressure gauges. The gauges show that the temperature is 288 K and the pressure is 107 kPa inside the container.

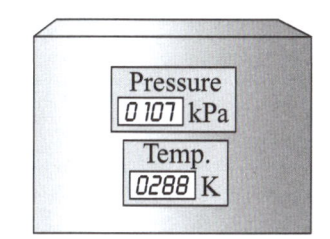

The container is heated so that the temperature of the gas inside it becomes 405 K.
Calculate the pressure that will be shown on the pressure gauge.

(3 marks)

Revision Summary for Section 5

A small but perfectly formed section — jam-packed with maths and scary calculations. If you've learnt all the formulas it should be a doddle. Double-check you have learnt them all by having a go at these...

1) What is the relationship between the density, mass and volume of a substance?
2)* Calculate the volume of 2 kg of water (density = 1000 kg/m^3).
3) How would you measure the density of an unknown liquid in the lab?
4) Draw a formula triangle containing pressure, force and area.
5)* What pressure does a woman weighing 600 N exert on the floor if her high-heeled shoes have an area of 5 cm^2 touching the floor?
6) What is the formula used to work out a pressure difference?
7) Describe how the particles are arranged and move in:
    a) a solid,   b) a liquid,   c) a gas.
8) Explain what happens to particles in a substance during:
    a) melting,   b) boiling,   c) evaporation.
9) What is Brownian motion?
10) How does Brownian motion support particle theory?
11) What temperature is 'absolute zero' in
    a) kelvins,   b) degrees Celsius?
12) Why is there an absolute zero temperature?
13) How does the temperature of a gas (in kelvins) relate to its kinetic energy?
14) What happens to the pressure of a gas in a sealed container if you increase the temperature?
15)* 500 cm^3 of a fixed mass of gas at 50 kPa is forced into a 100 cm^3 container. What is the new pressure of the gas (assuming the temperature is kept constant)?
16)* Another 500 cm^3 of gas is kept sealed in its container at 50 kPa, but is then heated from a temperature of 290 K to 300 K. What is the new pressure of the gas?

*Answers on page 189.

SECTION 5 — SOLIDS, LIQUIDS AND GASES

Section 6 — Magnetism and Electromagnetism

Magnets and Magnetic Fields

I think magnetism is an attractive subject, but don't get repelled by the exam — revise.

Magnets Produce Magnetic Fields

1) All magnets have two poles — north and south.
2) A magnetic field is a region where magnetic materials (e.g. iron) experience a force.
3) Magnetic field lines (or "lines of force") are used to show the size and direction of magnetic fields. They always point from NORTH to SOUTH. 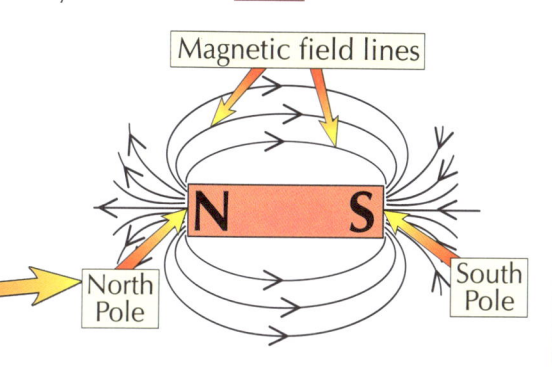
4) Placing the north and south poles of two permanent bar magnets near each other creates a uniform field between the two magnets.

Use Compasses and Iron Filings to show Magnetic Field Patterns

1) Compasses and iron filings align themselves with magnetic fields.
2) You can use multiple compasses to see the magnetic field lines coming out of a bar magnet or between two bar magnets.  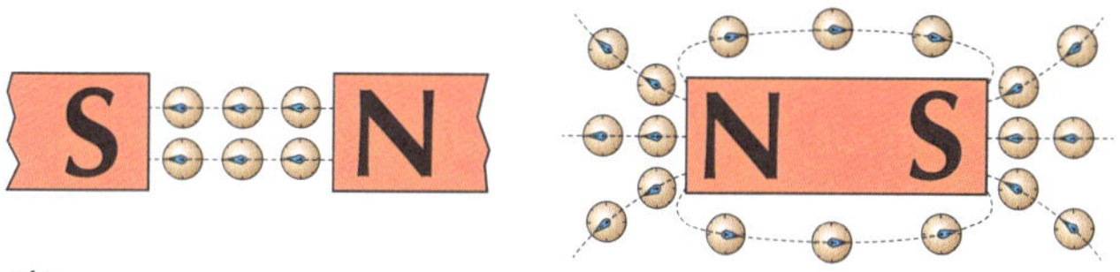
3) If you don't have lots of compasses, you can just use one and move it around (trace its position on some paper before each move if it helps).
4) You could also use iron filings to see magnetic field patterns. Just put the magnet(s) under a piece of paper and scatter the iron filings on top.

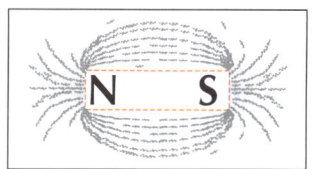

Magnetism can be Induced

1) Magnets affect magnetic materials and other magnets.
2) Like poles repel each other and opposite poles attract.

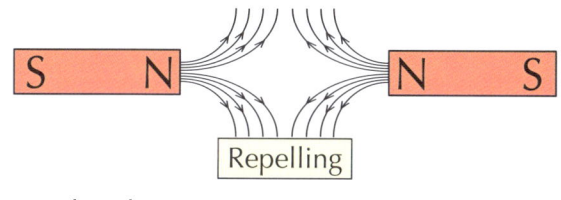

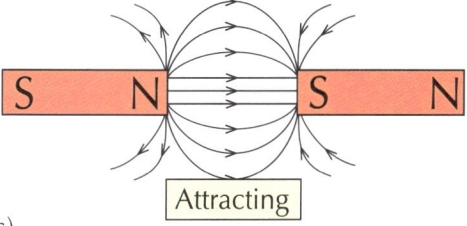

3) Both poles attract magnetic materials (that aren't magnets).
4) When a magnet is brought near a magnetic material then that material acts as a magnet.
5) This magnetism has been induced by the original magnet.
6) The closer the magnet and the magnetic material get, the stronger the induced magnetism will be.

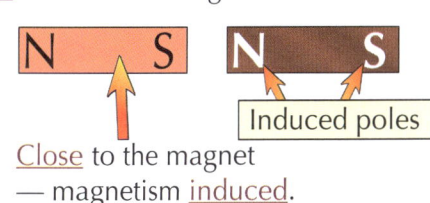

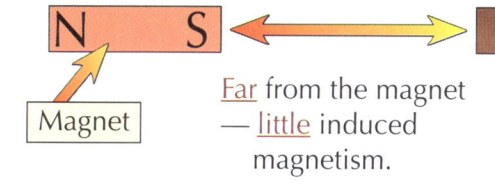

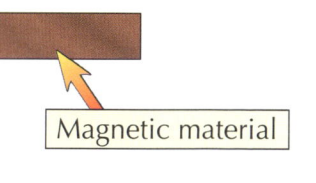

Electromagnetism

Permanent magnets are great, but it would be really handy to be able to turn a magnetic field on and off. Well, it turns out that when electric current flows it produces a magnetic field — problem solved.

A Current-Carrying Wire Creates a Magnetic Field

1) An electric current in a material produces a magnetic field around it.
2) The larger the electric current, the stronger the magnetic field.
3) The direction of the magnetic field depends on the direction of the current.

The Magnetic Field Around a Straight Wire

1) There is a magnetic field around a straight, current-carrying wire.
2) The field is made up of concentric circles with the wire in the centre.

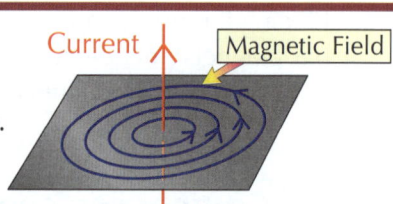

The Magnetic Field Around a Flat Circular Coil

1) The magnetic field in the centre of a flat circular coil of wire is similar to that of a bar magnet.
2) There are concentric ellipses (stretched circles) of magnetic field lines around the coil.

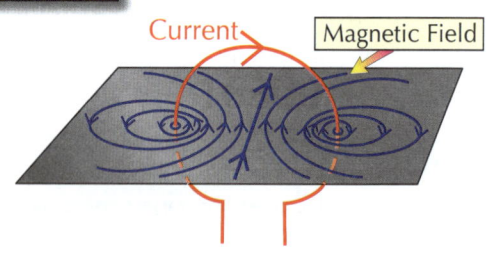

The Magnetic Field Around a Solenoid

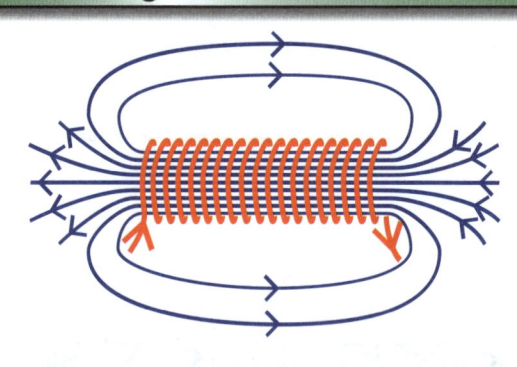

1) The magnetic field inside a current-carrying solenoid (a coil of wire) is strong and uniform.
2) Outside the coil, the field is just like the one around a bar magnet.
3) This means that the ends of a solenoid act like the north pole and south pole of a bar magnet. This type of magnet is called an ELECTROMAGNET.

Magnetic Materials can be 'Soft' or 'Hard'

1) A magnetic material is considered 'soft' if it loses its induced magnetism quickly, or 'hard' if it keeps it permanently.
2) Iron is an example of a soft magnetic material. Steel is an example of a hard magnetic material.
3) Iron is used in transformers because of this property — it needs to magnetise and demagnetise 50 times a second (mains electricity in the UK runs at 50 Hz) — see p. 118.
4) You can increase the strength of the magnetic field around a solenoid by adding a magnetically "soft" iron core through the middle of the coil.

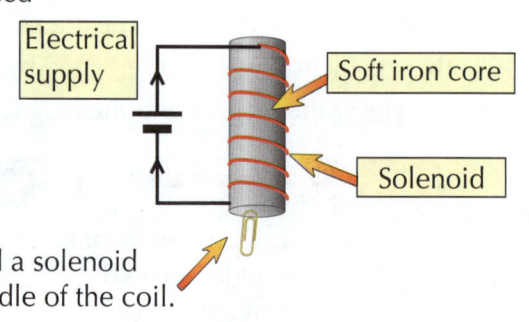

The Motor Effect

The motor effect can happen when you put a current-carrying wire in a magnetic field.

A Current in a Magnetic Field Experiences a Force

When a current-carrying wire is put between magnetic poles, the two magnetic fields affect one another. The result is a force on the wire. This can cause the wire to move.

Paper 2

> This is because charged particles (e.g. electrons in a current) moving through a magnetic field will experience a force, as long as they're not moving parallel to the field lines.

This is an aerial view. The red dot represents a wire carrying current "out of the page" (towards you).

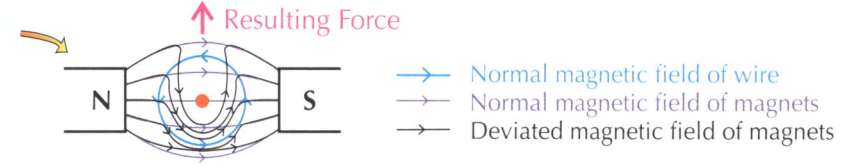

↑ Resulting Force
→ Normal magnetic field of wire
→ Normal magnetic field of magnets
→ Deviated magnetic field of magnets

1) To experience the full force, the wire has to be at 90° to the magnetic field. If the wire runs along the magnetic field, it won't experience any force at all. At angles in between, it'll feel some force.

2) The force always acts in the same direction relative to the magnetic field of the magnets and the direction of the current in the wire.

3) A good way of showing the direction of the force is to apply a current to a set of rails inside a horseshoe magnet (shown opposite). A bar is placed on the rails, which completes the circuit. This generates a force that rolls the bar along the rails.

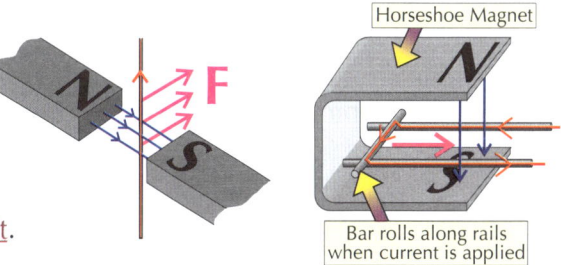

4) The magnitude (strength) of the force increases with the strength of the magnetic field.

5) The force also increases with the amount of current passing through the conductor.

6) Reversing the current or the magnetic field also reverses the direction of the force.

Fleming's Left-Hand Rule Tells You Which Way the Force Acts

1) They could test if you can do this, so practise it.
2) Using your left hand, point your First finger in the direction of the Field and your seCond finger in the direction of the Current.
3) Your thuMb will then point in the direction of the force (Motion).

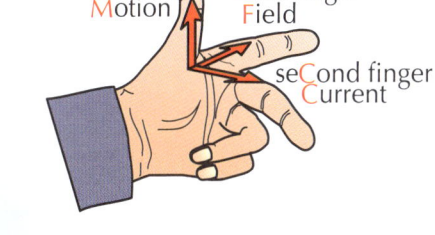

thuMb — Motion
First finger — Field
seCond finger — Current

EXAMPLE: Which direction is the force on the wire?

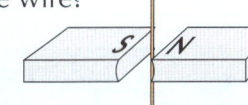

ANSWER:
1) Draw in current arrows (+ve to –ve). 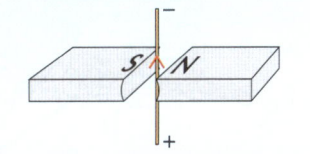
2) Fleming's LHR. 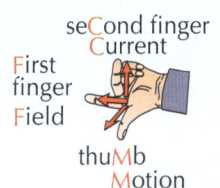
   seCond finger Current
   First finger Field
   thuMb Motion
3) Draw in direction of force (motion).

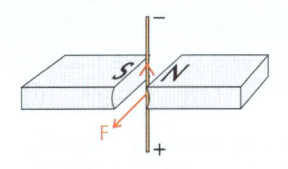

SECTION 6 — MAGNETISM AND ELECTROMAGNETISM

Electric Motors and Loudspeakers

Aha — one of the favourite exam topics of all time. Read it. Understand it. Learn it.

A Simple D.C. Electric Motor

4 Factors which Speed it up

1) More CURRENT
2) More TURNS on the coil
3) STRONGER MAGNETIC FIELD
4) A SOFT IRON CORE in the coil

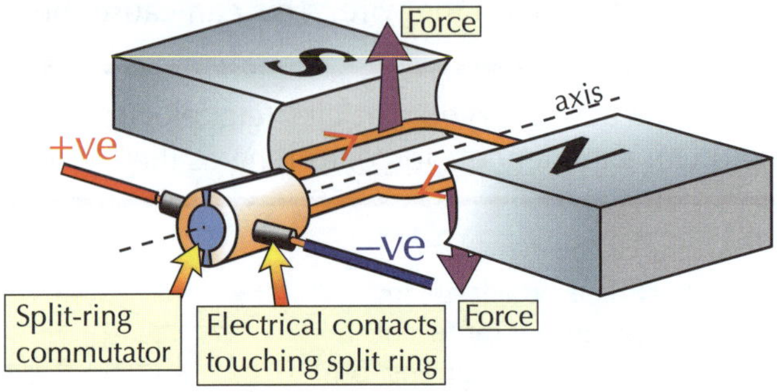

1) The diagram shows the forces acting on the two side arms of the coil.
2) These forces are just the usual forces which act on any current in a magnetic field.
3) Because the coil is on a spindle and the forces act one up and one down, it rotates.
4) The split-ring commutator is a clever way of swapping the contacts every half turn to keep the motor rotating in the same direction.
5) The direction of the motor can be reversed either by swapping the polarity of the d.c. supply or swapping the magnetic poles over.
6) The speed can be increased by adding more turns to the coil, increasing the current, increasing the strength of the magnetic field or by adding a soft iron core.
7) You can use the left-hand rule to work out which way the coil will turn.

EXAMPLE: Is the coil turning clockwise or anticlockwise?

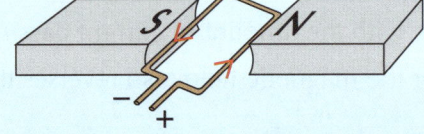

ANSWER:
1) Draw in current arrows (+ve to –ve).
2) Fleming's LHR on one arm (I've used the right-hand arm). 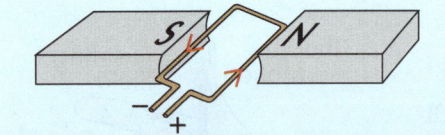 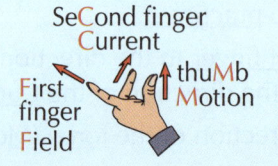
   SeCond finger — Current
   First finger — Field
   thuMb — Motion
3) Draw in direction of force (motion).
   So — the coil is turning anticlockwise. 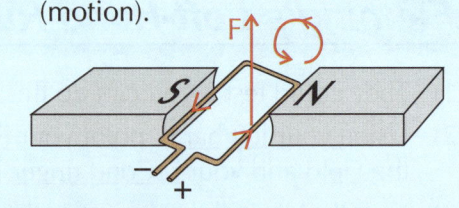

Loudspeakers Work Because of the Motor Effect

1) A.c. electrical signals from an amplifier are fed to a coil of wire in the speaker, which is wrapped around the base of a cone.
2) The coil is surrounded by a permanent magnet, so the a.c. signals cause a force on the coil and make it move back and forth.
3) These movements make the cone vibrate and this creates sounds.

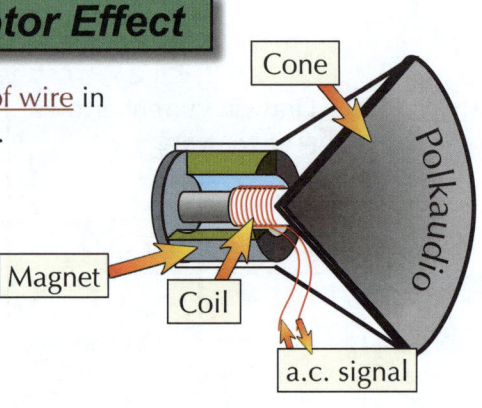

SECTION 6 — MAGNETISM AND ELECTROMAGNETISM

Electromagnetic Induction

Generators use a pretty cool piece of physics to make electricity from the movement of a turbine. It's called electromagnetic (EM) induction — which basically means making electricity using a magnet.

> **ELECTROMAGNETIC INDUCTION:**
> The creation of a **VOLTAGE** (and maybe current) in a wire which is experiencing a **CHANGE IN MAGNETIC FIELD**.

The Dynamo Effect — Move the Wire or the Magnet

1) Using electromagnetic induction to transform kinetic energy (energy of moving things) into electrical energy is called the dynamo effect. (In a power station, this kinetic energy is provided by the turbine.)

2) There are two different situations where you get EM induction:
   a) An electrical conductor (a coil of wire is often used) moves through a magnetic field.
   b) The magnetic field through an electrical conductor changes (gets bigger or smaller or reverses).

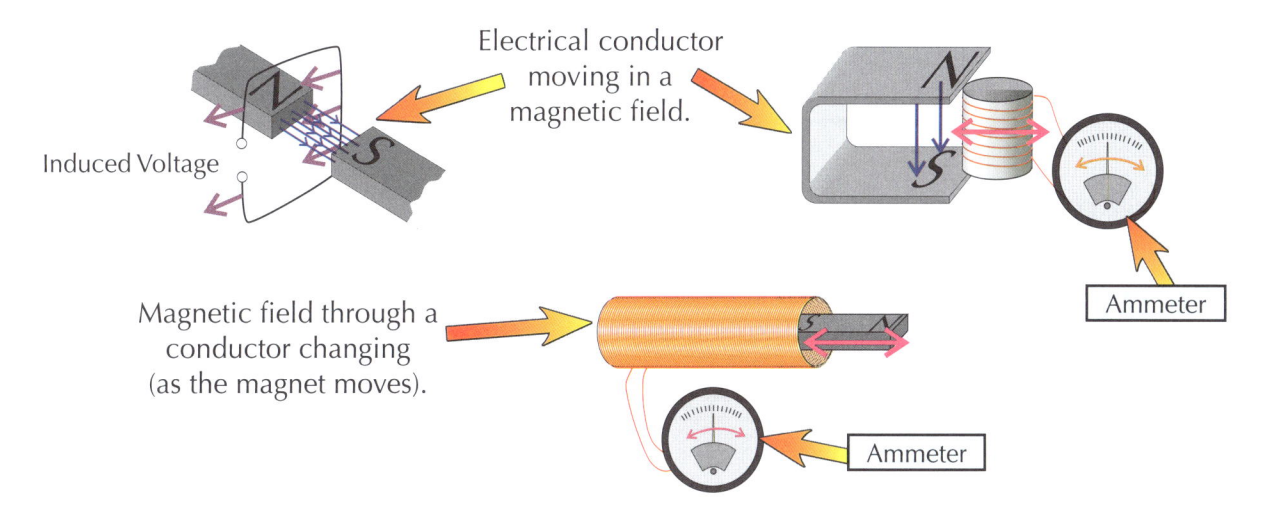

Induced Voltage

Electrical conductor moving in a magnetic field.

Magnetic field through a conductor changing (as the magnet moves).

Ammeter

Ammeter

3) You can test this by connecting an ammeter to a conductor and moving the conductor through a magnetic field (or moving a magnet through the conductor). The ammeter will show the magnitude and direction of the induced current.

4) If the direction of movement is reversed, then the induced voltage/current will be reversed too.

> **To get a bigger voltage, you can increase...**
> 1) The **STRENGTH** of the **MAGNET**
> 2) The **number of TURNS** on the **COIL**
> 3) The **SPEED** of movement

Think about the simple electric motor — you've got a current in the wire and a magnetic field, which causes movement. Well, a generator works the opposite way round — you've got a magnetic field and movement, which induces a current.

Electromagnetic induction transforms kinetic to electrical energy

Kinetic energy is the energy of moving things. In a power station, kinetic energy is generated by a turbine. Electromagnetic induction then transforms this kinetic energy into electrical energy.

Electromagnetic Induction

Power stations use a.c. generators to produce electricity — it's just a matter of turning a coil in a magnetic field. Yes, it really is that simple — now you just need to learn it.

A.C. Generators — Just Turn the Coil and There's a Current

You've already met generators and electromagnetic induction — this is a bit more detail about how a simple generator works.

1) Generators rotate a coil in a magnetic field (or a magnet in a coil).

2) Their construction is pretty much like a motor.

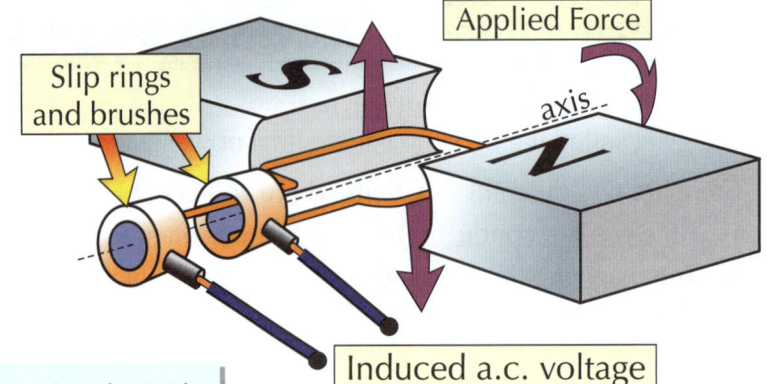

3) As the coil spins, a current is induced in the coil. This current changes direction every half turn.

4) Instead of a split-ring commutator, a.c. generators have slip rings and brushes so the contacts don't swap every half turn.

5) This means they produce a.c. voltage, as shown by these CRO displays. Note that faster revolutions produce not only more peaks but higher overall voltage too.

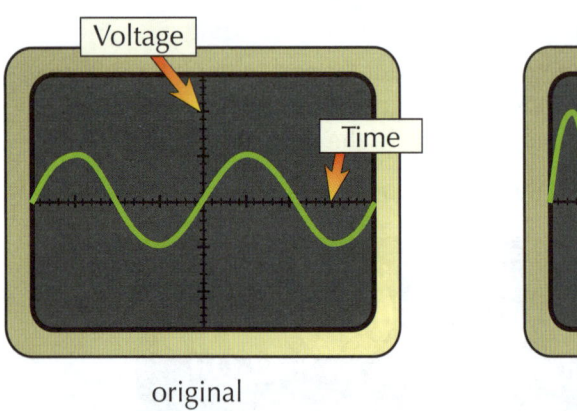

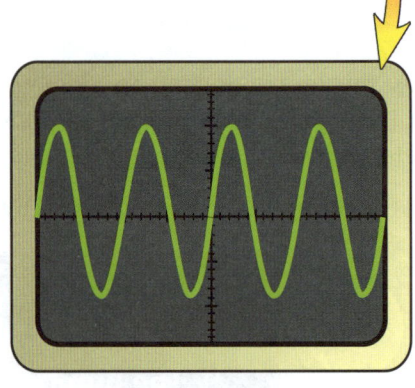

original   faster revs

6) Power stations use a.c. generators to produce electricity — they just get the energy needed to turn the coil or magnetic field in different ways.

EM induction — works whether the coil or the field is moving

Induction's simple enough: conductor + magnetic field + movement = voltage (and current if there's a circuit). So you have no excuse not to learn it. It will probably come up in your exam.

Transformers

Transformers use electromagnetic induction to either increase or decrease the voltage. Watch out though — they only work with an alternating current.

Transformers Change Alternating Voltages

1) Transformers change the size of the voltage of an alternating current.

2) They all have two coils, the primary and the secondary, joined with an iron core.

3) When an alternating voltage is applied across the primary coil, the magnetically soft (iron) core magnetises and demagnetises quickly. This induces an alternating voltage in the secondary coil (page 116).

4) The ratio between the primary and secondary voltages is the same as the ratio between the number of turns on the primary and secondary coils.

STEP-UP TRANSFORMERS step the voltage up. They have more turns on the secondary coil than the primary coil.

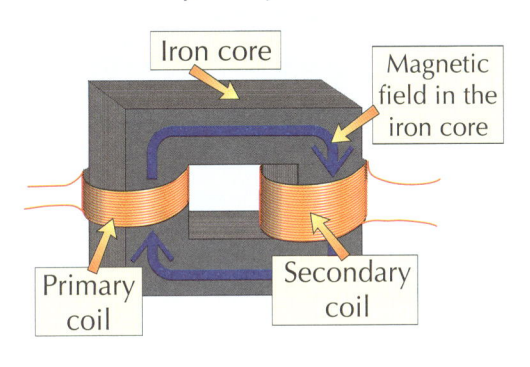

STEP-DOWN TRANSFORMERS step the voltage down. They have more turns on the primary coil than the secondary.

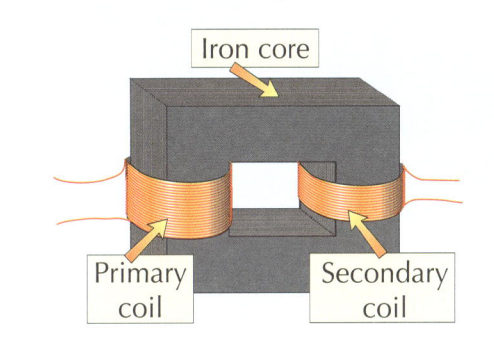

The Transformer Equation — Use it Either Way Up

You can calculate the output voltage from a transformer if you know the input voltage and the number of turns on each coil.

$$\frac{\text{Input (Primary) Voltage}}{\text{Output (Secondary) Voltage}} = \frac{\text{Number of turns on Primary}}{\text{Number of turns on Secondary}}$$

$$\frac{V_P}{V_S} = \frac{N_P}{N_S}$$

OR

$$\frac{V_S}{V_P} = \frac{N_S}{N_P}$$

This equation can be used either way up — there's less rearranging to do if you put whatever you're trying to calculate (the unknown) on the top.

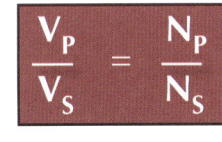

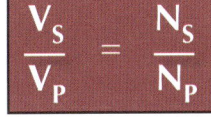

Step up to the task of learning this page

Transformers are pretty easy — their name tells you almost exactly what they do. The transformer equation is a bit trickier, but you may get a question on it in the exam, so it's well worth learning.

Transformers

Transformers are needed to change the voltage of electricity produced in power stations, before it can be transported through the National Grid to be used at home or in factories.

Transformers are Nearly 100% Efficient So "Power In = Power Out"

The formula for power supplied is: Power = Voltage × Current or: P = V × I.

So you can rewrite input power = output power as:

$$V_p I_p = V_s I_s$$

V_p = primary voltage V_s = secondary voltage
I_p = primary current I_s = secondary current

Transformers Make Transmitting Mains Electricity More Efficient

Step-up and step-down transformers are used when transmitting electricity across the country:

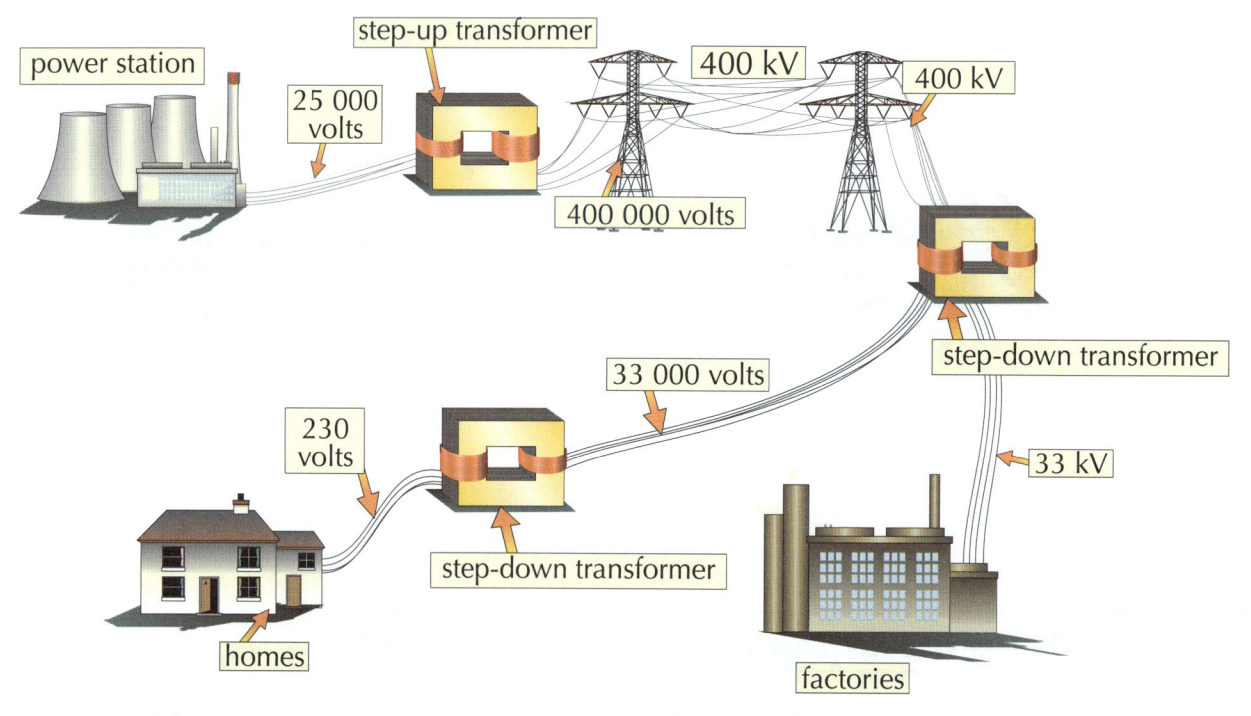

- power station → 25 000 volts → step-up transformer → 400 000 volts → 400 kV → 400 kV → step-down transformer → 33 kV → factories
- 33 000 volts → step-down transformer → 230 volts → homes

1) The voltage produced by power stations is too low to be transmitted efficiently. Power = VI, so the lower the voltage the higher the current for a given amount of power, and current causes wires to heat up.

2) A step-up transformer is used to boost the voltage before it is transmitted.

3) Step-down transformers are used at the end of the journey to reduce the voltage so it's more useful and safer to use.

Read this page and transform into a Physics whizz

See — transformers are really useful. Without them we would be sitting in a dark home, with no lights, and that would be really rubbish. So give transformers some credit and revise them for your exam.

SECTION 6 — MAGNETISM AND ELECTROMAGNETISM

Warm-Up and Exam Questions

There were lots of new ideas for you to tackle in that section. Try these questions and see what has stuck.

Warm-Up Questions

1) Draw a diagram to show the magnetic field around a single bar magnet.
2) Iron is a soft magnetic material. What does this mean?
   Give an example of a hard magnetic material.
3) What is electromagnetic induction?
4) How does a step-up transformer differ from a step-down transformer?

Exam Questions

1   A student draws the magnetic field lines between
    four bar magnets, as shown in the diagram on the right.

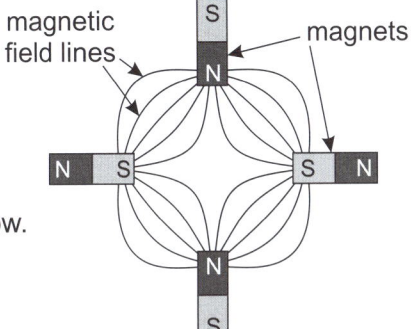

    a) Describe an experiment that the student could
       have done to show this magnetic field pattern.
       (2 marks)

    b) The student arranges two of the magnets as shown below.

       [N S] [N S]

       PAPER 2
       i) Describe the magnetic field in the shaded region between the dotted lines.
          (1 mark)

       PAPER 2
       ii) State whether there will be a force of attraction, repulsion,
           or no force between the two magnets. Explain your answer.
           (2 marks)

2   Iron and steel are both magnetic materials.

    a) Describe what is meant by a **magnetic material**.
       (1 mark)

    b) The head of an iron nail is placed close to the north pole of a bar magnet.
       The head of the nail is attracted towards the bar magnet until they touch and it
       sticks to the magnet. Explain what causes this to happen.
       (2 marks)

3   A student uses the rotation of a hamster wheel to power a battery charger.

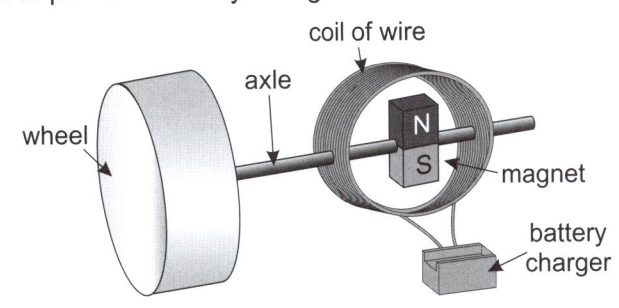

    a) Explain how rotating the wheel
       creates a voltage across the
       battery charger.
       (2 marks)

    b) Give **two** ways the voltage
       created across the battery
       charger could be increased.
       (2 marks)

SECTION 6 — MAGNETISM AND ELECTROMAGNETISM

Exam Questions

c) The student makes the following claim.

> My hamster will charge the battery if it runs in either direction round the wheel.

Do you agree or disagree? Explain your answer.

(1 mark)

4 The diagram shows an experiment where a current is passed through a wire in a magnetic field.

a) A force acts on the loop of wire causing it to move.
   i) Explain why this happens.
   (1 mark)
   ii) State the direction in which the loop will move.
   (1 mark)

b) i) State what effect increasing the current will have on the force on the loop of wire.
   (1 mark)
   ii) Give **two** ways in which the direction that the force acts could be reversed in this experiment.
   (2 marks)

[PAPER 2]

c) The diagram on the right shows a free-rolling conducting bar on a set of fixed conducting bars in a magnetic field. All of the conducting bars have a current flowing through them.

Explain, in terms of electron movement, why the free-rolling conducting bar doesn't move.
(2 marks)

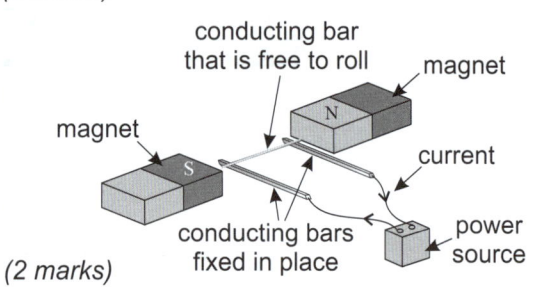

5 A student is building a simple d.c. motor. He starts by putting a loop of current-carrying wire that is free to rotate about an axis in a magnetic field, as shown in the diagram.

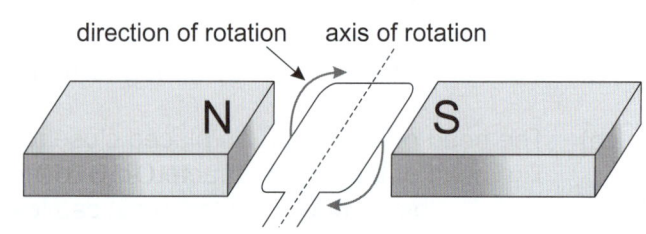

a) Copy the diagram and add an arrow to show the direction of the current in the wire.
(1 mark)

b) The starting position of the loop is shown in the diagram. Explain why the motor will stop rotating in the same direction after 90° of rotation from its start position.
(1 mark)

c) Suggest and explain how the student could get the motor to keep rotating in the same direction.
(2 marks)

d) Give **one** way the motor could be made to rotate faster.
(1 mark)

Section 6 — Magnetism and Electromagnetism

Exam Questions

6. The diagram shows the parts inside an earphone. Sound waves are caused by mechanical vibrations. Explain how the earphone uses an a.c. supply to produce sound waves.

   (4 marks)

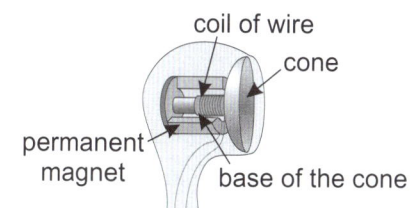

PAPER 2

7. An electromagnet is used by a crane to lift, move and drop iron and steel.

   a) Describe the basic structure of an electromagnet.
   (1 mark)

   b) Describe the shape of the magnetic field that an electromagnet produces. You may use a sketch to help with your answer.
   (2 marks)

   c) When a current is passed through the electromagnet, an iron bar on the ground nearby is attracted to it. When the current is stopped, the bar drops back to the ground. Explain why this happens.
   (4 marks)

PAPER 2

8. A student is investigating a transformer. He uses it to power a spotlight, and measures the quantities shown in the table below.

Voltage across primary coil (V)	Current in primary coil (A)	Voltage across secondary coil (V)
240	0.25	12

   a) State the equation linking power, current and voltage.
   (1 mark)

   b) Calculate the input power to the primary coil when using the spotlight.
   (2 marks)

   c) Calculate the current in the secondary coil when using the spotlight. Assume the transformer is 100% efficient.
   (3 marks)

PAPER 2

9. The National Grid is a network that transmits electricity around the country. The diagram shows a step-up transformer used in the National Grid. The secondary coil has 16 times more turns on it than the primary coil.

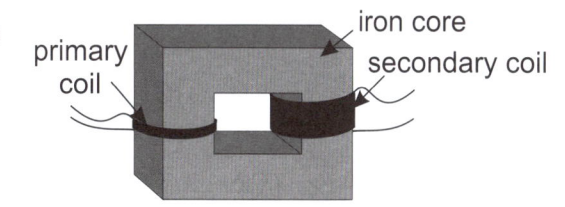

   a) Explain how transformers are used in the National Grid to transmit electricity from power stations efficiently and supply the electricity to the consumer safely.
   (3 marks)

   b) i) State the equation linking the number of turns on the primary and secondary coils of a transformer and the voltages across the primary and secondary coils.
   (1 mark)

   ii) The voltage across the primary coil is 25 000 V. Calculate the voltage across the secondary coil.
   (4 marks)

   c) Explain why a transformer wouldn't work if a direct current was supplied to the primary coil.
   (3 marks)

Revision Summary for Section 6

Another section conquered — congratulations. Now all you need to do is just answer a few more questions. If you can't answer them, you haven't revised enough. It's probably better to find out now than when you're sat in the exam though, so have a bash at these questions and see how you do.

1) Sketch a diagram showing how you can produce a uniform magnetic field using two bar magnets.
2) Briefly describe an experiment to investigate the magnetic field pattern around a permanent bar magnet.
3) What type of field is produced by an electric current in a conductor?
4) Sketch the magnetic field produced by:
   a) A straight wire. b) A flat loop of wire. c) A solenoid.
5) What is an electromagnet?
6) What is the difference between hard and soft magnetic materials?
7) What will happen to a charged particle moving through a magnetic field?
8) Name two factors that increase the strength of the force on a current-carrying wire in a magnetic field.
9) Briefly describe how to use the left-hand rule to predict the direction of the force on a current-carrying wire in a magnetic field.
10) What's the motor effect?
11) What's a split-ring commutator used for in an electric motor?
12) Sketch a labelled diagram of a loudspeaker and briefly explain how it works due to the motor effect.
13) Briefly describe how a voltage can be induced using a coil of wire and a magnet.
14) Give three factors you could change to increase the size of an induced voltage.
15) Sketch a labelled diagram of an a.c. generator and briefly explain how it works.
16) Sketch a diagram of a step-up transformer.
17) How does a transformer change the voltage of an electricity supply?
18)* A transformer has 10 turns on the primary coil and 50 turns on the secondary coil. If the primary voltage is 30 V, what will the secondary voltage be?
19)* The power output of a transformer is 6000 W. If the input voltage is 30 000 V, what is the input current?
20) How are transformers used in the transmission of electricity across long distances?

*Answers on page 190.

Atoms and Isotopes

Before you get stuck into nuclear radiation, you need to know a bit about atoms and isotopes.

At the Centre of Every Atom is a Nucleus

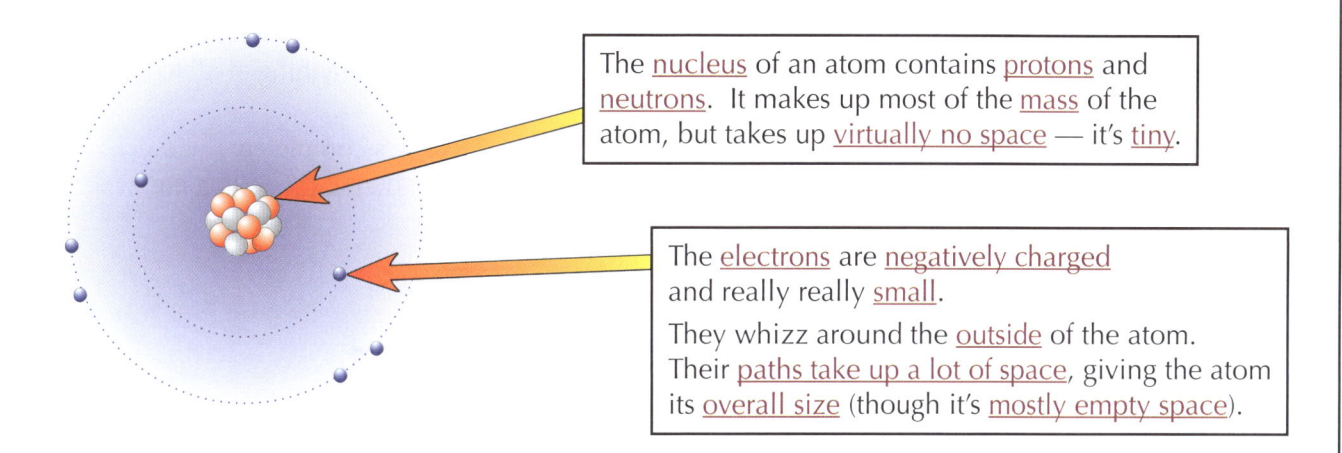

The nucleus of an atom contains protons and neutrons. It makes up most of the mass of the atom, but takes up virtually no space — it's tiny.

The electrons are negatively charged and really really small.
They whizz around the outside of the atom. Their paths take up a lot of space, giving the atom its overall size (though it's mostly empty space).

1) The number of protons in the nucleus is called the atomic number, or proton number.
2) The total number of protons and neutrons in the nucleus is called the mass number, or nucleon number.

Isotopes are Atoms with Different Numbers of Neutrons

1) Many elements have a few different isotopes. Isotopes are atoms with the same number of protons (i.e. the same atomic number) but a different number of neutrons (so a different mass number).

E.g. there are two common isotopes of carbon.
The carbon-14 isotope has two more neutrons than 'normal' carbon (carbon-12).

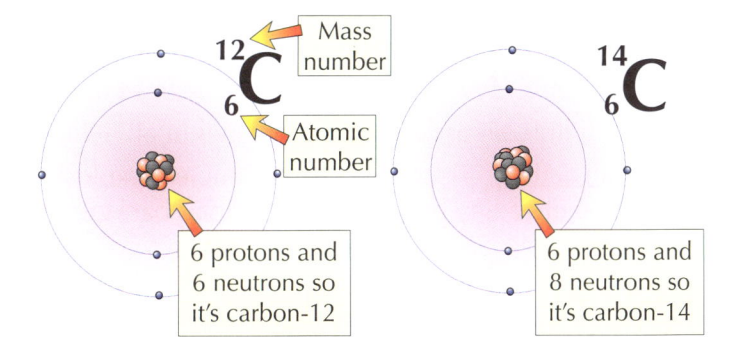

$^{12}_{6}C$ — Mass number / Atomic number
6 protons and 6 neutrons so it's carbon-12

$^{14}_{6}C$
6 protons and 8 neutrons so it's carbon-14

2) Usually each element only has one or two stable isotopes — like carbon-12. The other isotopes tend to be radioactive — the nucleus is unstable, so it decays (breaks down) and emits radiation. Carbon-14 is an unstable isotope of carbon.

You can get different isotopes of the same element

This isotope business can be confusing at first, but remember... it's the number of protons which decides what element it is, then the number of neutrons decides what isotope of that element it is.

Radioactivity

The nuclei of unstable isotopes decay and emit radiation (see previous page). Although you can't see it, nuclear radiation is all around us all the time. And that's what this page is all about.

Radioactive Decay is a Random Process

1) The nuclei of unstable isotopes break down at random. If you have 1000 unstable nuclei, you can't say when any one of them is going to decay, and you can't do anything at all to make a decay happen.
2) Each nucleus just decays quite spontaneously in its own good time. It's completely unaffected by physical conditions like temperature or by any sort of chemical bonding etc.
3) When the nucleus does decay it spits out one or more of the three types of radiation — alpha, beta and gamma (see next page).
4) In the process, the nucleus often changes into a new element.

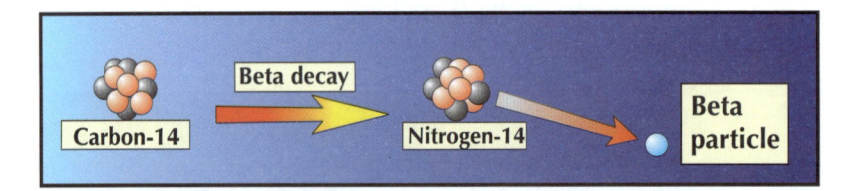

Background Radiation is Everywhere All the Time

There's (low-level) background nuclear radiation all around us all the time. It comes from:

- substances here on Earth — some radioactivity comes from air, food, building materials, soil, rocks...
- radiation from space (cosmic rays) — these come mostly from the Sun,
- living things — there's a little bit of radioactive material in all living things,
- radiation due to human activity — e.g. fallout from nuclear explosions, or nuclear waste (though this is usually a tiny proportion of the total background radiation).

Nuclear Radiation Causes Ionisation

1) Nuclear radiation causes ionisation by bashing into atoms and knocking electrons off them. Atoms (with no overall charge) are turned into ions (which are charged) — hence the term "ionisation".
2) There's a pattern: the further the radiation can penetrate before hitting an atom and getting stopped, the less damage it will do along the way and so the less ionising it is.
3) We can detect ionising radiation with photographic film or a Geiger-Muller detector.

SECTION 7 — RADIOACTIVITY AND PARTICLES

The Three Kinds of Radioactivity

Alpha, beta and gamma are three types of ionising radiation. You need to remember <u>what</u> they are, how well they <u>penetrate</u> materials, and their <u>ionising</u> power.

Alpha Particles are Helium Nuclei $^{4}_{2}He$

1) Alpha particles are made up of <u>2 protons and 2 neutrons</u> — they're <u>big</u>, <u>heavy</u> and <u>slow-moving</u>.

2) They therefore <u>don't penetrate</u> far into materials but are <u>stopped quickly</u>.

3) Because of their size they're <u>strongly ionising</u> (see previous page), which means they <u>bash into a lot of atoms</u> and <u>knock electrons off</u> them before they slow down, which creates lots of ions.

4) Because they're electrically <u>charged</u> (with a positive charge), alpha particles are <u>deflected</u> (their <u>direction changes</u>) by <u>electric</u> and <u>magnetic fields</u>.

5) Emitting an alpha particle <u>decreases</u> the <u>atomic</u> number of the nucleus by <u>2</u> and the <u>mass</u> number by <u>4</u> (see page 123 for more).

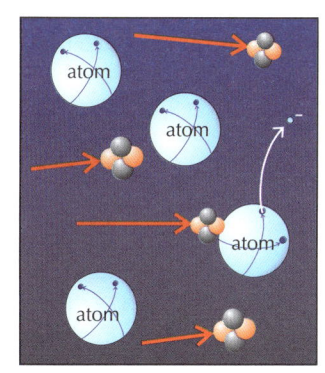

Beta Particles are Electrons $^{0}_{-1}e^{-}$

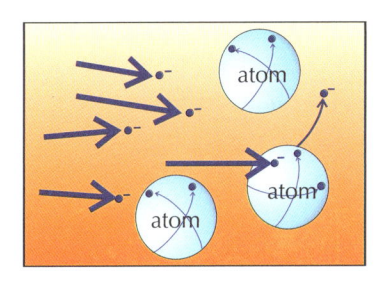

1) A beta particle is an <u>electron</u> which has been emitted from the <u>nucleus</u> of an atom when a <u>neutron</u> turns into a <u>proton</u> and an <u>electron</u>.

2) When a <u>beta particle</u> is emitted, the number of <u>protons</u> in the nucleus increases by 1. So the <u>atomic</u> number <u>increases</u> by <u>1</u> but the <u>mass</u> number <u>stays the same</u> (p.123).

3) They move <u>quite fast</u> and they are <u>quite small</u>.

4) They <u>penetrate moderately</u> before colliding and are <u>moderately ionising</u> too.

5) Because they're <u>charged</u> (negatively), beta particles are <u>deflected</u> by electric and magnetic fields.

Gamma Rays are Very Short Wavelength EM Waves

1) In a way, gamma (γ) rays are the <u>opposite of alpha particles</u>. They have <u>no mass</u> — they're just <u>energy</u> (in the form of an EM wave — see p. 56).

2) They can <u>penetrate a long way</u> into materials without being stopped.

3) This means they are <u>weakly ionising</u> because they tend to <u>pass through</u> rather than collide with atoms. But eventually they <u>hit something</u> and do <u>damage</u>.

4) Gamma rays have <u>no charge</u>, so they're <u>not</u> <u>deflected</u> by electric or magnetic fields.

5) Gamma emission always happens after beta or alpha decay. You <u>never</u> get <u>just gamma</u> rays emitted.

6) Gamma ray emission has <u>no effect</u> on the atomic or mass numbers of the isotope (p. 123). If a nucleus has <u>excess energy</u>, it loses this energy by emitting a gamma ray.

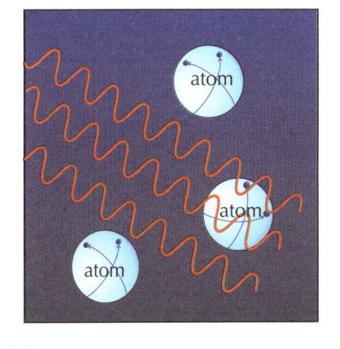

Radioactivity and Nuclear Equations

A bit more on how well the three types of ionising radiation penetrate materials (including air), and then some stuff on nuclear equations. Well it is Physics — there was bound to be an equation somewhere...

You Can Identify Radioactivity by its Penetrating Power

1) Alpha particles are blocked by paper, skin or a few centimetres of air.
2) Beta particles are stopped by thin metal.
3) Gamma rays are blocked by thick lead or very thick concrete.

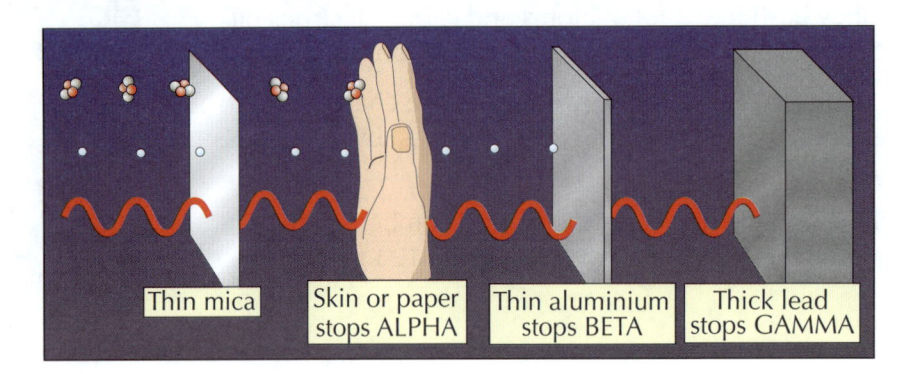

| Thin mica | Skin or paper stops ALPHA | Thin aluminium stops BETA | Thick lead stops GAMMA |

Balancing Nuclear Equations

1) You can write equations for nuclear reactions — just like you can for chemical reactions.
2) The total of the atomic and mass numbers has to be the same on both sides of the equation:

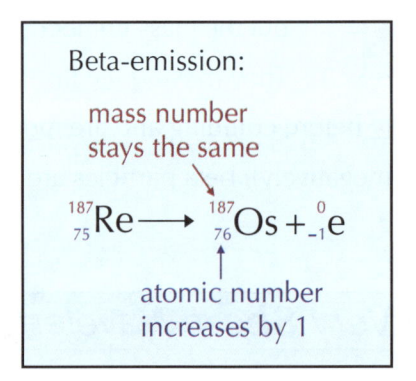

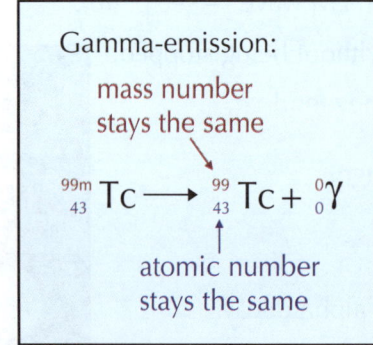

Alpha-emission:

mass number decreases by 4

$$^{226}_{88}Ra \longrightarrow {}^{222}_{86}Rn + {}^{4}_{2}He$$

atomic number decreases by 2

Beta-emission:

mass number stays the same

$$^{187}_{75}Re \longrightarrow {}^{187}_{76}Os + {}^{0}_{-1}e$$

atomic number increases by 1

Gamma-emission:

mass number stays the same

$$^{99m}_{43}Tc \longrightarrow {}^{99}_{43}Tc + {}^{0}_{0}\gamma$$

atomic number stays the same

Gamma- and alpha-emission:

mass number decreases by 4 — γ makes no difference

$$^{238}_{92}U \longrightarrow {}^{234}_{90}Th + {}^{4}_{2}He + {}^{0}_{0}\gamma$$

atomic number decreases by 2 — γ makes no difference

Like chemical equations, nuclear equations should be balanced
You might get asked to complete a balanced nuclear equation in the exam — so make sure you can.

SECTION 7 — RADIOACTIVITY AND PARTICLES

Alpha Scattering

Back in the day, a Greek fella called Democritus in the 5th Century BC thought that <u>all matter</u> was made up of <u>tiny</u> lumps called "atomos". And that's about as far as the theory got until the 1800s...

Rutherford Scattering and the Demise of the Plum Pudding

1) In 1804 <u>John Dalton</u> agreed with Democritus that matter was made up of <u>tiny spheres</u> ("atoms") that couldn't be broken up. He reckoned that <u>each element</u> was made up of a <u>different type</u> of "atom".

2) Nearly 100 years later, J J Thomson discovered that <u>electrons</u> could be <u>removed</u> from atoms. So Dalton's theory wasn't quite right (atoms could be broken up). Thomson suggested that atoms were <u>spheres of positive charge</u> with tiny negative electrons <u>stuck in them</u> like plums in a <u>plum pudding</u>.

3) That "plum-pudding" theory didn't last very long though. In 1909 <u>Hans Geiger</u> and <u>Ernest Marsden</u> tried firing <u>alpha particles</u> at <u>thin gold foil</u>.

4) Most of the particles just went <u>straight through</u>, and were detected when they hit a <u>zinc sulfide screen</u> and gave off a tiny flash of light (this is called a scintillation).

5) But the odd alpha particle came <u>straight back</u> at them, which was frankly a bit of a <u>shocker</u>.

Rutherford came up with a Nuclear Model of the Atom

Ernest Rutherford, Geiger and Marsden's boss, used their results to come up with a <u>nuclear model</u> of the atom.

1) If the <u>plum-pudding model</u> was right, alpha particles would just <u>pass straight through</u> the gold foil.

2) The fact that some of the alpha particles <u>bounced back</u> meant that inside the atoms there must be <u>small positively charged nuclei</u>, which <u>repel</u> the passing alpha particles, so Rutherford's nuclear model of the atom says:

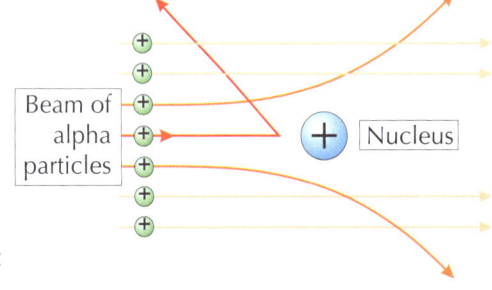

> - <u>Most</u> of the <u>mass</u> must be concentrated at the <u>centre</u>, and most of an atom is <u>empty space</u>.
> - The nucleus must be <u>small</u> since very few alpha particles are deflected by much.
> - It must be <u>positive</u> to repel the positively charged alpha particles.

3) The <u>faster</u> an alpha particle's travelling, the <u>less</u> it will be deflected by a nucleus.

4) The <u>more positively charged</u> a nucleus is (i.e. the higher the atomic number), the <u>more</u> an alpha particle will be deflected.

5) The <u>closer</u> an alpha particle passes to the <u>nucleus</u>, the more it will be <u>deflected</u>.

Atoms are mostly empty space

Rutherford used Geiger and Marsden's observations to come up with a new, clear model of the atom. And jolly useful it is too. Make sure you know Rutherford's nuclear model inside out for your exams.

Warm-Up and Exam Questions

Well, it's time to test what you know. If you've learnt everything on the previous few pages, you should be able to answer every single one of these questions. Better get started...

Warm-Up Questions

1) What is the nucleon number of a nucleus?
2) What is the name of an atom that has been ionised?
3) Explain why alpha radiation is so strongly ionising.
4) Name the type of nuclear radiation whose particles are electrons.
5) Name the type of nuclear radiation that is a type of electromagnetic wave.
6) Who's gold-foil experiment led Rutherford to come up with the nuclear model of the atom?
7) Describe Rutherford's nuclear model of the atom.

Exam Questions

1   Iodine-131 ($^{131}_{53}$I) is an unstable isotope of iodine.

   a) i)   Copy and complete the table for an atom of iodine-131.

Particle	Charge	Number present in an atom of iodine-131
Proton	positive	
Neutron	zero	
Electron		53

(3 marks)

      ii) Name the particle(s) found in the nucleus of an atom.

(1 mark)

   b)   What is meant by the term **isotopes**?

(1 mark)

   c)   Iodine-131 is a waste product of some nuclear power plants and it contributes to the low level of radiation that is present all around us all the time.

      i)   Give the name of this low level of radiation.

(1 mark)

      ii) Give **two** natural sources of this low level of radiation.

(2 marks)

   d)   Name **three** types of radiation that can be given out when unstable nuclei decay.

(3 marks)

Exam Questions

2. Alpha, beta and gamma radiation sources were used to pass radiation through thin sheets of paper and aluminium. A detector was used to measure where radiation had passed through the sheets. The results are shown below.

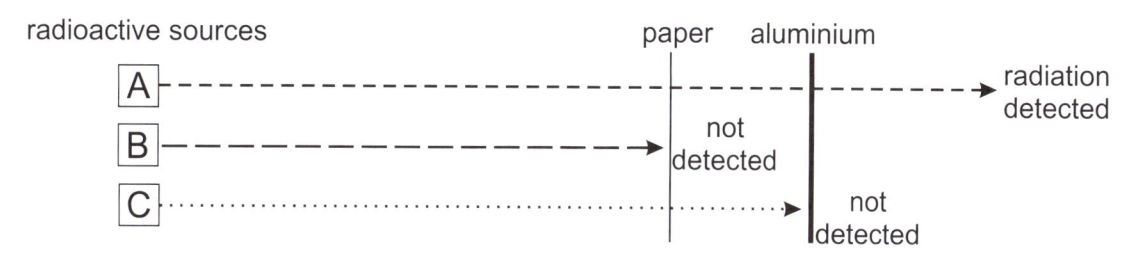

   a) State the type of radiation that source C produces. Explain your answer.
   (2 marks)

   b) Give **one** example of a detector that could have been used to detect the radiation.
   (1 mark)

3. Alpha particles are fired towards a gold nucleus ($^{197}_{79}$Au) and a silver nucleus ($^{107}_{47}$Ag) as shown in the diagram below. The amount of deflection of the alpha particles is measured.

   a) State which nucleus will deflect the alpha particles more. Explain your answer.
   (1 mark)

   b) The speed of the alpha particles directed at the gold nucleus is increased. Describe what effect this will have on how much the particles are deflected by the gold nucleus.
   (1 mark)

   c) The beam of alpha particles is moved so that it doesn't pass as close to the gold nucleus. Describe what effect this will have on how much the particles are deflected by the gold nucleus.
   (1 mark)

4. Nuclear equations show what is produced when unstable nuclei decay.
   a) i) Draw the symbol for a beta particle.
      (2 marks)

      ii) Describe what happens to the atomic number and the mass number of a nucleus when it undergoes beta decay.
      (2 marks)

   b) i) Describe what happens to the atomic number and the mass number of a nucleus when it undergoes gamma decay.
      (2 marks)

      ii) Copy and complete this nuclear equation, which shows a polonium isotope decaying by alpha and gamma emission.

      $$^{\ldots}_{\ldots}\text{Po} \rightarrow ^{195}_{82}\text{Pb} + ^{\ldots}_{\ldots}\alpha + ^{\ldots}_{\ldots}\gamma$$

      (4 marks)

Half-Life

Half-life is the time it takes for a radioactive material to lose half of its radioactivity. Simple really.

The Radioactivity of a Sample Always Decreases Over Time

1) This is pretty obvious when you think about it. Each time a decay happens and an alpha or beta particle or gamma ray is given out, it means one more radioactive nucleus has disappeared.

2) Obviously, as the unstable nuclei all disappear, the activity as a whole will decrease. So the older a sample becomes, the less radiation it will emit.

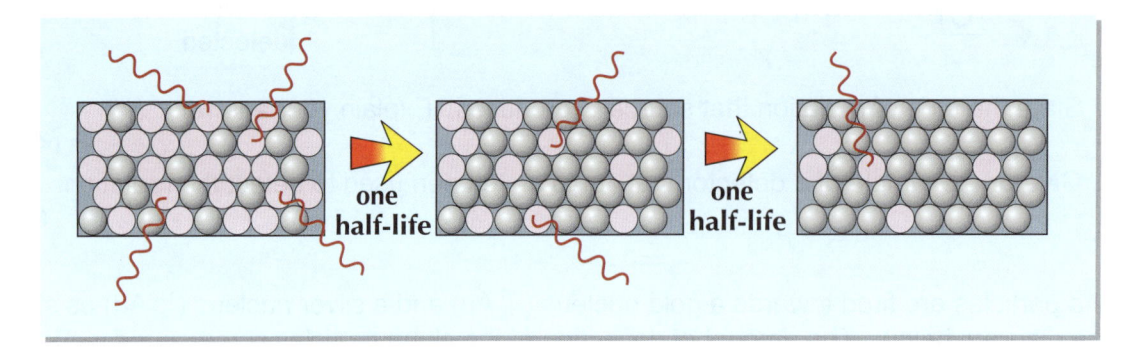

3) How quickly the activity drops off varies a lot. For some isotopes it takes just a few hours before nearly all the unstable nuclei have decayed, whilst others last for millions of years.

4) The problem with trying to measure this is that the activity never reaches zero, which is why we have to use the idea of half-life to measure how quickly the activity drops off.

5) Learn this important definition of half-life:

Half-life is the time taken for half of the radioactive atoms now present to decay.

Another definition of half-life is:

"The time taken for the activity (or count rate) to fall by half."

You can use either of these two definitions.

6) A short half-life means the activity falls quickly, because lots of the nuclei decay quickly.

7) A long half-life means the activity falls more slowly because most of the nuclei don't decay for a long time — they just sit there, basically unstable, but kind of biding their time.

Make sure you've learnt a definition of half-life

Isotopes can have very different half-lives. E.g. uranium-235 (used in nuclear power stations) has a half-life of 700 million years, while the half-life of fluorine-18 (used in hospitals) is less than 2 hours.

Half-Life

This page is about how to tackle the two main types of half-life questions.

Do Half-Life Questions Step by Step

Half-life is maybe a little confusing, but the calculations are straightforward so long as you do them slowly, STEP BY STEP. Like this one:

EXAMPLE:

> The activity of a radioisotope is 640 Bq.
> Two hours later it has fallen to 40 Bq. Find the half-life of the sample.

Radioactivity is measured in becquerels (Bq). 1 Bq is 1 decay per second.

ANSWER: You must go through it in short simple steps like this:

INITIAL count:		after ONE half-life:		after TWO half-lives:		after THREE half-lives:		after FOUR half-lives:
640	(÷2)→	320	(÷2)→	160	(÷2)→	80	(÷2)→	40

Notice the careful step-by-step method, which tells us it takes four half-lives for the activity to fall from 640 to 40. Hence two hours represents four half-lives, so the half-life is 30 minutes.

Measuring the Half-Life of a Sample Using a Graph

1) This can only be done by taking several readings of a source's activity, usually using a Geiger-Muller (G-M) detector. The results can then be plotted as a graph, which will always be shaped like the one below.

2) The half-life is found from the graph, by finding the time interval on the bottom axis corresponding to a halving of the activity on the vertical axis. Easy peasy really.

3) One trick you need to know is about the background radiation, which also enters the G-M detector and gives false readings.

4) Measure the background activity first and then subtract it from every reading you get, before plotting the results on the graph.

5) Realistically, the only difficult bit is actually remembering about that for your exam, should they ask you about it. They could also test that idea in a calculation question.

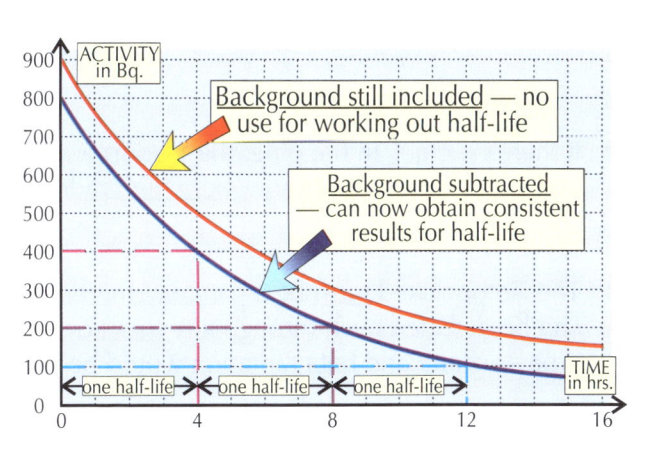

Remember: 1 Bq is 1 decay per second

There are lots of things the examiner could ask you to do when it comes to calculating a half-life in the exam. As long as you've learnt this page though, and take the questions step by step, you'll be fine.

SECTION 7 — RADIOACTIVITY AND PARTICLES

Uses of Nuclear Radiation

Nuclear radiation can be really useful — but you've got to be careful about what isotope you use.

Medical Tracers Use Beta or Gamma Radiation

Beta and gamma will penetrate the skin and other body tissues. This makes them suitable as medical tracers:

1) A source which emits beta or gamma radiation is injected into the patient (or swallowed). The radiation penetrates the body tissues and can be detected externally. As the source moves around the body, the radiographer uses a detector to monitor its progress or to get a 'snapshot' of its distribution.

2) A computer converts the reading to an on-screen display showing where the radiation is coming from. Doctors use this method to check whether the organs of the body are working as they should.

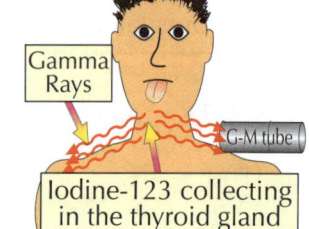

3) The radioactive source has to have a short half-life, so you can use less of the radioactive source but still get a reading on your detector.

4) An alpha source would be worse than useless as a medical tracer — useless because it would be stopped by the body's tissues, so you'd never detect it externally, and worse than useless because its strong ionising power makes alpha radiation really harmful if it gets inside you (see page 134).

Gamma Radiation is Used in Industrial Tracers

If you're looking for a leak in an underground pipe, you could dig it up, or you could use gamma rays...

1) You squirt a γ-source into the pipe, let it flow along, and go along the outside with a detector.

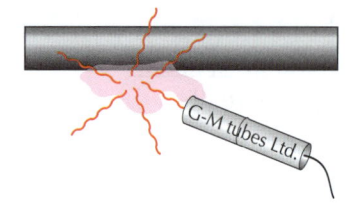

2) Gamma radiation will penetrate through a metal pipe, but some of it gets absorbed — exactly how much depends on the thickness of the pipe and what it's made of.

3) If there's a crack in the pipe, the γ–source will collect outside the pipe, and your detector will show extra high radioactivity at that point.

4) The isotope used must be a gamma emitter, so that the radiation can be detected even through any rocks or earth surrounding the pipe — alpha and beta radiation would be too easily blocked.

5) It should also have a short half-life so as not to cause a long-term hazard if it collects somewhere.

Choose your source carefully
To make use of radiation, you've got to match the requirements of the job to your source's properties.

SECTION 7 — RADIOACTIVITY AND PARTICLES

More Uses of Nuclear Radiation

Yep, there are even more ways in which nuclear radiation has proved itself useful. Take a look...

Radioactive Dating of Rocks and Archaeological Specimens

1) The discovery of radioactivity and the idea of half-life (see p. 130-131) gave scientists their first opportunity to accurately work out the age of rocks, fossils and archaeological specimens.

2) By measuring the amount of a radioactive isotope left in a sample, and knowing its half-life, you can work out how long the thing has been around.

Uranium and Potassium-40 Can be Used to Date Rocks

1) Igneous rocks contain radioactive uranium which has a ridiculously long half-life.

2) It eventually decays to become stable isotopes of lead, so a clue to a rock sample's age is the relative proportions of uranium and lead isotopes.

3) Igneous rocks also contain radioactive potassium-40, some of which decays to stable argon gas. So you can date rocks by comparing the relative proportion of potassium-40 to trapped argon gas.

Carbon-14 Helps to Date Archaeological Specimens

1) Carbon-14 makes up about 1/10 000 000 (one ten-millionth) of the carbon in the air. This level stays fairly constant in the atmosphere.

2) The same proportion of C-14 is also found in living things. When they die, the C-14 becomes trapped inside wood, bones, wool etc. C-14 is a beta-emitting radioactive isotope, so the C-14 inside them decays over time and its radioactivity decreases.

3) Comparing the activity of the sample to living tissue lets you make an estimate of how many half-lives of C-14 have passed. This gives you an idea of how long ago the animal or plant died.

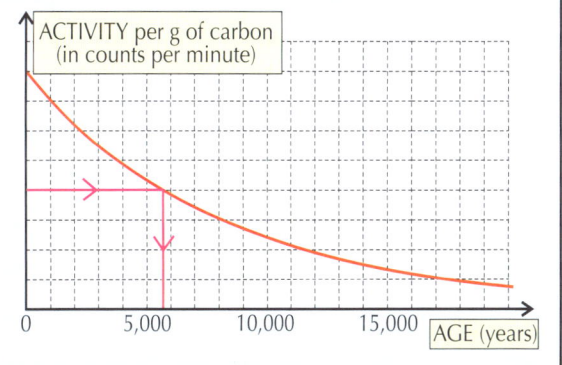

4) The ratio of C-14 to C-12 in living materials is fixed, so comparing the ratio in the sample can also help you estimate the age.

Radiation is Also Used to Treat Cancer

1) Radiation can cause cancer (see next page), but it can also be used to treat it.

2) Once cancer's started, patients can be given radiotherapy to kill the cancer cells and stop them dividing.

3) This involves using a high dose of gamma rays, carefully directed to zap the cells in the tumour while minimising the dose to the rest of the body.

Risks from Nuclear Radiation

Radiation's dangerous and useful at the same time — it can both cause and cure cancer, for instance.

Ionising Radiation Can Damage Cells and Tissues

1) Beta and gamma can penetrate the skin and soft tissues to reach the delicate organs inside the body. This makes beta and gamma sources more hazardous than alpha when outside the body. If they get inside the body (by being swallowed or breathed in, say), their radiation mostly passes straight out without doing much damage.

2) Alpha radiation can't penetrate the skin, but it's very dangerous if it gets inside the body. Alpha sources do all their damage in a very localised area.

The properties of alpha, beta and gamma are on page 125.

3) When radiation enters your body, it will collide with molecules in your cells. These collisions cause ionisation, which damages or destroys the molecules.

4) Lower doses tend to cause minor damage without killing the cell. This can cause mutations in cells which then divide uncontrollably — this is cancer.

5) Higher doses tend to kill cells completely, causing radiation sickness if a large part of your body is affected at the same time.

6) The extent of the harmful effects depends on how much exposure you have to the radiation, and its energy and penetration.

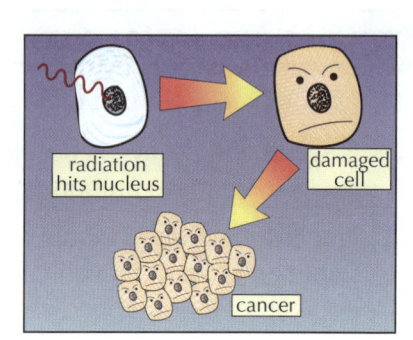

Radioactive Waste is Difficult to Dispose of Safely

1) Most radioactive waste from nuclear power stations and hospitals is 'low-level' (slightly radioactive) — things like clothing, syringes, etc. This kind of waste can be disposed of by burying it in secure landfill sites.

2) High-level waste is the really dangerous stuff — a lot of it stays highly radioactive for tens of thousands of years, and so has to be treated very carefully. It's often sealed into glass blocks, which are then sealed in metal canisters. These could then be buried deep underground.

3) However, it's difficult to find suitable places to bury high-level waste. The site has to be geologically stable (e.g. not suffer from earthquakes), since big movements in the rock could disturb the canisters and allow radioactive material to leak out. If this material gets into the groundwater, it could contaminate the soil, plants, rivers, etc., and get into our drinking water.

Use Protection if You're Working with Radioactive Materials

It's important to minimise your exposure when you're working with radioactive sources.

1) Never allow skin contact with a source, and always hold it with tongs and at arm's length.
2) Keep the source pointed away from the body and avoid looking directly at it.
3) Store radioactive sources in a sealed lead box whenever they're not being used.

If You Regularly Work with Radioactivity, Take Extra Precautions

1) Medical workers who use radioactivity need to wear lead aprons and stand behind lead screens during procedures.
2) Industrial nuclear workers wear full protective suits to prevent tiny radioactive particles being inhaled or lodging on the skin or under fingernails etc.
3) Workers can also use remote-controlled robot arms to carry out tasks in highly radioactive areas.

SECTION 7 — RADIOACTIVITY AND PARTICLES

Nuclear Fission

Most power stations get the energy they need to drive the generators by burning fuel (e.g. coal) or from the natural motion of something (e.g. waves, tides). Nuclear power stations do it a bit differently...

Nuclear Power Stations use Nuclear Fission

1) Nuclear fission is the splitting of an atom, which releases energy.
2) Nuclear power stations are powered by nuclear reactors (see below). In a nuclear reactor, nuclear fission is carried out in a controlled chain reaction — uranium or plutonium atoms split up, releasing loads of energy.

You Can Split More than One Atom — Fission Chain Reactions

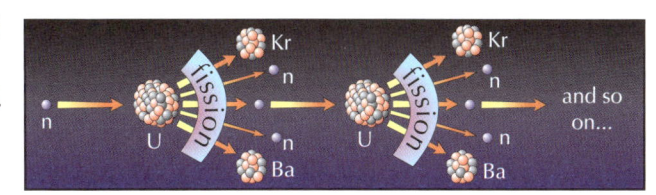

1) The "fuel" that's split in a nuclear reactor (and bombs — a nuclear bomb is an uncontrolled fission chain reaction) is usually uranium-235.
2) If a slow-moving neutron gets absorbed by a uranium-235 nucleus, the nucleus can split.
3) Each time a uranium-235 (U-235) nucleus splits up, it spits out a small number of neutrons. These might go on to hit other uranium-235 nuclei, causing them to split and release even more neutrons, which hit even more nuclei... and so on and so on. This process is known as a chain reaction.
4) When uranium-235 splits in two it will form two new daughter nuclei. These daughter nuclei are lighter elements than uranium.
5) These new nuclei are usually radioactive because they have the "wrong" number of neutrons in them. This is the big problem with nuclear power — it produces huge amounts of radioactive waste which is very difficult and expensive to dispose of safely — see previous page.
6) Each nucleus splitting gives out a lot of energy — this energy is in the form of kinetic energy of the fission products (the daughter nuclei and the neutrons).
7) This energy can be converted to heat energy in a reactor, by collisions with other atoms.

Inside a Gas-Cooled Nuclear Reactor

This is a gas-cooled nuclear reactor, but there are many other kinds.

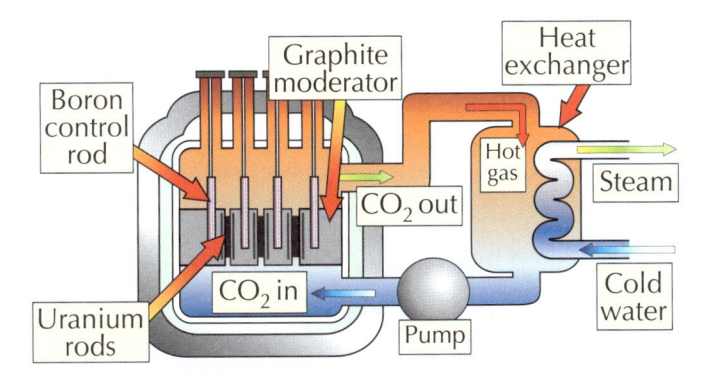

1) Free neutrons in the reactor 'kick-start' the fission process.
2) The atoms produced then collide with other atoms, causing the temperature in the reactor to rise.
3) The moderator, usually graphite or water, slows neutrons so that they can successfully collide with uranium nuclei and sustain the chain reaction.
4) Control rods, often made of boron, limit the rate of fission by absorbing excess neutrons.
5) A gas, typically carbon dioxide (CO_2), is pumped through the reactor to carry away the heat generated.
6) The gas is then passed through a heat exchanger, where it gives its energy to water. This water is heated and turned into steam, which turns a turbine, which turns a generator, generating electricity.

Warm-Up and Exam Questions

Right. More questions to help you find out what you know. And more importantly, what you don't...

Warm-Up Questions

1) What units is radioactivity measured in?
2) Name the two types of radiation that can be used in medical tracers.
3) How could you use gamma rays to detect a leak in an underground pipe?
4) Why is it important that sites where high-level radioactive waste is buried are geologically stable?

Exam Questions

1   A radioactive isotope sample has a half-life of 40 seconds.

   a) i)   The initial activity of the sample is 8000 Bq.
            Calculate the activity after 2 minutes. Give your answer in becquerels.

   (2 marks)

       ii) Calculate the number of whole minutes it would
            take for the activity to fall below 200 Bq.

   (3 marks)

   b) Chang and Paul are discussing half-lives.

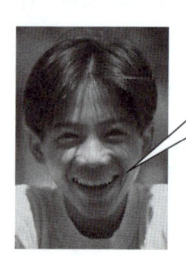

   Chang: "A sample of the same size but of a different isotope would have the same half-life."

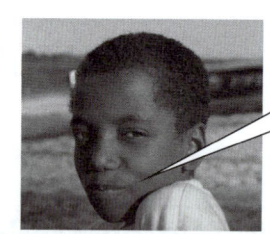

   Paul: "A sample of the same size but of a different isotope would have a different half-life."

   Which student is correct? Explain your answer.

   (1 mark)

2   Some people are exposed to higher than average levels of ionising radiation while at work.

   a) Explain why exposure to ionising radiation can be dangerous.

   (2 marks)

   b) Radiotherapists in hospitals use some types of radiation
       as part of **radiotherapy** treatment.

       i)   Describe what is meant by radiotherapy.

   (2 marks)

       ii) Describe **one** precaution that should be taken by radiotherapists to minimise
            their radiation exposure.

   (2 marks)

       iii) Some radiotherapists have to handle radioactive sources in a laboratory.
            Describe **two** safety precautions that should be taken when handling
            radioactive sources.

   (2 marks)

SECTION 7 — RADIOACTIVITY AND PARTICLES

Exam Questions

3. Iodine-123 is commonly used as a tracer in medicine.

   a) Describe how iodine-123 can be used to detect whether the thyroid gland is absorbing iodine as it normally should do.
   (2 marks)

   b) Explain why alpha emitters cannot be used as tracers in medicine.
   (4 marks)

   c) The table shows the properties of three other radioisotopes.

      State which of these would be best to use as a medical tracer. Explain your answer.

Radioisotope	Half-life	Type of emission
technetium-99m	6 hours	gamma
phosphorus-32	14 days	beta
cobalt-60	5 years	beta/gamma

      (2 marks)

4. An ancient wooden artefact was found to have 1 part carbon-14 to 80 000 000 parts carbon. The half-life of carbon-14 is 5730 years and the ratio of carbon-14:carbon in living things is 1:10 000 000. Calculate the amount of time that has passed since the wood was living material. Give your answer in years.
   (3 marks)

5. Nuclear fission takes place in nuclear reactors. The diagram shows the basic structure of a gas-cooled nuclear reactor.

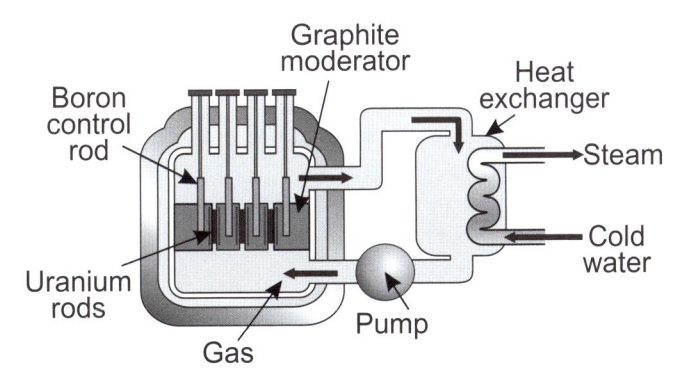

   a) Give **one** fuel that can be used in a nuclear reactor.
   (1 mark)

   b) i) Describe what happens during a single nuclear fission event and the products formed.
      (4 marks)

      ii) Explain how nuclear fission can be used to produce energy continuously in a nuclear reactor, and how part of the nuclear reactor is designed to help this happen.
      (3 marks)

   c) Explain the purpose of the control rods in a nuclear reactor.
   (1 mark)

Revision Summary for Section 7

Now a reward for ploughing through loads of pages of pretty intense science — a page of lovely Revision Summary questions. Okay, I know you've already answered a fair few questions, but it's absolutely vital to check that you've learnt all the right stuff.

1) List the three particles that make up an atom.
2) What is the atomic number of a nucleus?
3) What is the mass number of a nucleus?
4) What are isotopes of an element?
5) Briefly describe what background radiation is and where it comes from.
6) Give two ways you can detect ionising radiation.
7) Describe what alpha, beta and gamma radiation are.
8) Which is the most ionising out of alpha, beta and gamma radiation?
9) What type of radiation is stopped by paper?
10)*Balance the following nuclear reaction equations:

   a) $^{131}_{53}I \longrightarrow ^{...}_{...}Xe + ^{0}_{-1}e$ b) $^{241}_{95}Am \longrightarrow ^{...}_{...}Np + ^{4}_{2}He$ c) $^{14}_{6}C \longrightarrow ^{14}_{7}N + ^{...}_{...}$

11) a) Describe Geiger and Marsden's gold foil experiment.
    b) Describe how the results of this experiment helped Rutherford devise a new model of the atom.
12) What is the half-life of an isotope?
13)*Calculate the half-life of a sample of copper-64 with an activity at the start of the experiment of 400 Bq, and an activity 1 day later of 100 Bq.
14) Briefly describe three uses of nuclear radiation.
15) Why is nuclear radiation dangerous to living organisms?
16) Explain why radioactive waste is difficult to dispose of safely.
17) What are the products of the nuclear fission of uranium-235?
18) Briefly describe how a chain reaction is set up in a nuclear reactor.
19) What job do control rods and moderators do in a nuclear reactor?

*Answers on page 191.

Describing Experiments

139

Experimental Know-How

Scientists need to know how to plan and carry out scientific experiments. Unfortunately, the examiners think you should be able to do the same. But don't worry — that's what this section's all about.

You Might Get Asked Questions on Reliability and Validity

1) RELIABLE results come from experiments that give the same data:

   - each time the experiment is repeated (by you),
   - each time the experiment is reproduced by other scientists.

2) VALID results are both reliable AND come from experiments that were designed to be a fair test.

In the exam, you could be asked to suggest ways to improve the reliability or validity of some experimental results. If so, there are a couple of things to think about:

1) Controlling Variables Improves Validity

1) A variable is something that has the potential to change, e.g. temperature.
   In a lab experiment you usually change one variable and measure how it affects another variable.

   > EXAMPLE: you might change only the surface colour of a beaker to find out how quickly it loses heat after being filled with hot water.

2) To make it a fair test, everything else that could affect the results should stay the same — otherwise you can't tell if the thing you're changing is causing the results or not.

   > EXAMPLE continued: you need to keep the initial temperature of the water the same, or you won't know whether the rate of heat loss is caused by the beaker's colour or the temperature of the water.

3) The variable you CHANGE is called the INDEPENDENT variable.
4) The variable you MEASURE is called the DEPENDENT variable.
5) The variables that you KEEP THE SAME are called CONTROL variables.

   EXAMPLE continued: Independent variable = surface colour of the beaker
   Dependent variable = temperature of the water
   Control variables = initial temperature of the water, volume of water, beaker material, etc.

6) Because you can't always control all the variables, you often need to use a CONTROL EXPERIMENT — an experiment that's kept under the same conditions as the rest of the investigation, but doesn't have anything done to it. This is so that you can see what happens when you don't change anything at all.

2) Carrying Out Repeats Improves Reliability

To improve reliability you need to repeat any measurements you make and calculate the mean (average). You need to repeat each measurement at least three times.

Getting reliable and valid results is very important

You might be asked to suggest what variables need to be controlled in an experiment. E.g. you know that heat radiation is affected by surface colour and initial temperature, so these variables need to be kept constant (providing you're not investigating one of them). You might also need to say how you'd control the variables, e.g. surface colour can be kept constant by using the same beaker each time.

Experimental Know-How

You Might Have to Suggest Ways to Make an Experiment Safer

1) It's important that experiments are safe. If you're asked to suggest ways to make an experiment safer, you'll first need to identify what the potential hazards might be. Hazards include things like:

- Radioactivity, e.g. too much exposure can damage skin cells.
- Springs, e.g. a taut spring can get detached or snap, so you need to protect your eyes.
- Electricity, e.g. faulty electrical equipment could give you a shock.

2) Then you'll need to suggest ways of reducing the risks involved with the hazard, e.g.

- If you're stretching a metal spring using weights, make sure it's clamped firmly and that you don't apply too much force. This way it won't snap or flick up into your face.

You Could be Asked About Accuracy...

1) It's important that results are ACCURATE.
Really accurate results are those that are really close to the true figure.

2) The accuracy of your results usually depends on your method.

E.g. say you wanted to measure how long a ball takes to roll down a slope of varying length. You could count how long it takes in your head, but it's almost impossible to count in exact seconds, even if you think you're really good at it. You also wouldn't be able to count in tenths or hundredths of seconds, so you'd have to estimate if it was 2.3 or 2.7 seconds. It would be more accurate to use a stopwatch, pressing the button whenever the ball passes a mark drawn on the slope.

3) There is always some uncertainty in your results. The larger the value of a result, the less the result is affected by the uncertainty and the more accurate the result will be.

E.g. say you want to measure the time a feather takes to fall a certain distance, it'll take some time to press stop (say 0.2 s). If you measure 0.5 s, the uncertainty of 0.2 s is large compared to the result. However, if you measure 5 s, the uncertainty's smaller compared to the result, so it'll be more accurate.

4) To make sure your results are as accurate as possible, you also need to make sure you're measuring the right thing and that you don't miss anything that should be included in the measurements.

E.g. if you want to know the length of a wire, you need to start measuring from '0 cm' on the ruler, not the very end of the ruler (or your measurement will be a few mm too short).

...And Precision

1) Results also need to be PRECISE. Precise results are those taken using sensitive instruments that measure in small increments, e.g. using a ruler with a millimetre scale gives more precise data than using a ruler with a scale in centimetres.

2) By recording your results to a greater number of decimal places, you'll increase their precision, e.g.

In some exam questions, you'll be told how precise to be in your answer. So if you're told to give an answer to 2 decimal places, make sure you do or you could lose marks.

Repeat	Data set 1	Data set 2
1	12	11.98
2	14	14.00
3	13	13.01

The results in data set 2 are more precise than those in data set 1.

Safety first — goggles on before you read this book...

Sometimes you'll be asked to describe how you'd carry out your own experiment in the exam. All this stuff about reliability and what not will apply then too. So make sure you learn it and write it down.

Drawing Graphs and Interpreting Results

If you're presented with some results from an experiment you've got to know what to do with them.

You Should Be Able to Identify Anomalous Results

1) Most results vary a bit, but any that are totally different are called anomalous results.
2) They can be caused by human errors, e.g. by a mistake made when measuring, or by an outside factor affecting the experiment, e.g. a cold draught affecting a temperature reading.
3) You could be asked to identify an anomalous result in the exam and suggest what caused it — just look for a result that doesn't fit in with the rest (e.g. it's too high or too low) then try to figure out what could have gone wrong with the experiment to have caused it.
4) If you're calculating an average, you can ignore any anomalous results.

You Need to Be Able to Draw Graphs...

In the exam, you might be asked to draw a graph or bar chart from a set of results.
If you're not told which one to go for, here's how you decide:

1) If the independent variable is categoric (comes in distinct categories, e.g. colours, metals) you should use a bar chart to display the data.
2) If the independent variable is continuous (can take any value within a range, e.g. length, volume, time) you should use a line graph to display the data.

Here are a few useful tips for drawing line graphs:

- Remember to label the axes and include the units.
- The dependent variable (the thing you measure) goes on the y-axis (the vertical one).
- The independent variable (the thing you change) goes on the x-axis (the horizontal one).
- When plotting points, use a sharp pencil and make a neat little cross (don't do blobs).
- If you're told to join up the points using a straight line, use a ruler to draw a neat line between each point.
- If you're told to draw a line of best fit, try to draw the line through or as near to as many points as possible, ignoring anomalous results. This graph shows a line of best fit.

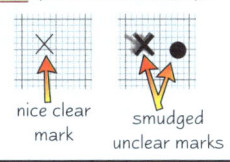

Make sure you fill at least half of the space you're given to draw a graph.

...And Interpret Them

1) A graph is used to show the relationship between two variables — you need to be able to look at a graph and describe this relationship. For example, the graph above shows that as voltage increases, so does the current.
2) You also need to be able to read information off a graph. In this example, if you wanted to know what the current was at 11 V, you'd draw a vertical line up from the x-axis at 11 V and a horizontal line across to the y-axis. This would tell you that the current at 11 V was around 9.7 mA.

You might have to describe the results in a table too...

...or pick out an anomalous result from one. You'll also be expected to do basic maths, like calculating a mean (add everything together and divide by the total number of values) or a percentage.

Describing Experiments

Planning Experiments and Evaluating Conclusions

In the exam, you could be asked to plan or describe how you'd carry out an experiment. The experiment might be one you've already come across or you might be asked to come up with an experiment of your own to test something. You might also be asked to say what you think of someone else's conclusion.

You Need to Be Able to Plan a Good Experiment

Here are some general tips on what to include when planning an experiment:

1) Say what you're measuring (i.e. what the dependent variable is going to be).
2) Say what you're changing (i.e. what the independent variable is going to be) and describe how you're going to change it.
3) Describe the method and the apparatus you'd use.
4) Describe what variables you're keeping constant (your control variables) — and how you're going to do it.
5) Say that you need to repeat the experiment at least three times, to make the results more reliable.
6) Say whether you're using a control or not.

Here's an idea of the sort of thing you might be asked in the exam and what you might write as an answer.

Exam-style Question:

1 Describe an investigation to find how the type of surface under a wood block affects the force needed to slide the block across the surface. (6)

Example Answer:

Set up a wood block with a hook firmly attached to the centre of one of the faces, so that a newton meter can be attached. Choose three different surfaces to place the block on, making sure they're all flat and horizontal.

Take a newton meter and calibrate it by suspending masses from it with a known weight and writing down the force shown. This will ensure its readings are accurate.

You could use a spirit level to make sure the surfaces are flat and horizontal.

Place the wood block on the first surface you're testing, and hook a newton meter onto the block. Pull gently on the block using the newton meter in the horizontal direction until the block starts to move. Write down the force shown on the newton meter at this point. Repeat this experiment at least three times and calculate an average reading, discounting any anomalous results.

Do the same again for each type of surface you're investigating. Between testing each surface, suspend one of the weights used for the initial calibration from the newton meter and check the reading is still the same. This will show whether the newton meter is still giving accurate readings.

Drawing a diagram of your experiment might be helpful.

You Could Be Asked to Evaluate a Conclusion

1) In the exam, you could be given an experimental conclusion and asked to evaluate it.
2) This just means saying whether or not you think evidence from the experiment supports the conclusion — and why.

Plan your way to exam success...

The number of marks available for a question like this will vary, but it'll usually be around five or six. This means you'll have to write an extended answer. Think about what you're going to say beforehand and in what order — that way you're less likely to forget something important.

DESCRIBING EXPERIMENTS

Practice Papers

Once you've been through all the questions in this book, you should feel pretty confident about the exams. As final preparation, here is a set of **practice papers** to really get you set for the real thing. These papers are designed to give you the best possible preparation for your exams.

Candidate Surname

Candidate Forename(s)

Centre Number

Candidate Number

Certificate International GCSE

Physics
Paper 1P

Practice Paper
Time allowed: 2 hours

You must have:
- A ruler.
- A calculator.

Total marks:

Instructions to candidates
- Use **black** ink to write your answers.
- Write your name and other details in the spaces provided above.
- Answer **all** questions in the spaces provided.
- In calculations, show clearly how you worked out your answers.
- You will need to answer some questions by placing a cross in a box, like this: ☒
  To change your answer, draw a line through the box like this: ~~☒~~
  Then mark your new answer as normal.

Information for candidates
- The marks available are given in brackets at the end of each question.
- There are 120 marks available for this paper.
- You might find the equations on page 182 useful.

Advice for candidates
- Read all the questions carefully.
- Write your answers as clearly and neatly as possible.
- Keep in mind how much time you have left.

Answer **all** questions

1 At the start of a roller coaster ride a carriage is raised by a chain lift through a vertical height of 40 m to point A, as shown in the diagram. It is stopped at point A and then released to follow the track through points B, C and D.

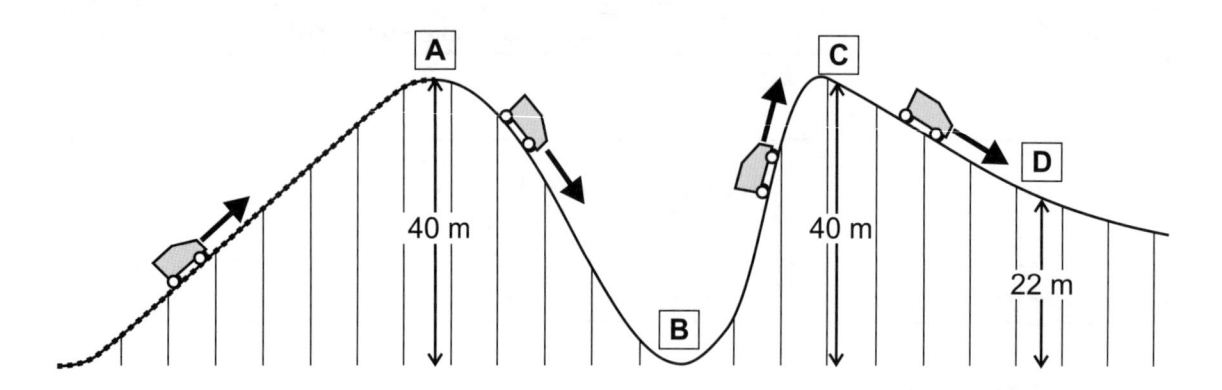

(a) (i) At which two points does the carriage have the same gravitational potential energy?
Place a cross (x) in the appropriate box to indicate your answer.

☐ B and D

☐ A and C

☐ C and D

☐ A and D

[1]

(ii) At which point does the car have the greatest kinetic energy?
Place a cross (x) in the appropriate box to indicate your answer.

☐ A

☐ B

☐ C

☐ D

[1]

(iii) What will happen to the car between points B and C?
Place a cross (x) in the appropriate box to indicate your answer.

☐ It will travel at a steady speed.

☐ It will reach its terminal velocity.

☐ It will decelerate.

☐ It will accelerate.

[1]

PRACTICE PAPER 1P

(b) The mass of the carriage and the people in it is 1500 kg.
The Earth's gravitational field strength is 10 N/kg.

(i) State the equation linking gravitational potential energy, mass, height and gravitational field strength.

....
[1]

(ii) Calculate the gain in gravitational potential energy (in kJ) of the carriage and people as they are raised by the chain lift to point A.

Gain in gravitational potential energy = ... kJ
[2]

(c) A different type of roller coaster uses a spring system to launch the carriage forward. The springs used are elastic objects. State what is meant by an **elastic object**.

....
....
[1]
[Total 7 marks]

2 The diagram below shows a generator that is used to produce electricity in a coal-fired power station. The generator contains a coil of wire in a magnetic field.

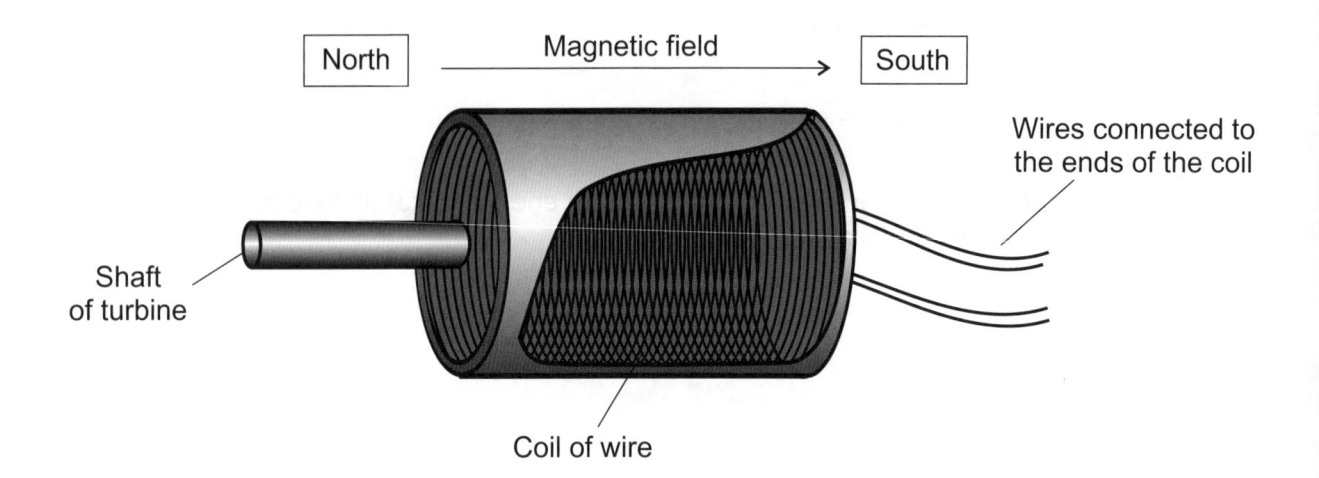

(a) Describe how a voltage can be induced across a coil of wire in a magnetic field.

....

....

....
[1]

(b) Suggest **two** ways that the amount of energy generated by this generator could be increased.

1. ....

....

2. ....

....
[2]

(c) (i) State the equation linking efficiency, useful energy output and total energy input.

....
[1]

(ii) The generators in the power station produce a combined 180 MJ of electrical energy per second. However, the power station also wastes 415 MJ of energy every second, mainly as heat and sound. Calculate the efficiency of the power station.
Give your answer to an appropriate number of significant figures.

Efficiency = ...
[3]

(d) Coal-fired power stations are one of the many types of power station that supply the UK alternating current (a.c.) mains supply.

State what is meant by **alternating current (a.c.)**.

....
....
[1]

(e) Burning fossil fuels such as coal is a reliable method of generating a lot of electricity relatively cheaply.

Describe the disadvantages of burning coal to generate electricity.

....
....
....
....
[4]
[Total 12 marks]

Turn over ▶

3 Hot water tanks, like the one shown below, are used to heat and store water.

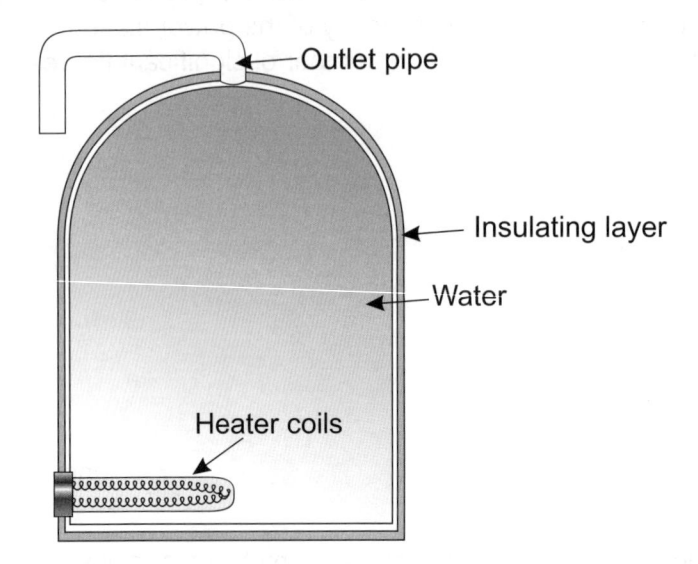

The heater coils have a current of 12 A flowing through them and a voltage of 230 V across them.

(a) Calculate the amount of energy transferred from the coils to the water in 30 s.

Energy transferred = ... J
[2]

(b) Describe how heat is transferred from the coils throughout the water in the tank.

....

....

....

....

....
[4]

A student wanted to model how the thickness of the insulating layer on a water tank affects how quickly the water in a tank cools.

She carried out an investigation to test how the thickness of a cotton wool jacket affects its ability to insulate. She used the following apparatus and method:

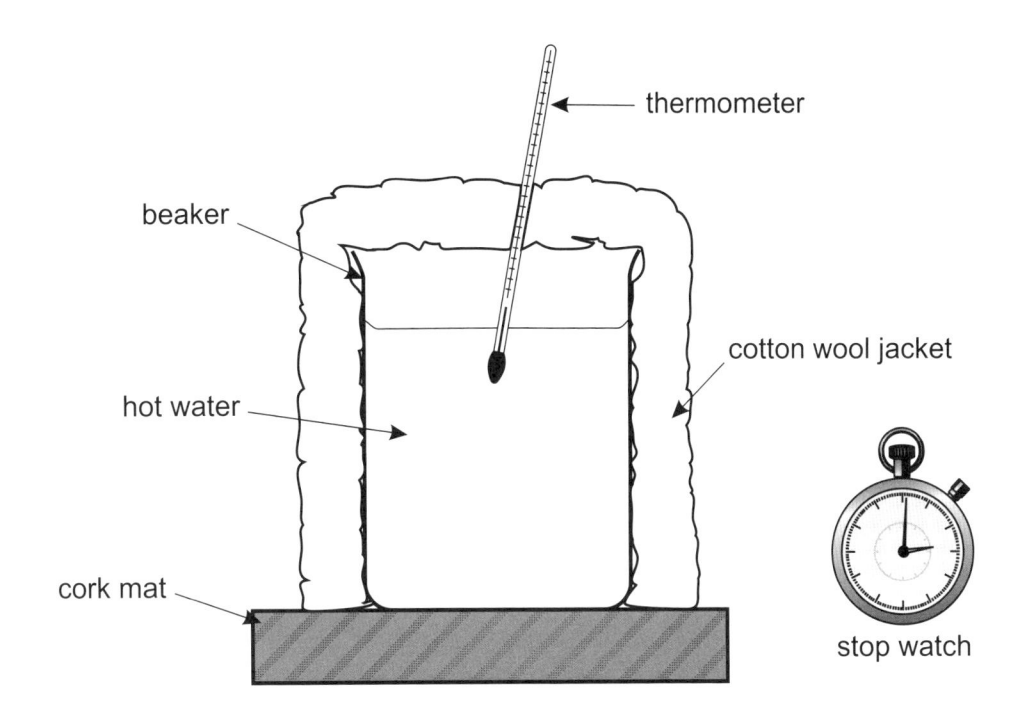

- Put 200 cm³ of boiling water in the glass beaker.
- Fit a 1 cm thick cotton wool jacket over the beaker.
- Put a thermometer into the beaker through the cotton wool jacket.
- Start the stop watch when the temperature cools to 95 °C.
- Record the temperature after three minutes.
- Repeat the experiment using jackets of 2, 3, 4 and 5 cm thickness.

(c) (i) Give **two** ways the student could make her results more precise.

1. ....

2. ....
[2]

(ii) Describe how the student could process her repeated results to get one value for the final water temperature after 3 minutes for each insulating layer.

....

....
[1]

Turn over ▶

PRACTICE PAPER 1P

(iii) The student's results are shown in the sketch below.

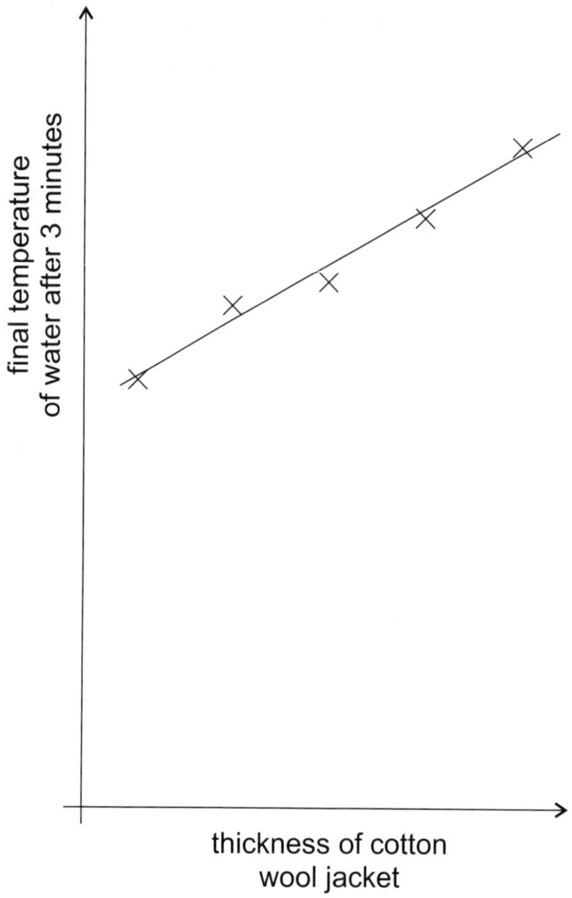
final temperature
of water after 3 minutes
thickness of cotton
wool jacket

Use the graph to write a suitable conclusion for this investigation.

....

....

[1]

[Total 10 marks]

4 A driving instructor has been looking at the Highway Code. He has found the following data about thinking and braking distances for a car travelling on dry roads at various speeds.

Speed (m/s)	Thinking distance (m)	Braking distance (m)
9	6	6
13	9	14
18	12	24
22	15	38
27	18	55
31	21	75

(a) Calculate the stopping distance for a speed of 13 m/s.

Stopping distance = ... m
[1]

(b) The data in the table was obtained by observing a large number of drivers.
Explain why it was sensible to collect the data this way.

....

....

....
[2]

(c) Describe the different factors, other than speed, that can increase the stopping distance of a car. State whether each one affects the thinking distance or the braking distance.

....

....

....

....

....

....
[5]
[Total 8 marks]

Turn over ▶

PRACTICE PAPER 1P

5 An artificial satellite orbits the Earth in an almost circular path, as shown in the diagram. It takes 1 day to orbit the Earth.

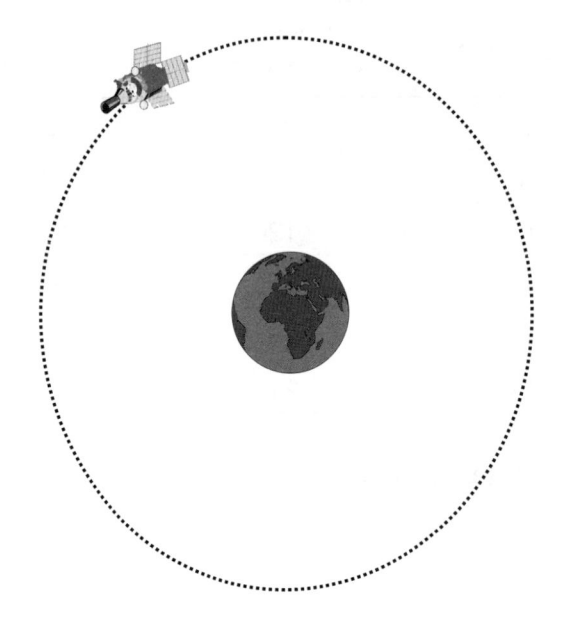

(a) Which of the following also orbits the Earth?
Place a cross (x) in the appropriate box to indicate your answer.

☐ a planet
☐ a star
☐ a moon
☐ a comet

[1]

(b) Name the force that keeps the satellite in orbit around the Earth.

....
[1]

(c) The satellite has an orbital speed of 3080 m/s. Calculate the radius of the satellite's orbit.

Radius = ... m
[3]

PRACTICE PAPER 1P

(d) The satellite sends microwave signals and visible light waves to Earth.

Describe the similarities and differences between visible light and microwaves.

....

....

....

....

....
[4]
[Total 9 marks]

Turn over ▶

6 A student measures the activity of a radioactive sample. He uses a detector to measure the activity of the sample every minute. His results are shown in the table.

Time (minutes)	0	1	2	3	4	5	6
Activity (becquerels)	80	60	45	34	25	19	14

(a) Give **two** dangers of exposure to ionising radiation.

1. ....

2. ....
[2]

(b) Suggest **one** piece of equipment that could have been used to measure the activity of the sample.

....
[1]

(c) (i) Use this data to draw a graph on the grid below.
Draw a curved line of best fit.
[5]

(ii) Use the graph to find the half-life of this radioactive sample.

Half-life = ... min
[2]

PRACTICE PAPER 1P

(d) After the experiment is finished the radioactive source is put into storage in another part of the building. The detector still picks up background radiation in the laboratory.

Give **four** sources that may contribute to this background radiation.

1. ....

....

2. ....

....

3. ....

....

4. ....

....
[4]

(e) (i) Another radioactive isotope, radium-226, decays by alpha emission.
Fill in the blanks in the reaction below to show the alpha emission.

$$^{226}_{88}Ra \rightarrow ^{222}_{....}Rn + ^{....}_{2}\alpha$$

[1]

(ii) How many protons does the radium-226 (Ra) nucleus shown in part (i) have?
Place a cross (x) in the appropriate box to indicate your answer.

☐ 226

☐ 138

☐ 88

☐ 222

[1]
[Total 16 marks]

Turn over ▶

7 A student wanted to know how the current flowing through a filament lamp changes with the voltage across it. He set up this circuit.

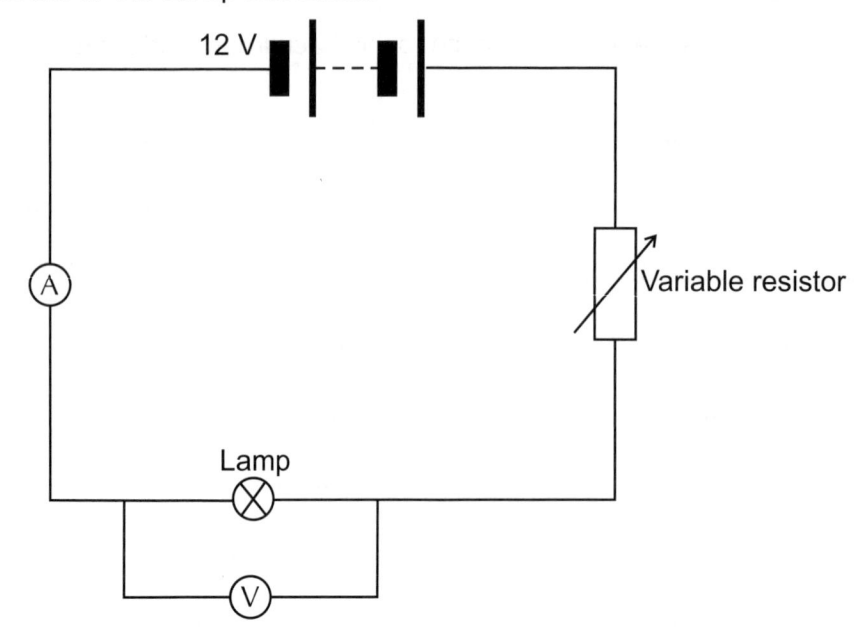

He used a variable resistor to change the voltage across the lamp.

Here is the graph he plotted of his results.

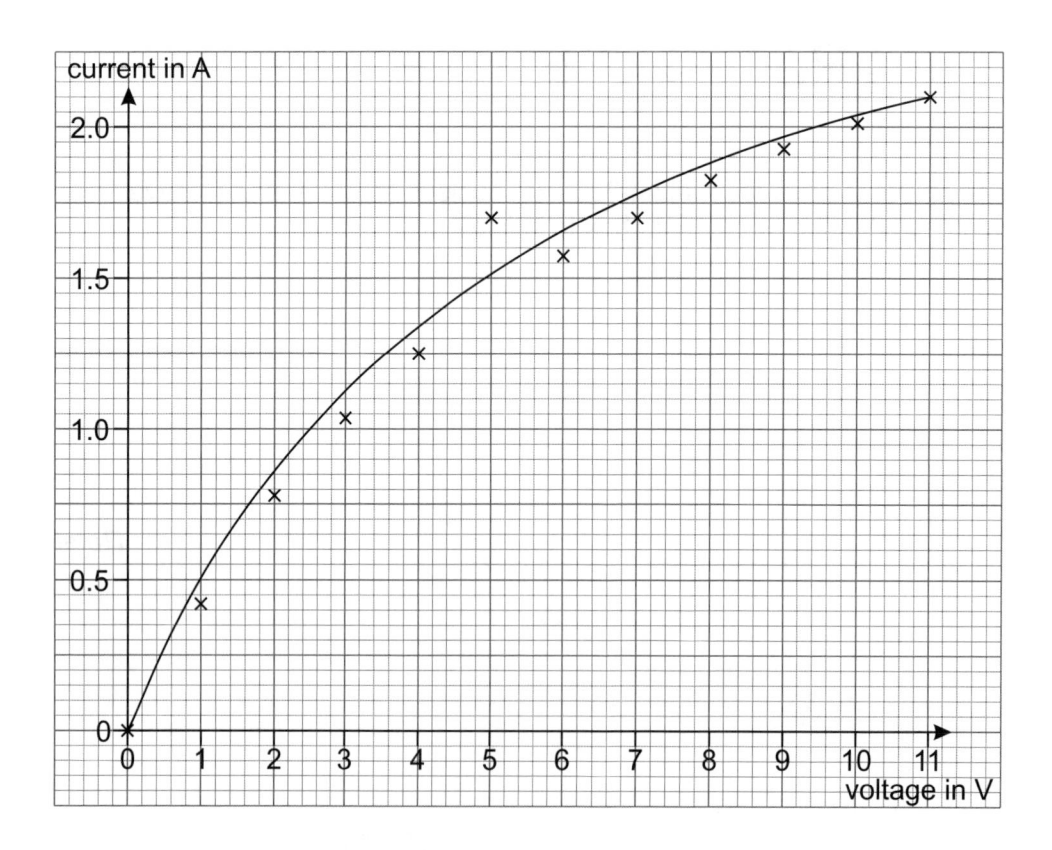

(a) Give the dependent variable in this experiment.

....
[1]

(b) (i) Describe what the student has done wrong when drawing a line of best fit.

....

....
[1]

(ii) State the equation linking voltage, current and resistance.

....
[1]

(iii) The student corrects his line of best fit and uses it to work out that when the voltage across the lamp is 5 V, the current through it is 1.4 A.
Calculate the resistance of the lamp when the voltage across it is 5 V.

Resistance = ... unit ....
[3]

(c) The student makes the following claim.

"The resistance of a filament bulb is constant."

Do you agree or disagree? Use the graph to explain your answer.

....

....

....
[2]
[Total 8 marks]

Turn over ▶

PRACTICE PAPER 1P

8 An engineering student has made a simple electric motor as shown in the diagram.

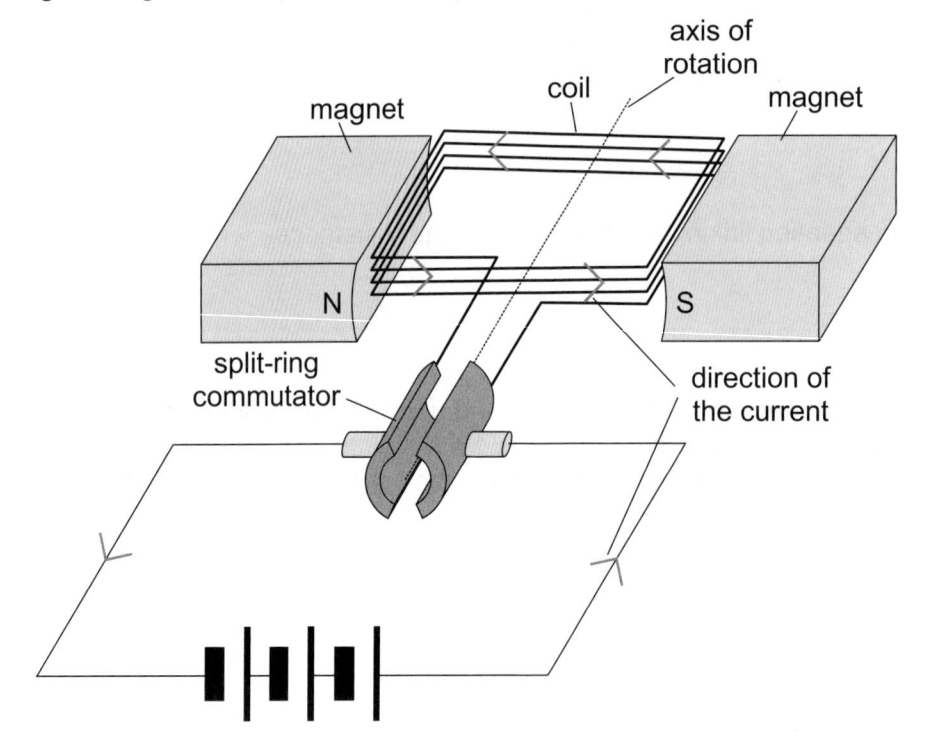

The split-ring commutator changes the direction of the current every half turn so that the motor will continue to rotate in the same direction.

(a) The direction of the current is shown. State which direction the coil will rotate in.

....
[1]

(b) Explain how the coil of wire in a simple electric motor turns.

....

....

....
[2]

(c) The engineering student decides to make some changes to his motor.

Suggest **two** ways that he could speed up the rotation of the motor.

1. ....

....

2. ....

....
[2]
[Total 5 marks]

PRACTICE PAPER 1P

9 A hydraulic system is shown in the diagram below.

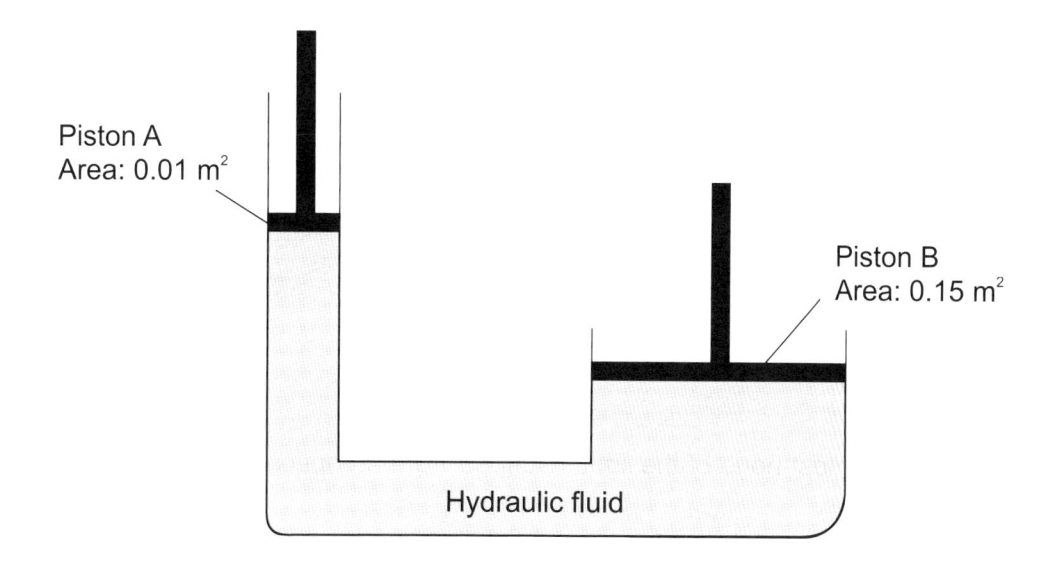

(a) Explain why there is a force on piston B when a force is applied to piston A.

....

....

....

....
[3]

(b) (i) Show that the force on piston B is 375 N when a force of 25 N is applied to piston A.

[4]

(ii) Explain why the pressure is slightly different at piston A and piston B when the hydraulic system is in the position shown in the diagram.

....

....
[1]

[Total 8 marks]

Turn over ▶

10 Optical fibres, such as the one shown below, are used in medicine.

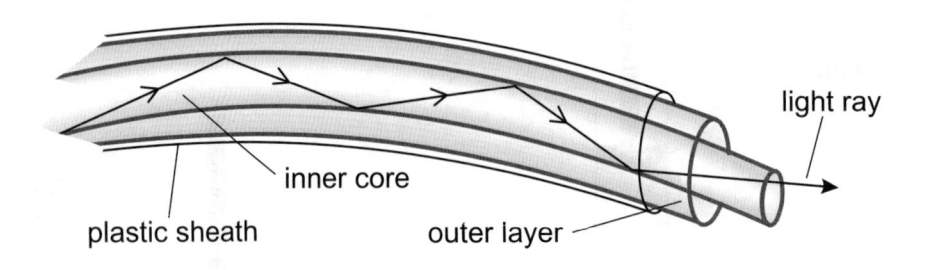

(a) Explain why almost none of the light 'escapes' from an optical fibre as a light ray travels along it.

....

....

....
[2]

(b) Describe an experiment to find the refractive index of a rectangular block of the material used to make optical fibres.

....

....

....

....

....
[4]

(c) The refractive index of the material is 1.5. Light is shone into a semi-circular block of the same material at different angles. As shown in the diagram, an angle, θ, is reached at which the light refracts along the flat boundary between the block and the air.

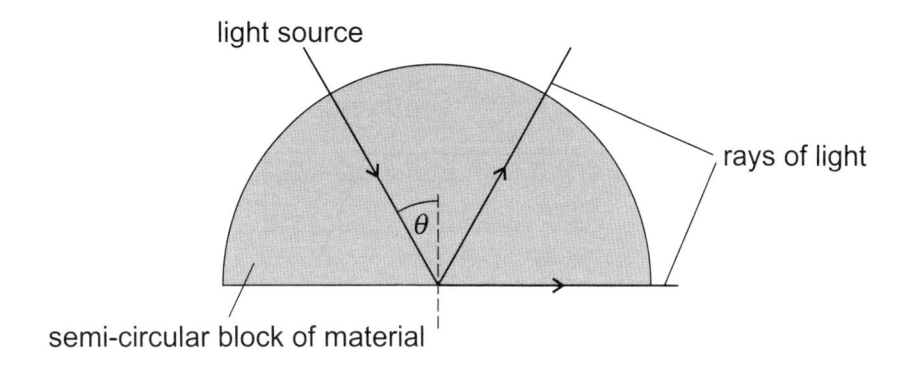

light source

rays of light

semi-circular block of material

Calculate the angle θ.

θ = ... °

[4]

[Total 10 marks]

11 This question is about velocity-time graphs.

(a) The velocity-time graph shows the motion of a vehicle as it travels along a flat, straight road before braking and stopping at a set of traffic lights.

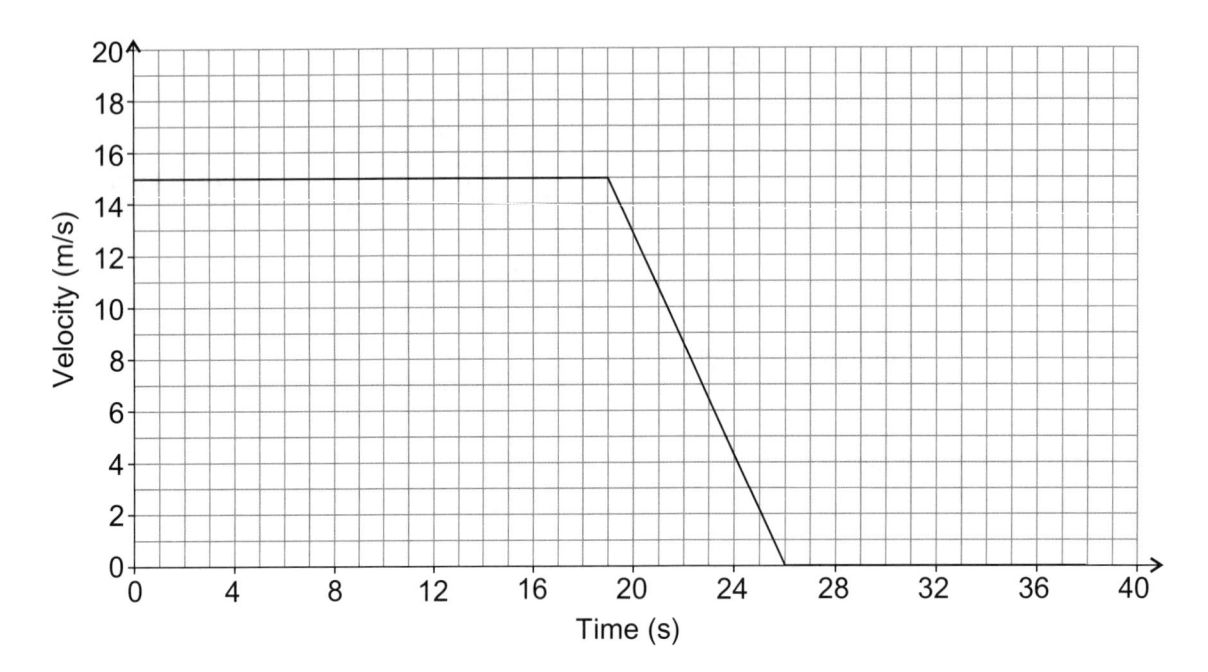

(i) Calculate the total distance travelled by the car in the first 28 seconds.

Total distance travelled = ... m
[2]

(ii) Describe what happens to the temperature of the car brakes when they are applied to slow the car down. Explain why this happens.

....

....

....
[2]

PRACTICE PAPER 1P

(b) This velocity-time graph shows the motion of a skydiver jumping from an aeroplane.

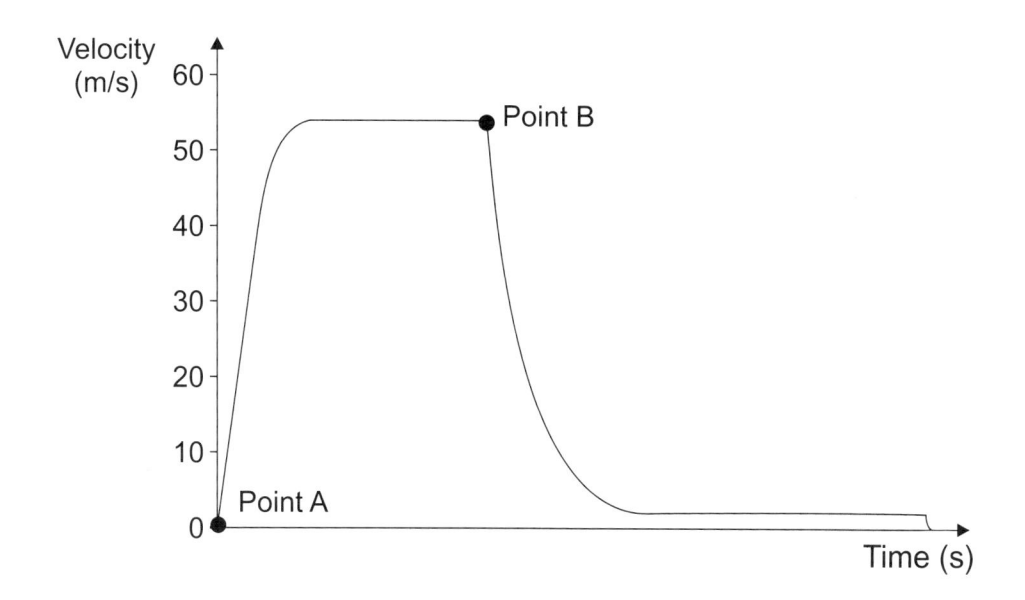

(i) Describe the motion of the skydiver from point A to point B on the graph, in terms of the forces acting on him.

....

....

....

....

....

....
[4]

(ii) At point B, the skydiver opens his parachute.
Explain why this causes the change in his velocity.

....

....

....
[2]
[Total 10 marks]

12 Pollen grains move around randomly when suspended in water, as shown in the diagram.

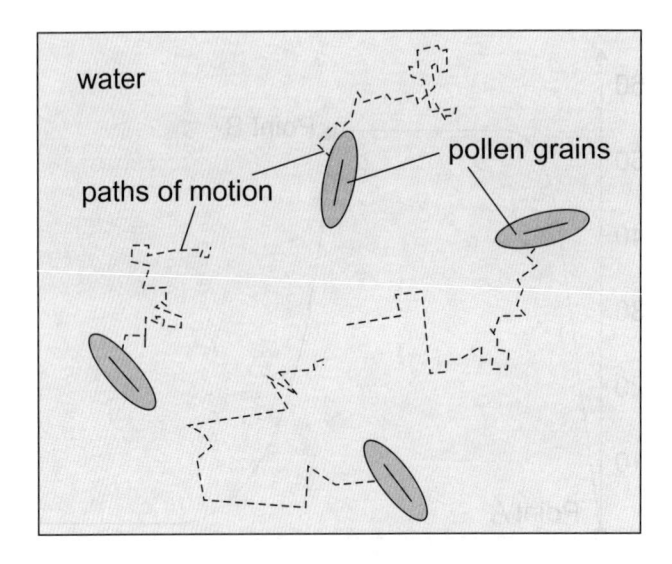

(a) State the name given to this type of motion.

....
[1]

(b) Explain what causes the pollen grains to move in this way.

....
....
....
....
....
[3]

(c) Give the name of the theory that this motion is evidence for.

....
[1]
[Total 5 marks]

13 A microwave oven can be used for heating food quickly.

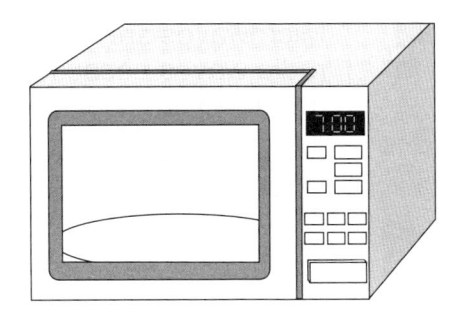

(a) Describe how the microwave oven heats food.

....

....

....

....
[3]

(b) (i) State the equation linking frequency, wavelength and speed.

....
[1]

(ii) A microwave uses microwaves with a frequency of 2.5×10^9 Hz that travel at 3.0×10^8 m/s. Calculate the wavelength of these microwaves.

Wavelength = ... m
[2]

(c) (i) Mobile phones work by transmitting and receiving microwave signals. Explain why some people are concerned about using microwaves in this way.

....

....

....
[2]

Turn over ▶

(ii) A student is discussing the dangers of microwaves and radio waves.

> Microwaves are more dangerous than radio waves because they have a lower frequency and so transfer less energy.

Do you agree or disagree? Explain your answer.

....

....

....
[3]

d) Give **one** other use of microwaves.

....
[1]
[Total 12 marks]

[Total for paper 120 marks]

Candidate Surname	Candidate Forename(s)

Centre Number	Candidate Number

Certificate International GCSE

Physics
Paper 2P

Practice Paper
Time allowed: 1 hour

You must have:
- A ruler.
- A calculator.

Total marks:

Instructions to candidates
- Use **black** ink to write your answers.
- Write your name and other details in the spaces provided above.
- Answer **all** questions in the spaces provided.
- In calculations, show clearly how you worked out your answers.
- You will need to answer some questions by placing a cross in a box, like this: ☒
  To change your answer, draw a line through the box like this: ☒
  Then mark your new answer as normal.

Information for candidates
- The marks available are given in brackets at the end of each question.
- There are 60 marks available for this paper.
- You might find the equations on page 182 useful.

Advice for candidates
- Read all the questions carefully.
- Write your answers as clearly and neatly as possible.
- Keep in mind how much time you have left.

Answer all questions

1 A fire engine speeds past an observer.
Sound waves are emitted from the fire engine's siren as it travels.

(a) (i) Which of the following describes the **amplitude** of a wave?
Place a cross (x) in the appropriate box to indicate your answer.

☐ The height of the wave, from a trough to a crest.

☐ The length of the wave, from a crest to a crest.

☐ The height of the wave, from the rest position to a crest.

☐ The length of the wave, from a trough to a crest.

[1]

(ii) Which of the following describes the **frequency** of a wave?
Place a cross (x) in the appropriate box to indicate your answer.

☐ The number of complete waves passing a certain point per second.

☐ The number of complete waves passing a certain point per minute.

☐ The number of crests and troughs passing a certain point per minute.

☐ The number of crests and troughs passing a certain point per second.

[1]

(b) Describe the direction of oscillations relative to the direction of energy transfer for a sound wave.

....

....
[1]

(c) The siren sounds quieter as the fire engine gets further away from the observer. Suggest what this tells you about the amplitude of the sound waves reaching the observer.

....

....
[1]

(d) The fire engine drives round a corner. The observer can no longer see the fire engine, but she can still hear its siren.

Some of the sound waves the observer hears are reflected off buildings. Name and describe the other property of waves that allows her to hear the fire engine's siren.

....

....

....
[2]
[Total 6 marks]

Turn over ▶

2 The body panels of a plane are painted with a spray gun that gives the paint droplets a negative static charge. The body panels are given a positive static charge.

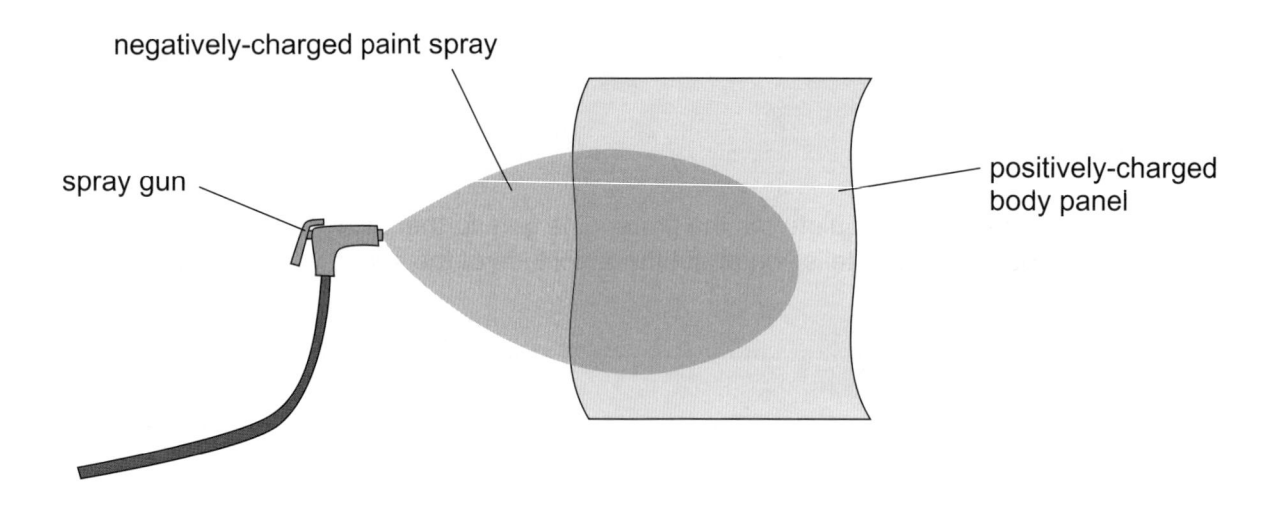

(a) (i) Explain why the spray gun produces a fine, even spray of paint.

....
....
....
[1]

(ii) This method leaves an even coverage of paint on the body panels, including areas that are not directly facing the spray gun. Explain why this happens.

....
....
....
....
[2]

(b) When a plane is being refuelled, fuel is pumped into a tank in the wing of the plane. The tank and wing are made from metal, which is an electrical conductor, and connected to earth.

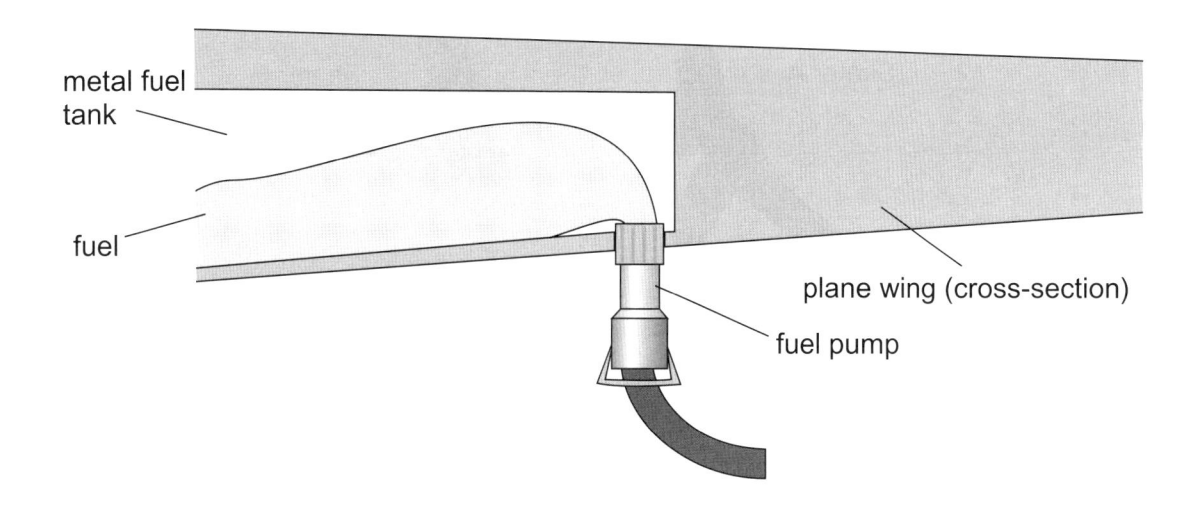

Describe, in terms of particle transfer, how a static charge could build up on the fuel tank during refuelling if the tank were made from an electrical insulator. Explain why a build-up of static charge on the fuel tank could be dangerous.

....

....

....

....

....

[3]

[Total 6 marks]

3 Two skaters are taking part in a figure skating contest.
The diagram below shows their velocity and mass at one point in their routine.

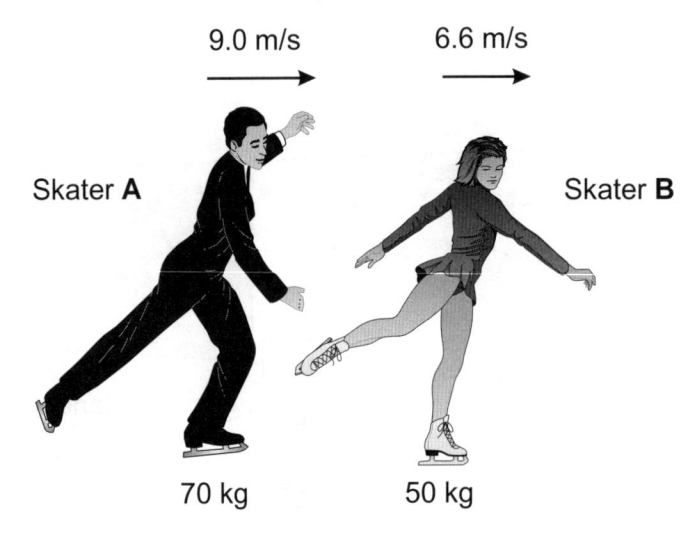

Skater A: 9.0 m/s, 70 kg
Skater B: 6.6 m/s, 50 kg

(a) State the equation linking momentum, mass and velocity.

....
[1]

(b) Complete the table below to show the momentum of each skater.

	Mass (kg)	Velocity (m/s to the right)	Momentum (kg m/s to the right)
Skater A	70	9.0	
Skater B	50	6.6	

[2]

(c) The skaters continue at the same velocity until Skater A catches up with skater B and holds on to her. They continue to move in the same direction.

Calculate their velocity immediately after skater A begins to hold skater B.

Velocity = ... m/s
[2]

(d) During the routine, the skaters come to a stop. Skater A then pushes skater B away from him with a force of 100 N.

(i) Describe the reaction force that skater B exerts on skater A.

....

....
[1]

(ii) State the equation linking unbalanced force, mass and acceleration.

....
[1]

(iii) Calculate skater B's acceleration due to this force and state the correct unit. Assume there are no frictional forces acting on her.

Acceleration = ... unit ....
[3]
[Total 10 marks]

Turn over ▶

4 The pie chart shows the proportions of a country's electricity generated by different resources.

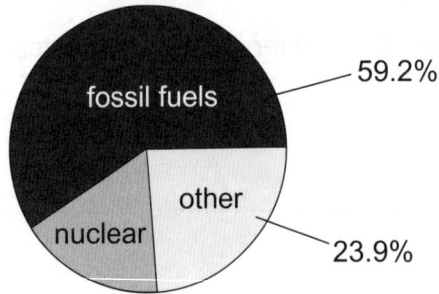

- fossil fuels — 59.2%
- other — 23.9%
- nuclear

(a) Calculate the proportion of the country's electricity that comes from nuclear power.

Proportion from nuclear power = ...%
[1]

(b) Describe the advantages and disadvantages of using nuclear power to generate electricity compared to burning fossil fuels.

....
....
....
....
....
[4]

(c) Nuclear fuel emits ionising radiation and precautions must be taken while handling it.

(i) Describe the damage that can be done by ionising radiation to living organisms.

....
....
....
[2]

(ii) Suggest **one** precaution workers in nuclear power stations could take when handling sources of ionising radiation to minimise the risk to their health.

....
....
[1]

[Total 8 marks]

5 The volume of a fixed mass of gas depends on its pressure and temperature.

(a) A student performs an experiment to show how the volume and pressure of a gas are related. She takes several readings of the volume of a fixed mass of gas at different pressures, making sure the temperature of the gas is kept constant. Her results are shown in the table below.

Pressure (kPa)	Volume (cm³)
10	5.0
20	4.0
30	3.3
40	2.8
50	0.6
60	2.0
70	1.8

(i) Name **one** control variable in the student's experiment.

....
[1]

(ii) Explain why control variables need to be kept constant in experiments such as this.

....
....
[1]

Turn over ▶

PRACTICE PAPER 2P

(b) (i) Use the grid to plot a graph of the results in the table.
Draw a curved line of best fit.

[5]

(ii) One of the results in the experiment is anomalous. Circle this result on the graph.

[1]

(iii) Using the graph, describe the relationship between the pressure and volume of the gas at a constant temperature.

....

....

[1]

PRACTICE PAPER 2P

(c) The graph shows how the volume of a gas is affected by changes in temperature, at a constant pressure.

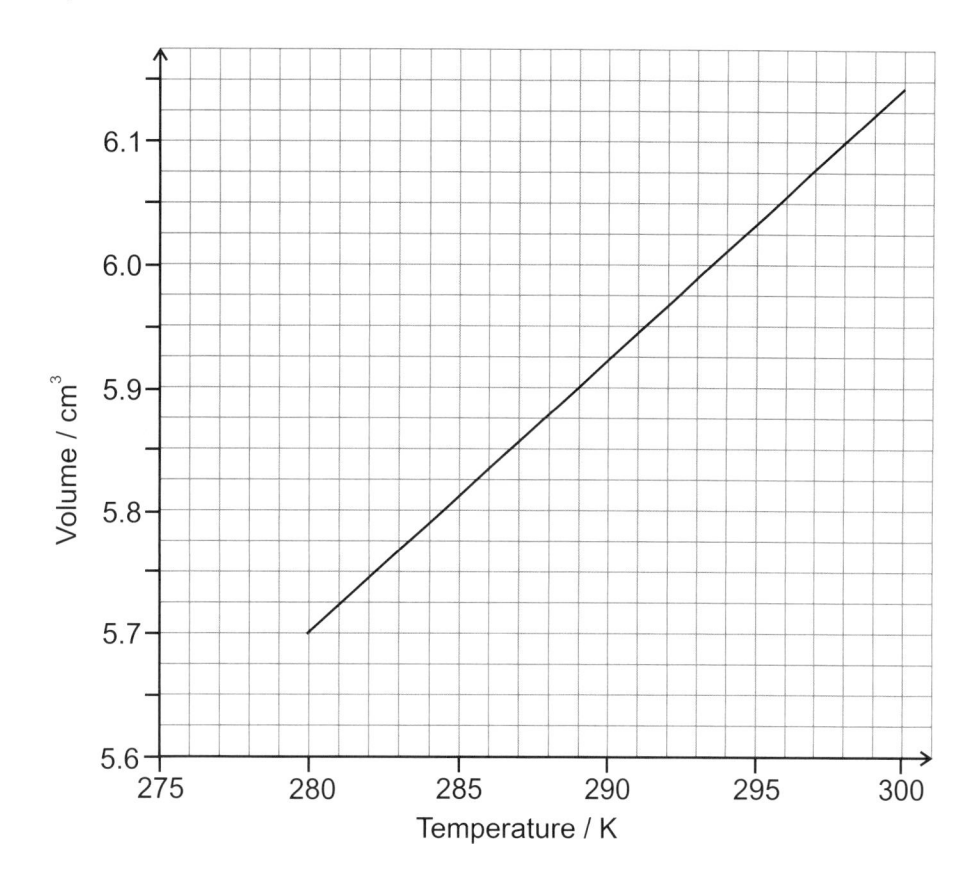

(i) Using the graph, describe the relationship between the temperature and volume of the gas at a constant pressure.

....
....
[1]

(ii) Use the graph to estimate the volume of the gas at 25 °C.

Volume of gas = ... cm³
[2]
[Total 12 marks]

6 The generator in a power station produces an alternating voltage of 25 kV.
This is changed to 400 kV by the transformer shown.

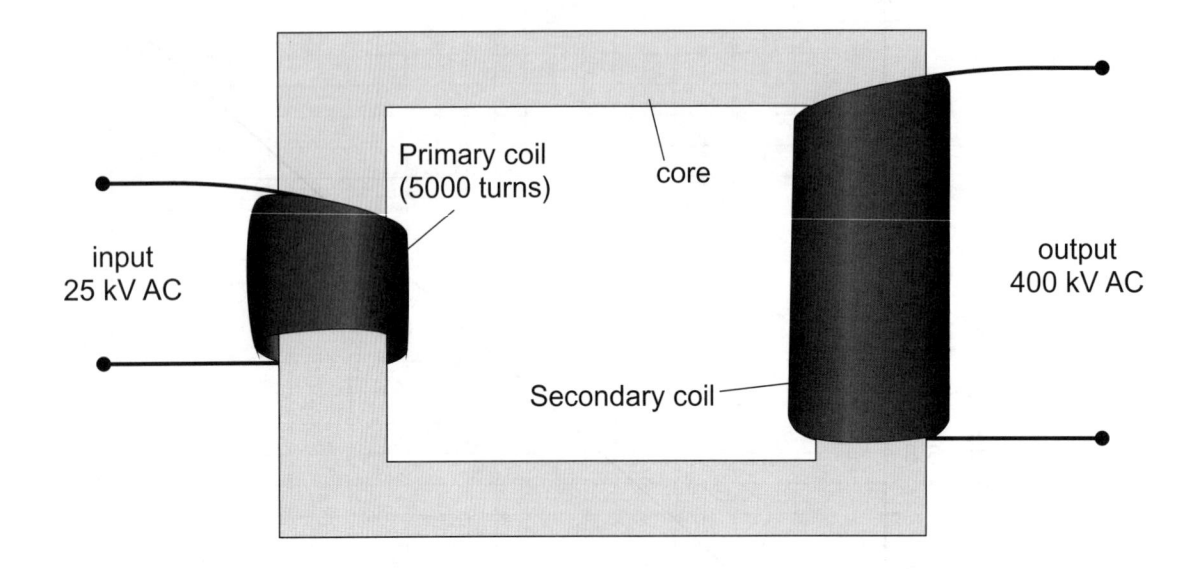

(a) What type of transformer is shown in the diagram?
Place a cross (x) in the appropriate box to indicate your answer.

☐ Step-left transformer
☐ Step-up transformer
☐ Step-right transformer
☐ Step-down transformer

[1]

(b) (i) State the equation linking the number of turns on the primary coil, the number of turns on the secondary coil, the input voltage and the output voltage for a transformer.

....
[1]

(ii) The primary coil has 5000 turns.
Calculate the number of turns on the secondary coil.

Number of turns = ...
[3]

PRACTICE PAPER 2P

(c) (i) State the equation linking the input power and the output power in terms of the current and voltage across each coil of a 100% efficient transformer.

....
[1]

(ii) The output current of this transformer is 250 A.
Calculate the input current, assuming the transformer is 100% efficient.

Input current = ... A
[2]

(d) Explain how transformers are used to reduce energy loss from the cables that make up the National Grid, while ensuring that consumers are supplied with electricity at a useful and relatively safe voltage.

....

....

....

....
[3]
[Total 11 marks]

7 A construction worker is using a crane with an electromagnet to pick up a metal load.

(a) What is an electromagnet?

....

....
[1]

(b) The electromagnet is shown in the diagram.

(i) Sketch magnetic field lines to show the magnetic field around the electromagnet.
[1]

(ii) Explain why it is important for the core to be made from a magnetically soft material.

....

....
[1]

(c) The diagram shows all the forces acting on the crane as it carries a metal anvil.

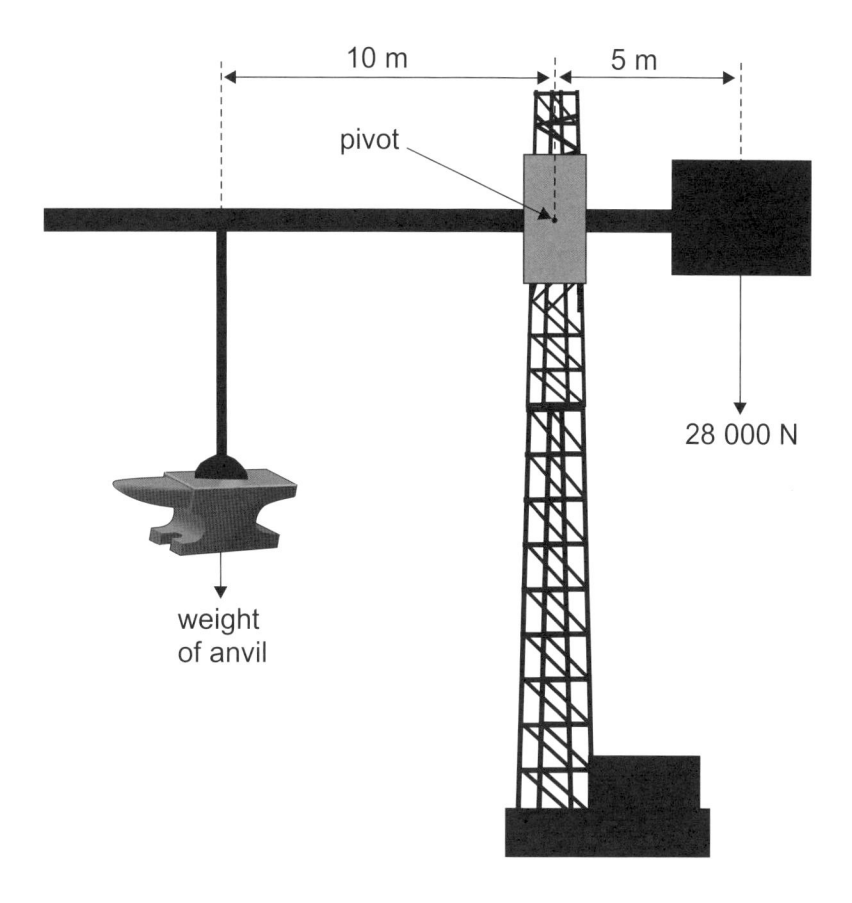

(i) State the equation linking the moment of a force, the force and the perpendicular distance from the line of action of the force to the pivot.

....
[1]

(ii) Use the information on the diagram to calculate the weight of the anvil if the system is balanced.

Weight = ... N
[3]
[Total 7 marks]

[Total for paper 60 marks]

PRACTICE PAPER 2P

Useful Equations

Here are some equations you might find useful when you're doing the practice papers — you'll be given these equations in the real exams.

orbital speed = $\dfrac{2\pi \times \text{orbital radius}}{\text{time period}}$	$v = \dfrac{2 \times \pi \times r}{T}$
energy transferred = current × voltage × time	$E = I \times V \times t$
frequency = $\dfrac{1}{\text{time period}}$	$f = \dfrac{1}{T}$
power = $\dfrac{\text{work done}}{\text{time taken}}$	$P = \dfrac{W}{t}$
power = $\dfrac{\text{energy transferred}}{\text{time taken}}$	$P = \dfrac{W}{t}$
pressure × volume = constant	$p_1 \times V_1 = p_2 \times V_2$

Assume the acceleration due to gravity is $g = 10$ m/s^2

PAPER 2

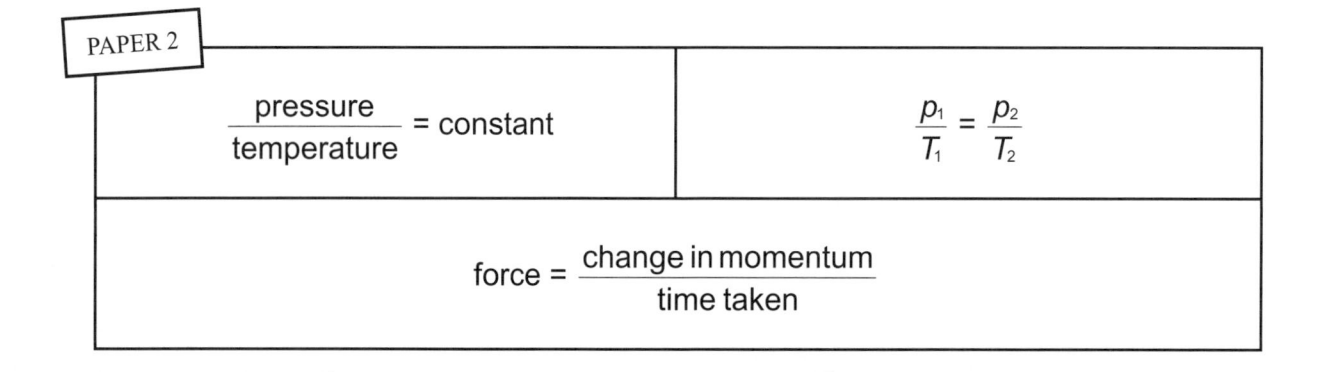

$\dfrac{\text{pressure}}{\text{temperature}}$ = constant	$\dfrac{p_1}{T_1} = \dfrac{p_2}{T_2}$
force = $\dfrac{\text{change in momentum}}{\text{time taken}}$	

Answers

Pages 6-7

Warm-Up Questions

1) Velocity is a measure of how fast something is going, and in what direction. Speed is just how fast something is travelling.
2) time = distance/speed
   = 125/6.5
   = **19.2 s** (to 3 s.f.)
3) m/s^2
4) acceleration
5) units of mass = kg, units of weight = N

Exam Questions

1 a) average speed = $\frac{\text{distance moved}}{\text{time taken}}$ ($s = \frac{d}{t}$) *(1 mark)*

   b) average speed = $\frac{1500}{300}$ = **5 m/s**

   (2 marks if answer correct, otherwise 1 mark for correct substitution of values into the equation.)

   c) $a = \frac{v-u}{t} \Rightarrow t = \frac{v-u}{a} = \frac{10-2}{2.4}$ = **3.3 s** (to 2 s.f.)

   (4 marks if answer correct, otherwise 1 mark for using the correct equation, 1 mark for correct rearrangement of the equation and 1 mark for correct substitution of values into the equation.)

2 a) 300 s *(1 mark)*

   b) Yes — the gradient of the graph shows the student's speed *(1 mark)* and the gradient for this part of the journey is constant (it's a straight line) *(1 mark)*.

   c) average speed = $\frac{\text{distance moved}}{\text{time taken}} = \frac{450}{300}$ = **1.5 m/s**

   (3 marks if answer correct, otherwise 1 mark for using the correct equation and 1 mark for correct substitution of values in the equation.)

   d) E.g. 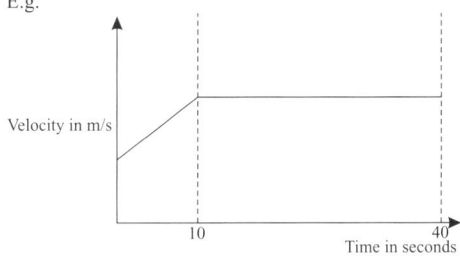

   [Graph: Velocity in m/s vs Time in seconds, showing sloped line from 0 to 10 s, then horizontal line from 10 to 40 s]

   (3 marks available — 1 mark for a straight, sloped line showing the initial acceleration, 1 mark for a straight horizontal line showing the constant speed, and 1 mark for plotting a horizontal line for roughly 3 times the time the sloped line is plotted over.)

3 a) i) Travelling at a steady velocity (20 m/s) *(1 mark)*.

   ii) E.g. Slowing down / (increasing) deceleration *(1 mark)*.

   b) Distance travelled = area under graph
      = (60 − 40) × (20 − 0)
      = **400 m**

   (3 marks for the correct answer, otherwise 1 mark for attempting to find the area under the graph between 40 and 60 seconds, 1 mark for correctly showing (60 − 40) × 20 or 20 × 20.)

   c) Acceleration = gradient = $\frac{20-0}{40-0}$ = **0.5 m/s^2**

   (3 marks for the correct answer, otherwise 1 mark for attempting to find the gradient, 1 mark for dividing a correct change in velocity by a correct change in time in the time range 0 − 40 s.)

   d) Velocity in m/s

   [Graph showing velocity vs time line continuing from previous, with dip around 80-100s and rising line between 100 and 140s, horizontal between 140 and 200s]

   (1 mark for a straight line with a positive gradient between 100 and 140 seconds, 1 mark for a straight horizontal line between 140 and 200 seconds.)

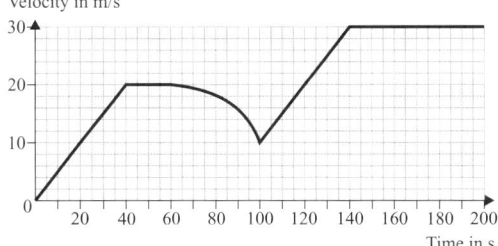

4 a) i) Weight = mass × gravitational field strength ($W = m \times g$) *(1 mark)*

   ii) $W = m \times g \Rightarrow g = \frac{W}{m} = \frac{19.6}{2}$
       = **9.8 newtons per kilogram (N/kg)**

   (3 marks if answer correct, otherwise 1 mark for correct rearrangement of the equation and correct substitution of values into the equation, and 1 mark for correct unit. Allow m/s^2 as a correct unit.)

   b) The weight would be smaller *(1 mark)* as the gravitational field strength, g, is lower on the moon *(1 mark)*.

Pages 13-14

Warm-Up Questions

1) Gravity/weight.
2) Forces of attraction or repulsion between two charged objects.
3) friction/drag/air resistance
4) When the resistance force on an object is equal to the accelerating force.

Exam Questions

1 a) i) In the opposite direction to the thrust. *(1 mark)*

   ii) As the speed increases, the drag force increases *(1 mark)*.

   b) Any one of, e.g. reaction force *(1 mark)* (from the road) acting upwards on the truck *(1 mark)*. / Weight/gravitational force *(1 mark)* acting straight downwards *(1 mark)*.

2 a) As the initial height increases, the bounce height increases / they're (directly) proportional *(1 mark)*.

   b) E.g. drop the ball from a fixed height *(1 mark)* and measure the height of each successive bounce *(1 mark)*.

3 a) Dirk is not correct. There are actually multiple forces acting on the object *(1 mark)*, but the forces in each direction are balanced *(1 mark)*.

   If you answered Jenny, you receive no marks for this question regardless of the reasoning.

   b) When an object falls, resistive forces (e.g. air resistance) act on it in the opposite direction to its motion *(1 mark)*. Eventually these balance the downward force of an object's weight *(1 mark)*.

   c) The ball with the lower weight. Air resistance increases with velocity *(1 mark)*, and the air resistance at any given velocity will be the same on each ball (because they're the same size) *(1 mark)*. So air resistance will balance the lower-weight ball's weight at a lower velocity, giving a lower terminal velocity *(1 mark)*.

   If you answered the ball with the larger mass, you receive no marks for this question regardless of the reasoning.

4 a) i) slowly *(1 mark)*

   ii) larger *(1 mark)*

   b) E.g. repeating the experiment with steel balls with different masses *(1 mark)* and using the same parachute throughout *(1 mark)*.

   You get one mark here for describing a way of changing the mass and one mark for describing how you'd control an independent variable that isn't being tested.

Pages 21-22

Warm-Up Questions

1) If all the forces on an object are balanced, then it will stay still, or else if it's already moving, it will continue to move at the same velocity.
2) A car full of people has a larger mass than a car that's less full, so with the same brakes it will take longer to stop. Other factors that increase stopping distance include any two from: e.g. how fast the vehicle is going / how good the brakes are / how good the grip is / tiredness of the driver / influence of alcohol/drugs on driver.
3) The total momentum after a collision is the same as the total momentum before a collision (as long as no external forces act).

Exam Questions

1 a) $F = m \times a \Rightarrow a = \frac{F}{m} = \frac{200}{2500}$ = **0.08 m/s^2**

   (3 marks if answer correct, otherwise 1 mark for using the correct equation, and 1 mark for correct rearrangement of the equation and correct substitution of values into the equation.)

b) i) $F = m \times a = 10 \times 29 = $ **290 N**
(2 marks if answer correct, otherwise 1 mark for correct substitution of values into the equation.)

ii) Force exerted on the van by the traffic cone = **290 N** *(1 mark)*
If the van exerts a force of 290 N on the traffic cone, the cone will exert the exact opposite force on the van. This is Newton's third law of motion.

iii) Assuming all of this force causes the van to decelerate:
$F = m \times a \Rightarrow a = \dfrac{F}{m} = \dfrac{290}{2500} = $ **0.116 m/s²**
(2 marks if answer correct, otherwise 1 mark for correct rearrangement of the equation and correct substitution of values into the equation.)

2 a) force = mass × acceleration ($F = m \times a$) *(1 mark)*

b) The maximum force of the engine in each scooter ($= m \times a$)
$= 127.5 \times 2.4$ *(1 mark)*
$= 306$ N *(1 mark)*
So, the mass of student B and her scooter $= \dfrac{F}{a}$
$= \dfrac{306}{1.70}$ *(1 mark)*
$= $ **180 kg** *(1 mark)*

3 a) A scalar quantity just has size (magnitude) / is just a number *(1 mark)*.
A vector quantity also has a direction *(1 mark)*.

b) force *(1 mark)*

c) 14 kg *(1 mark)*

4 a) Resultant force in the horizontal direction: $17 + 3 - 10 - 10 = 0$ N
Resultant force in the vertical direction:
$10 - 2 = $ **8 N** *(1 mark)* **up** *(1 mark)*

b) $20 - 5 - x = 0 \Rightarrow x = 20 - 5 = $ **15 N** *(1 mark)*
$y - 4 = 0 \Rightarrow y = $ **4** *(1 mark)*

5 a) i) momentum = mass × velocity ($p = m \times v$) *(1 mark)*

ii) $p = m \times v = 1200 \times 30$
$= $ **36 000 kilogram metres per second (kg m/s)**
(3 marks if answer correct, otherwise 1 mark for correct substitution of values into the equation and 1 mark for correct unit.)

b) i) force $= \dfrac{\text{change in momentum}}{\text{time taken}}$ *(1 mark)*

ii) force $= \dfrac{\text{change in momentum}}{\text{time taken}} = \dfrac{36\,000}{1.2} = $ **30 000 N**
(2 marks if answer correct, otherwise 1 mark for correct substitution of values into the equation. Allow full marks if an incorrect answer from part a) is used and the calculations are done correctly.)

6 a) $p = m \times v = 650 \times 15$
$= $ **9750 kilogram metres per second (kg m/s)**
(4 marks if answer correct, otherwise 1 mark for using the correct equation, 1 mark for correct substitution of values into the equation and 1 mark for correct unit.)

b) momentum before = momentum after
$[m_1 \times v_1] + [m_2 \times v_2] = [(650 + 750) \times v_{\text{after}}]$
$[650 \times 15] + [750 \times -10] = [(650 + 750) \times v_{\text{after}}]$
$9750 - 7500 = 1400 \times v_{\text{after}}$
$v_{\text{after}} = \dfrac{2250}{1400}$
$v_{\text{after}} = $ **1.6 m/s (to 2 s.f.)**
(4 marks if answer correct, otherwise 1 mark for equating momentum before and after, 1 mark for correct substitution of values into the equations for momentum of each vehicle and 1 mark for correct rearrangement of the equation(s). Allow full marks if an incorrect answer from part a) is used and the calculations are done correctly.)

c) The crumple zone increases the time taken by the car to stop/change its velocity *(1 mark)*. The time over which momentum changes is inversely proportional to the force acting, so this reduces the force *(1 mark)*.

Pages 30-31
Warm-Up Questions

1) E.g. hang a spring from a clamp, and measure its length. Add a known mass to the end of the spring, then measure the new length of the spring. The extension is the change in length between the new length and the original length, with no load. Keep adding masses until you have at least six measurements. Once you're done, repeat the experiment and calculate an average value for the length of the spring for each applied weight.

2) satellite, gravity

3) A collection of billions of galaxies (each of which are made of a large collection of stars).

Exam Questions

1 a) B *(1 mark)* — the force is at the furthest distance from the pivot and is acting in a direction perpendicular to the handle *(1 mark)*.

b) i) force *(1 mark)*
ii) gravity *(1 mark)*

c) i) moment = force × perpendicular distance from the line of action of the force to the pivot ($M = F \times d$) *(1 mark)*

ii) $M = F \times d = 45 \times 0.1 = $ **4.5 newton metres (Nm)**
(3 marks if answer correct, otherwise 1 mark for correct unit and 1 mark for correct substitution of values into the equation.)

2 Situation B. Rope 1 balances the moment applied by the box around rope 2 *(1 mark)* and so the further the box is from rope 2, the larger the force applied by rope 1 *(1 mark)*.
Award no marks for this question if you answered situation A.

3 shape / length / size *(1 mark)*, proportional *(1 mark)*, elastic *(1 mark)*.
There are quite a few things you could write for the first word — as long as your answer seems sensible give yourself the mark.

4 a) moment = force × perpendicular distance from the pivot
$= 2 \times 0.2 = $ **0.4 Nm**
(3 marks if answer correct, otherwise 1 mark for using the correct equation and 1 mark for correct substitution of values into the equation.)

b) clockwise moments about pivot = anticlockwise moments about pivot
force$_C$ × perpendicular distance$_C$ = 0.4 + 0.8
perpendicular distance$_C = \dfrac{0.4 + 0.8}{8} = $ **0.15 m**
(4 marks if answer correct, otherwise 1 mark for reference to balanced moments in each direction, 1 mark for correct substitution of values into the equation and 1 mark for correct rearrangement of the equation. Allow full marks if an incorrect answer from part a) is used and the calculations are done correctly.)

5 a) C *(1 mark)* — Comets usually have (highly) elliptical orbits *(1 mark)*.

b) 1.2 km/s — orbital speed only depends on the orbital radius and the time period. *(1 mark for the correct speed and the correct reason.)*

c) orbital speed $= \dfrac{2 \times \pi \times \text{orbital radius}}{\text{time period}}$
$= \dfrac{2 \times \pi \times 42\,000\,000}{(24 \times 60 \times 60)}$
$= $ **3100 metres per second (m/s)**
or 3.1 kilometres per second (km/s) (to 2 s.f.)
(3 marks if answer correct, otherwise 1 mark for correct substitution of values into the equation and 1 mark for correct unit.)

Revision Summary for Section 1 (page 32)

2) $a = \dfrac{(v - u)}{t}$ so $t = \dfrac{(v - u)}{a}$
$= (2.7 - 0) \div 0.5 = 5.4$ s

9) $W = mg = 25 \times 1.6 = 40$ N

17) $a = F \div m = 25\,000 \div 25 = 1000$ m/s²

20) $19\,000 - 13\,500 = 5500$ N

22) $m = p \div v = 14\,700 \div 15 = 980$ kg

24) Momentum after = momentum before
$= 25 \times 5 = 125$ kg m/s
Speed = momentum ÷ mass
$= 125 \div (25 + 37) = 2.02$ m/s (to 3 s.f.)

25) Change in momentum = force × time
$= 230 \times 10$
$= 2300$ kg m/s

26) Moment $= 290 \times 7.5 = 2175$ Nm

28) distance = moment ÷ force
$= 108 \div 27 = 4$ m

36) $T = 365 \times 24 \times 60 \times 60 = 3.15... \times 10^7$ s
$v = \dfrac{2 \times \pi \times r}{T}$
$= (2 \times 3.14... \times 1.5 \times 10^8) \div 3.15... \times 10^7$
$= 29.9$ km/s (to 3 s.f.) (or 29 900 m/s)

Pages 42-43

Warm-Up Questions

1) Energy is transferred to the resistor, which heats the resistor. Toasters contain a coil of wire with a high resistance. When a current passes through the coil, its temperature increases so much that it glows and gives off infrared (heat) radiation, which cooks the bread.
2) The current in the circuit increases.
3) Mains electricity is usually a.c. Batteries are usually d.c.

Exam Questions

1. a) Any two of: One of the plugs has a cracked casing *(1 mark)* which could expose live parts and give someone a shock if they touched them *(1 mark)*. / One cable is frayed *(1 mark)*, which could expose live parts and give someone a shock if they touched them *(1 mark)*. / One cable is very long and trailing on the floor *(1 mark)*. This could be a trip hazard *(1 mark)*. / There is water close to plug sockets/plug cables *(1 mark)*, which is dangerous as water can conduct electricity *(1 mark)*. / There is a child pushing a metal object into a plug socket *(1 mark)*, which is unsafe as metal conducts electricity and the child could get an electric shock *(1 mark)*.
   b) i) The kettle is double insulated. / Plastic is an (electrical) insulator *(1 mark)*. This means the casing doesn't conduct electricity, so it can never become live *(1 mark)*.
      ii) Disagree. When the toaster is working properly, no current should be flowing in the earth wire *(1 mark)*.

2. a) $E = I \times V \times t$ so $t = \dfrac{E}{I \times V} = \dfrac{828}{2.3 \times 12} = $ **30 s**
   (3 marks for correct answer, otherwise 1 mark for rearranging the equation and 1 mark for correctly substituting into the equation.)
   b) Disagree. The fuse should be rated as close as possible but just above the normal operating current *(1 mark)*. If the fuse is below the normal operating current it will blow straight away even if there is no fault *(1 mark)*.

3. a) If the LED is lit up, current is flowing in the circuit *(1 mark)*.
   b) i) E.g. both have a resistance that varies. / Both are affected by external conditions *(1 mark)*.
      ii) E.g. thermistors are affected by temperature whereas LDRs are affected by light intensity *(1 mark)*.

4. a) Power = current × voltage or $P = I \times V$
      (1 mark — accept any rearranged version of the same equation.)
   b) $I = \dfrac{P}{V} = \dfrac{2.8 \times 1000}{230} = 12.17...$ A = **12 amps (A) (to 2 s.f.)**
      (3 marks available for correct answer, otherwise 1 mark for correctly substituting into a correctly rearranged equation and 1 mark for giving the correct unit.)
   c) 13 A *(1 mark)*
   Remember that fuses should be rated as near as possible but just higher than the normal operating current, which is 12 A here.
   d) She should choose kettle B because it has the higher power rating *(1 mark)*. This means that it transfers more energy (to heat energy) per unit time, so it will boil the water faster *(1 mark)*.

5. a) resistor *(1 mark)*
   b) (component) D *(1 mark)*
   The graph with the shallowest gradient corresponds to the component with the highest resistance.
   c) $V = I \times R$ so $I = \dfrac{V}{R} = \dfrac{15}{0.75} = $ **20 A**
      (2 marks for correct answer, otherwise 1 mark for correctly substituting into the correct rearranged equation.)

Pages 51-52

Warm-Up Questions

1) A material that can conduct electric charge easily. E.g. copper, silver.
2) A material that doesn't conduct electric charge very well. E.g. plastic, rubber.

Exam Questions

1. a) i) E.g. if one fairy light breaks, the rest still light up *(1 mark)*.
      ii) $V = I \times R$ *(1 mark)*
          $R = \dfrac{V}{I} = \dfrac{12}{0.5} = $ **24 Ω**
          (2 marks for correct answer, otherwise 1 mark for correct substitution.)
      iii) It would increase *(1 mark)*.
   b) The windscreen wipers, headlights and air conditioning must all be wired in parallel *(1 mark)*.

2. a) i) Rate of flow of charge *(1 mark)*.
      ii) It is carried by negatively charged electrons *(1 mark)*.
   b) i) Charge = current × time or $Q = I \times t$
         (1 mark — accept any rearranged version of the same equation.)
      ii) $Q = I \times t = 5 \times (20 \times 60) = $ **6000 coulombs (C)**
         (4 marks for correct answer, otherwise 1 mark for calculating the time in seconds, 1 mark for correctly substituting and 1 mark for the correct unit.)
      iii) The current will be double the original current (i.e. 10 A) *(1 mark)*.
   c) Energy transferred per unit charge is also known as voltage. The battery has a voltage of 3 V or 3 J/C, so 3 J of energy is transferred by the battery per coulomb.
      (3 marks available — 1 mark for saying that voltage in V is energy transferred per coulomb, 1 mark for getting 3 and 1 mark for the correct units.)

3. a) When the cloth duster and the balloon are rubbed together, the friction causes electrons to be transferred *(1 mark)* from the balloon to the cloth *(1 mark)*.
   b) E.g. any of: Use a gold leaf electroscope *(1 mark)*. Hold the balloon close to the metal disc of the electroscope. If the balloon is charged the gold leaves will become charged and repel each other, causing them to rise *(1 mark)*. / Use a rod with a known charge *(1 mark)*. Bring it close to the balloon and look for attraction or repulsion *(1 mark)*.
   c) –1.5 µC *(1 mark)*. The same number of electrons that were lost by the balloon were gained by the cloth, so it should have an equal but opposite charge to the balloon *(1 mark)*.

4. a) Inside the printer are two metal plates that can have a voltage applied to them *(1 mark)*. The voltage gives the plates opposite charges, which causes the droplets passing between them to be deflected, as they are attracted by one and repelled by the other *(1 mark)*. The amount and direction of deflection can be controlled by changing the size and direction of the voltage *(1 mark)*.
   b) i) Light reflected off some parts (the white parts) of the original document onto the image plate *(1 mark)*.
      ii) The black parts of the document don't reflect light onto the plate, so the image plate keeps its positive charge in those places *(1 mark)*. A negatively-charged black powder *(1 mark)* is brought close to the plate and attracted to the positively-charged parts of it *(1 mark)*. Then a positively-charged piece of paper *(1 mark)* is brought close to the plate and the negatively-charged black powder is attracted to the paper *(1 mark)*.

5. a) It can cause a discharge spark *(1 mark)*, which can cause a fire or an explosion if it ignites fuel or fuel fumes *(1 mark)*.
   b) E.g. Make the nozzle out of metal *(1 mark)*.
      Connect the fuel nozzle to the fuel tank with an earthing strap *(1 mark)*.

Revision Summary for Section 2 (page 53)

8) a) $I = P \div V = 1100 \div 230 = 4.78$ A
      (to 3 s.f.) So the appropriate fuse is 5 A.
   b) $I = P \div V = 2000 \div 230 = 8.70$ A
      (to 3 s.f.) So the appropriate fuse is 13 A.
9) $I = E \div (V \times t)$
    $= (7.2 \times 1000) \div (20 \times (2 \times 60))$
    $= 3$ A
13) $R = V \div I = 12 \div 2.5 = 4.8$ Ω
20) $I = Q \div t = 80 \div 2 = 40$ A

Pages 61-62

Warm-Up Questions

1. a) The distance from one peak to the next.
   b) The height of the wave from rest to crest.
   c) The time it takes (in s) for one complete wave to pass a point.
2) In transverse waves, the vibrations are at 90° to the direction energy is transferred by the wave. In longitudinal waves, the vibrations are along the same direction as the wave transfers energy.
3) False
   All EM waves travel at the same speed through free space (a vacuum).

4) Infrared radiation
5) X-ray radiation is directed through the object onto a detector plate. The brighter bits are where fewer X-rays get through.
6) Gamma rays are a form of ionising radiation and can penetrate far into the human body. There they can cause cell mutation or destruction, leading to tissue damage or cancer. To reduce the risk when using them, e.g. exposure should be kept to a minimum.

Exam Questions

1. a) 2 hertz (Hz) (or s^{-1}) *(2 marks available — 1 mark for the correct value and 1 mark for the correct unit.)*

   b) i) $v = f \times \lambda$ *(1 mark — accept any rearranged version.)*

   ii) $v = f \times \lambda$ so $\lambda = \frac{v}{f} = \frac{0.5}{2} =$ **0.25 m**
   (2 marks for the correct answer — otherwise 1 mark for correctly rearranging the equation and substituting the correct values into the equation.)

   Remember, the wavelength of a wave is the distance from crest to crest.

   iii) $f = \frac{1}{T}$, so $T = \frac{1}{f} = \frac{1}{2} =$ **0.5 s**
   (2 marks for the correct answer — otherwise 1 mark for correctly rearranging the equation and substituting the correct values into the equation. Allow full marks if the incorrect value from part i) is used correctly to calculate the period.)

2. a) Waves bending and spreading out as they travel past edges or through gaps *(1 mark)*.

   b) i) Visible light has a very short wavelength compared to the size of a doorway *(1 mark)*, so its diffraction is too small to notice *(1 mark)*.
   Light does diffract a very small amount, but it's too small for us to notice.

   ii) Disagree. Radio waves have a much longer wavelength than visible light *(1 mark)*, so they will diffract a lot more through doorways *(1 mark)*.

3. a) Long-wave radio signals can bend (diffract) round the mountain and reach the house *(1 mark)* because they have a long wavelength *(1 mark)*.

   b) The TV signals reflect off the ionosphere *(1 mark)*.

   c) i) microwave radiation *(1 mark)*.

   ii) They are transmitted through the atmosphere into space, where they are picked up by a satellite receiver orbiting Earth *(1 mark)*. The satellite transmits the signal back to Earth in a different direction, where it is received by a satellite dish connected to the house *(1 mark)*.

4. a) gamma radiation *(1 mark)*.

   b) Treating the fruit with radiation kills the microbes in it *(1 mark)*, which means that it will stay fresh for longer *(1 mark)*.

5. a) Microwaves can cause internal heating of human body tissue *(1 mark)*.

   b) E.g. infrared also has a heating effect *(1 mark)* but it has a higher frequency than microwaves and carries more energy (so it will have a greater heating effect) *(1 mark)*.

6. a) Disagree. Almost all of the ultraviolet radiation is absorbed *(1 mark)* by a (phosphor) coating on the inside of the glass that emits visible light instead *(1 mark)*.

   b) A camera focuses light onto a light-sensitive film or electronic sensor *(1 mark)*. The camera can control how much light enters it by controlling how big the aperture is *(1 mark)*. The photographer can control how long the film or sensor is exposed to the light by changing the shutter speed *(1 mark)*.

Pages 69-70

Warm-Up Questions

1) a transverse wave
2) That when an incident ray passes into a material, $n = \frac{\sin i}{\sin r}$
3) E.g. draw around a rectangular glass block on a piece of paper and direct a ray of light through it at an angle. Trace the incident and emergent rays, remove the block, then draw in the refracted ray between them. Draw in the normal at 90° to the edge of the block, at the point where the ray enters the block. Use a protractor to measure the angle of incidence (i) and the angle of refraction (r), then calculate the refractive index using Snell's law.

Exam Questions

1. a) i) An imaginary line that is at right angles to the surface (at the point where the light hits the surface) *(1 mark)*.

   ii) The angle of incidence is equal to the angle of reflection *(1 mark)*.

   b) E.g.

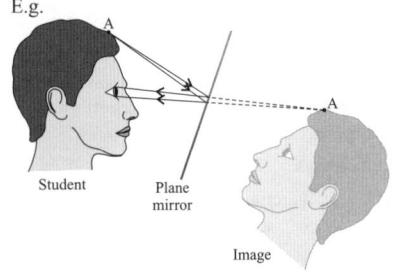

   (2 marks available — 1 mark for reflected rays drawn from point A on the student to the student's eyes, and 1 mark for virtual rays drawn from the point of reflection on the mirror to point A in the image. OR 1 mark for each correctly drawn ray from point A that is reflected in the mirror and ends at the eye.)

2. a) E.g.

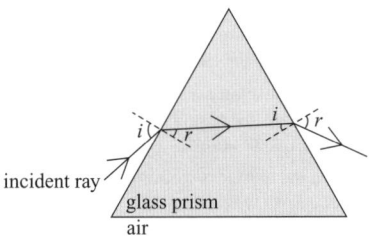

   (3 marks available — 1 mark for refracting the ray towards the normal upon entering the prism, 1 mark for refracting the ray away from the normal as it leaves the prism and 1 mark for correctly labelling all the angles of incidence and refraction.)

   b) E.g. Place the prism on a piece of paper and shine a ray of light at the prism. Trace the incident and emergent rays and the boundaries of the prism on the piece of paper *(1 mark)*. Remove the prism and draw in the refracted ray through the prism by joining the ends of the other two rays with a straight line *(1 mark)*. Draw in the normals using a protractor *(1 mark)* and use the protractor to measure i and r *(1 mark)*.

   c) i) White light is made up of different colours of light *(1 mark)*, which have different wavelengths and so refract by different amounts at each boundary of the prism *(1 mark)*.

   ii) The sides of a rectangular block are parallel *(1 mark)*, and so the rays of different colours of light bend by the same amount when they enter and leave the block and emerge parallel *(1 mark)*.

3. a) When light is incident at a boundary between materials at an angle greater than the critical angle, causing the light to be reflected back at the boundary (total internal reflection) *(1 mark)*.

   b) Bending an optical fibre sharply will result in a lot of light meeting the boundary at an angle that is smaller than or equal to than the critical angle *(1 mark)*. This means a lot of light will escape the optical fibre, so less light will be used to make the image *(1 mark)*.

4. a) $i = 45°$

   $n = \frac{\sin i}{\sin r}$ so $\sin r = \frac{\sin i}{n} = \frac{\sin 45°}{1.514} = 0.467...$
   So $r = \sin^{-1}(0.467...) =$ **27.84° (to 4 s.f.)**

   (4 marks for correct answer, otherwise 1 mark for using correct equation, 1 mark for correct substitution and 1 mark for correct rearrangement.)

   b) The separation happens when different colours refract by different amounts *(1 mark)*, but light doesn't refract when it crosses a boundary along the normal *(1 mark)*.

   c) Angle of incidence for violet light = $i = 45°$

   $\sin r = \frac{\sin i}{n} = \frac{\sin 45°}{1.528} = 0.4627...$
   $\Rightarrow r = \sin^{-1}(0.4627...) = 27.57°$ (to 4 s.f.)

   Then subtract this angle from the angle of refraction of red light to get:
   $\theta = 27.84 - 27.57 =$ **0.27°**

   (4 marks for correct answer, otherwise 1 mark for correct rearrangement of the equation to find r, 1 mark for correct angle of refraction of violet light and 1 mark for correctly subtracting one angle from the other. Allow the marks if the answer given to part a) is used correctly. Do not deduct marks for using an incorrect number of significant figures in calculations.)

5. a) The angle of incidence such that the angle of refraction is 90° (for light travelling from a denser material to a less dense material) *(1 mark)*.

b) It must be lower than 63.2° (the critical angle) as it is crossing the boundary *(1 mark)*.
c) It will be reflected back into the acrylic (total internal reflection) *(1 mark)*.
d) $n = \frac{1}{\sin C} = \frac{1}{\sin 41.8°} = \mathbf{1.50}$ **(to 3 s.f.)**
   (3 marks for correct answer, otherwise 1 mark for using the correct equation and 1 mark for substituting correct values into the equation. Deduct 1 mark for giving units.)

Page 75
Warm-Up Questions
1) An analogue signal can take any value within a certain range. A digital signal can only take two values.
2) a digital signal
3) longitudinal
4) 20-20 000 Hz
5) They are absorbed.
6) The louder a sound, the greater the amplitude of the sound wave.

Exam Question
1 a) i) The distance between the two microphones is 1 wavelength *(1 mark)* so use $v = f \times \lambda$ to calculate the speed of sound *(1 mark)*.
   ii) $v = f \times \lambda = 50 \times 6.8 = \mathbf{340}$ **metres per second (m/s)**
       (4 marks for correct answer, otherwise 1 mark for using the correct equation, 1 mark for substituting correct values into the equation and 1 mark for the correct units.)
   b) i) time period *(1 mark)*
      ii) One time cycle is 8 divisions long, so $T = 0.005 \times 8 = 0.04$ s
          $f = \frac{1}{T} = \frac{1}{0.04} = \mathbf{25\ Hz}$
          (2 marks for correct answer, otherwise 1 mark for substituting correctly into correct equation.)

Revision Summary for Section 3 (page 76)
3) $v = f \times \lambda = 50\ 000 \times 0.003 = 150$ m/s
13) $n = \sin i \div \sin r = 0.5 \div 0.34...$
    $= 1.5$ (to 2 s.f.)
14) A and D
15) $\sin C = 1 \div n$ so $C = \sin^{-1}(1 \div 1.35)$
    $= 48°$ (to 2 s.f.)

Pages 82-83
Warm-Up Questions
1) chemical energy
2) Energy can never be created or destroyed — it's only ever transferred from one form to another.
3) heat (energy)
4) Chemical energy to elastic potential energy and heat energy. Elastic potential energy to kinetic energy and heat energy.

Exam Questions
1

Device	Energy input	Useful energy output
A spring-loaded catapult	E.g. (elastic) potential energy	kinetic energy
A portable radio	chemical energy	sound energy
E.g. an electric heater	electrical energy	heat energy

(3 marks available — 1 mark for each correct answer)

2 a) light (energy) *(1 mark)*
   b) i) efficiency = $\frac{\text{useful energy output}}{\text{total energy input}}$ *(1 mark)*
      ii) efficiency = $\frac{\text{useful energy output}}{\text{total energy input}} = \frac{8}{20} = \mathbf{0.4}$ **(or 40%)**
          (2 marks if answer correct, otherwise 1 mark for correct substitution of values into the formula.)

c) efficiency = $\frac{\text{useful energy output}}{\text{total energy input}}$
   $\Rightarrow$ total energy input = $\frac{\text{useful energy output}}{\text{efficiency}}$
   $= \frac{10}{0.55} = \mathbf{18\ J}$ **(to 2 s.f.)**
   (2 marks if answer correct, otherwise 1 mark for correct rearrangement of the formula and correct substitution of values into the formula.)

d) Disagree — torch B has a lower energy input than torch A, i.e. it transfers less energy per second than torch A.
   (1 mark — allow the mark if an incorrect value from part c) has been used correctly.)
   You receive no marks for part d) if you agreed with the student's claim.

3 a) 10 J *(1 mark)*
   You know the total input energy is 200 J. The input energy arrow is 20 squares wide, so the value of each square must be 200 J ÷ 20 = 10 J.
   b) 50 J *(1 mark)*
   The useful energy arrow is 5 squares wide, and each square represents 10 J. So the amount of energy that's usefully transferred = 5 × 10 J = 50 J

4 a) E.g. heat energy/sound energy *(1 mark)*
   b) Gravitational potential energy of lifted weight
      $= 100 - 50 - 20 = 30$ kJ *(1 mark)*
   c) E.g.

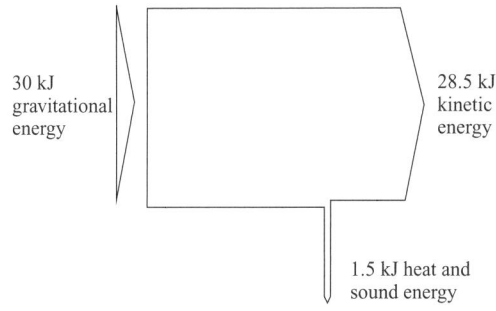

   30 kJ gravitational energy → 28.5 kJ kinetic energy; 1.5 kJ heat and sound energy

   (3 marks available — 1 mark for drawing a recognisable Sankey diagram, 1 mark for all of the arrows being drawn in roughly the correct proportions, 1 mark for all of the arrows being correctly labelled.)

Page 88
Warm-Up Questions
1) The transfer of heat energy by electromagnetic waves.
2) Vibrating particles pass on their extra kinetic energy to neighbouring particles. Gradually the extra kinetic energy (or heat) is passed all the way through the solid, causing a rise in temperature at the other side.
3) Because the particles in solids can't move.
4) Heat energy is transferred from the heater coils to the water by conduction. The particles near the coils get more energy, so they start moving around faster. This means there's more distance between them, i.e. the water expands and becomes less dense. This reduction in density means that hotter water tends to rise above the denser, cooler water. As the hot water rises it displaces (moves) the colder water out of the way, making it sink towards the heater coils. This cold water is then heated by the coils and rises — and so it goes on. You end up with convection currents going up, round and down, circulating the heat energy through the water.
5) Pockets of air trapped in the clothes and between layers reduce heat loss by conduction and convection. The material also absorbs some heat radiated out by our bodies, reducing heat loss by radiation.

Exam Questions
1 a) Conduction *(1 mark)* and radiation *(1 mark)*
   b) Flask C *(1 mark)*.
      There is a larger temperature difference between flask C and the surrounding gel *(1 mark)*.
      You receive no marks for part b) if you answered A or B.

2 a) i) conduction *(1 mark)*
      ii) E.g. it will help stop a convection current being set up in the air gap (and so reduce heat loss by convection). / It will reduce radiation across the gap (as it will absorb most of the heat radiated from the inside wall). / The foam and air trapped in it are both insulators, and so will help reduce heat loss by conduction from the home. *(1 mark for naming a type of heat transfer and correctly explaining how energy transfer is reduced.)*

b) E.g. any two from: Installing double glazing *(1 mark)* — the air gap between the layers of glass will help reduce the amount of energy being transferred through the window by conduction *(1 mark)*. / Fitting draught-proofing strips around the windows *(1 mark)* will help to reduce the amount of heat escaping as draughts *(1 mark)*. / Putting up curtains/buying thicker curtains *(1 mark)* — curtains will help to reduce the amount of warm air in a room reaching the window, and so reduce heat loss by conduction/radiation *(1 mark)*.

Page 92
Warm-Up Questions
1) The energy transferred when a force moves an object.
2) Power is the rate of doing work/the rate of energy transfer.
   Power = $\frac{\text{work done}}{\text{time taken}}$
3) kinetic energy = $\frac{1}{2}$ × mass × speed^2 (KE = $\frac{1}{2}$ × m × v^2)

Exam Questions
1 a) 50 joules (J) *(1 mark)*
   b) $W = F \times d \Rightarrow d = \frac{W}{F} = \frac{50}{250} = $ **0.2 m**
      (3 marks if answer correct, otherwise 1 mark for using the correct formula and 1 mark for the correct rearrangement and substitution of values into the formula.)

2 a) $P = \frac{W}{t} \Rightarrow W = P \times t = 150 \times (10 \times 60) = 90\,000$ J = **90 kJ**
      (2 marks if answer correct, otherwise 1 mark for correct rearrangement of the formula and correct substitution of values into the formula.)
   b) $W = F \times d = 155 \times 1.2 = $ **186 J**
      (2 marks if answer correct, otherwise 1 mark for correct substitution of values into the formula.)
   c) E.g. The maximum speed will increase. The motor has a higher power rating and so will transfer more chemical energy (from fuel) into kinetic energy (of the boat) each second. The boat will have to be refuelled more often because more energy is transferred per second. So more input energy from the fuel is needed, and so more fuel will be used per second.
      (4 marks available — 1 mark for saying the maximum speed would increase, 1 mark for supporting explanation. 1 mark for saying the boat would need to be refuelled more often, 1 mark for a supporting explanation)

3 a) KE = $\frac{1}{2}mv^2 = \frac{1}{2} \times 105 \times 2.39^2 = $ **300 J (to 3 s.f.)**
      (3 marks if answer correct, otherwise 1 mark for using the correct formula and 1 mark for correct substitution of values into the formula.)
   b) i) GPE = $m \times g \times h = 105 \times 10 \times 20.2 = $ **21 200 J (to 3 s.f.)**
         (3 marks if answer correct, otherwise 1 mark for using the correct formula and 1 mark for the correct rearrangement and substitution of values into the formula.)
      ii) It's converted to kinetic energy *(1 mark)*.

Pages 99-100
Warm-Up Questions
1) Burning coal releases sulfur dioxide, which causes acid rain. Acid rain can, e.g. harm trees/soils / impact on wildlife.
2) Nuclear energy is transferred into heat energy in nuclear reactions.
3) E.g. it doesn't produce greenhouse gases which contribute to global warming. There's still plenty of uranium left in the ground.

Exam Questions
1 a) wind *(1 mark)*
   b) The heat energy is used to turn the water into steam *(1 mark)*. The steam is used to drive turbines — transferring heat energy into kinetic energy *(1 mark)*. The turbine drives a generator — the kinetic energy of the generator is transferred into electrical energy *(1 mark)*.
   c) E.g. any two from:
      Burning natural gas releases a lot of energy for a relatively low cost *(1 mark)* / energy from natural gas doesn't rely on the weather or time of day (it's reliable) *(1 mark)* / no new technology or spending is needed to set up natural gas power stations — we have a lot already *(1 mark)*.

2 a) Kinetic energy *(1 mark)*.
   b) Disagree — the size of waves is variable and uncontrollable, and so this can be an unreliable method of generating electricity *(1 mark)*. The running costs are low, but wave power stations are initially expensive to set up *(1 mark)*.

3 a) A solar cell *(1 mark)*
   b) E.g. the cost of connecting solar cells to the National Grid is high compared to the amount of electricity they generate *(1 mark)*. It is often not practical to connect them to the National Grid. *(1 mark)*.

4 a) i) kinetic *(1 mark)*, kinetic *(1 mark)*, electrical *(1 mark)*.
      ii) Advantage — e.g.
          Wind farms have low running costs (as there are no fuel costs) *(1 mark)* / wind is a renewable resource (it won't run out) *(1 mark)* / wind farms cause no atmospheric pollution *(1 mark)*.
          Disadvantage — e.g.
          Some people think wind farms spoil the view/make too much noise *(1 mark)* / a lot of wind farms are needed to generate the same amount of electricity as a fossil fuel power station *(1 mark)* / wind speed varies, so they're not particularly reliable *(1 mark)* / wind farms usually require specific (remote) locations, so building and maintenance work is expensive *(1 mark)* / you can't increase the supply of electricity when demand is high *(1 mark)*.
   b) Advantage — e.g.
      Geothermal energy is a renewable resource *(1 mark)* / no fuel is required so there are low running costs *(1 mark)* / geothermal power stations have very little impact on the environment once set up *(1 mark)*.
      Disadvantage — e.g.
      There are high initial costs in drilling down several km *(1 mark)* / the cost of building a power station is often high compared to the amount of energy obtained *(1 mark)* / the possible locations for power stations are very limited *(1 mark)*.

5 a) The water's gravitational potential energy is converted to kinetic energy of the turbines *(1 mark)*, which is converted to electrical energy by a generator *(1 mark)*.
   b) E.g. any two from: they can cause the loss or destruction of habitats *(1 mark)* / rotting vegetation in dams releases methane *(1 mark)*.
   c) Pumped storage *(1 mark)*.
   d) E.g. any two from:
      They cause no atmospheric pollution *(1 mark)* / they use a renewable energy source *(1 mark)* / there are no fuel costs *(1 mark)* / maintenance and running costs are low *(1 mark)* / tides are regular and predictable, so this is a fairly reliable energy source *(1 mark)*.

Revision Summary for Section 4 (page 101)
2) Efficiency = 70 J ÷ 100 J = 0.7 = 70%
4) a) 80 J
   b) 20 J
   c) 80 J ÷ 100 J = 0.8 = 80%
10) Work done = force × distance moved
    = 535 × 12 = 6420 J
11) Power = W/t = 540 000/270 = 2000 W
12) KE = ½ × m × v^2 = ½ × 78 × 23^2
       = 20 600 J (to 3 s.f.)
14) GPE = m × g × h = 78 × 10 × 2 = 1560 J

Pages 108-109
Warm-Up Questions
1) Brownian motion
2) The average kinetic energy will increase by a factor of 3 (it will triple).
3) As gas particles move about, they randomly bang into each other or anything that gets in the way. When they collide with something they exert a force on it and their momentum and direction change. In a sealed container gas particles smash into the container walls and create an outward pressure.

Exam Questions
1 a) equal *(1 mark)*, greater *(1 mark)*
   b) i) pressure = $\frac{\text{force}}{\text{area}}$ ($p = \frac{F}{A}$) *(1 mark)*
      ii) pressure = $\frac{\text{force}}{\text{area}} = \frac{18}{0.45} = $ **40 Pa**
          (2 marks if answer correct, otherwise 1 mark for correct substitution of values into the equation.)

2 a) pressure difference = height × density × g ($p = h \times \rho \times g$) *(1 mark)*

b) i) density = $\frac{\text{mass}}{\text{volume}} = \frac{500}{0.5}$

= **1000 kilograms per metre cubed (kg/m³)**
(4 marks if answer correct, otherwise 1 mark for using correct equation, 1 mark for correct substitution and 1 mark for the correct unit.)

ii) $p = h \times \rho \times g \Rightarrow h = \frac{p}{\rho \times g} = \frac{240\,000}{1000 \times 10} =$ **24 m**

(3 marks if answer correct, otherwise 1 mark for correct rearrangement of the equation and 1 mark for correct substitution of values into the equation. Allow marks if incorrect value of density is used from part b) i))

The pressure given in the question was in kPa, so you have to convert it to Pa to do the calculation.

3 a) i) The average speed decreases *(1 mark)*.
   ii) The energy of the particles in a substance decreases with temperature *(1 mark)*. There is a minimum energy that the particles can have, so there is a minimum temperature *(1 mark)*.
   iii) –273 °C *(1 mark)*

b) i) –263 °C *(1 mark)*
   ii) 904 K *(1 mark)*

To convert from the Kelvin scale to the Celsius scale just subtract 273, and to convert from the Celsius scale to the Kelvin scale add 273.

4 a) The densities of each of the toy soldiers are the same, but their masses may vary *(1 mark)*.

b) i) The volume of the toy soldier *(1 mark)*.
   The mass of the toy soldier *(1 mark)*.
   ii) E.g. measure the mass of the toy soldier using the mass balance *(1 mark)*. Measure the volume of the soldier by first filling the measuring cylinder with enough water to submerge the toy soldier and taking a reading of the volume *(1 mark)*. Then submerge the toy soldier in the water and take another reading of the volume *(1 mark)*. Calculate the volume of the toy solder by subtracting the initial volume reading from the final volume reading *(1 mark)*. Divide the mass of the toy solider by the volume of the toy soldier to find the density *(1 mark)*.

With questions where you have to describe a method, make sure your description is clear and detailed. You could also pick up some of the marks by describing how you'd do repeats, take averages and other ways in which you'd make it a fair test — there's more on this in the Describing Experiments section.

5 a) Particles are held close together in a fixed, regular pattern *(1 mark)*. They vibrate about fixed positions *(1 mark)*.

b) i) melting *(1 mark)*
   ii) When the solid substance is heated the particles inside it gain energy and vibrate faster *(1 mark)*. When the temperature gets high enough, they start moving fast enough to overcome the forces of attraction between them and start moving around (i.e. the substance becomes a liquid) *(1 mark)*.

c) Evaporation *(1 mark)*. A liquid can evaporate at any temperature, whereas boiling happens only at the boiling point *(1 mark)*. Particles in the liquid can only evaporate if they are travelling in the right direction, fast enough to overcome the attractive forces of the other particles in the liquid, whereas when a liquid boils, all of the particles have enough energy to escape *(1 mark)*.

6 $p_1 V_1 = p_2 V_2 \Rightarrow p_2 = \frac{p_1 V_1}{V_2} = \frac{98 \times 0.014}{0.013} = 105.5$ kPa
= **110 kPa (to 2 s.f.)**

(3 marks if answer correct, otherwise 1 mark for correct rearrangement of the equation and 1 mark for correct substitution of values into the equation.)

7 $\frac{p_1}{T_1} = \frac{p_2}{T_2} \Rightarrow p_2 = \frac{p_1 \times T_2}{T_1} = \frac{107 \times 405}{288} =$ **150 kPa (to 3 s.f.)**

(3 marks if answer correct, otherwise 1 mark for correct rearrangement of the equation and 1 mark for correct substitution of values into the equation.)

Revision Summary for Section 5 (page 110)

2) Density = mass ÷ volume
   so volume = 2 ÷ 1000 = 0.002 m³

5) 5 cm² = 0.0005 m²
   Pressure = force ÷ area
   = 600 ÷ 0.0005 = 1 200 000 Pa = 1200 kPa

15) $p_1 V_1 = p_2 V_2$ so $50 \times 500 = p_2 \times 100$
    so $p_2 = (50 \times 500) \div 100 = 250$ kPa

16) $p_1 \div T_1 = p_2 \div T_2$ so $50 \div 290 = p_2 \div 300$
    so $p_2 = (50 \div 290) \times 300$
    = 51.7 kPa (to 3 s.f.)

Pages 119-121

Warm-Up Questions

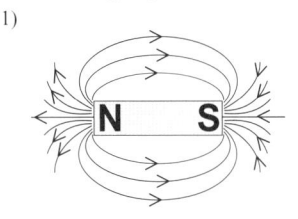

1) [diagram of magnetic field lines around a bar magnet with N and S poles]

2) It means it loses its induced magnetism quickly. Steel is an example of a hard magnetic material.

3) Electromagnetic induction is the creation of a voltage (and maybe a current) in a wire which is experiencing a change in magnetic field.

4) A step-up transformer increases the voltage of an alternating current. They have more turns on their secondary coil than their primary coil. A step-down transformer decreases the voltage. They have more turns on their primary coil.

Exam Questions

1 a) E.g. Put the magnets on a piece of paper and place many compasses in different places between the magnets to show the magnetic field at those points *(1 mark)*. The compasses will line up with the magnetic field lines *(1 mark)*.

You could also use iron filings to shown the pattern.

b) i) The field is uniform *(1 mark)*
   ii) Attraction *(1 mark)* — opposite poles are facing each other so there will be a force of attraction between them *(1 mark)*.

2 a) A material that is attracted by a magnet. / A material that becomes magnetised when placed in a magnetic field *(1 mark)*.

b) The north pole of the bar magnet induces a south/opposite pole in the head of the nail *(1 mark)* and the opposite poles attract each other *(1 mark)*.

3 a) As the wheel rotates, the magnet rotates inside the coil of wire *(1 mark)*. This creates a changing magnetic field in the coil of wire which induces a voltage *(1 mark)*.

b) Any two of: e.g. increase the strength of the magnet *(1 mark)*. / Increase the number of turns on the coil of wire *(1 mark)*. / Increase the speed of rotation of the magnet *(1 mark)*.

c) Agree. There will be a changing magnetic field through the wire when the magnet rotates in either direction *(1 mark)*.

4 a) i) A current-carrying wire in a magnetic field experiences a force *(1 mark)*.
   ii) upwards *(1 mark)*

b) i) The force will increase *(1 mark)*.
   ii) Reversing the direction of the magnetic field/moving the magnet so that the loop wraps around the other pole *(1 mark)*. Reversing the direction of the current/direction that the wire wraps round the magnet *(1 mark)*.

c) The electrons that form the current through the bar are moving parallel to the magnetic field *(1 mark)* so they (and the bar) will experience no force *(1 mark)*.

5 a) E.g.

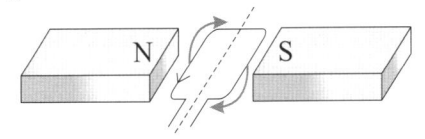

[diagram showing N and S magnets with a loop of wire and current direction indicated]

(1 mark for any indication that the current goes anticlockwise.)

b) After 90° the force on the top arm will act upwards and the force on the bottom arm will act downwards, so the forces will oppose the rotation of the loop *(1 mark)*.

c) By swapping the direction of the current/contacts every half turn (using a split-ring commutator) *(1 mark)* so the forces on the loop always act in a way that keeps the loop rotating *(1 mark)*.

d) Any of: Increase the current *(1 mark)*. / Increase the number of turns on the loop *(1 mark)*. / Increase the strength of the magnetic field *(1 mark)*.

6 When the a.c. current flows through the coil of wire in the magnetic field of the permanent magnet, the coil of wire experiences a force *(1 mark)*. The force causes the coil, and so the cone, to move *(1 mark)*. The a.c. current is constantly changing direction so the force on the coil is constantly changing so the cone vibrates back and forth *(1 mark)*. The vibrations cause the air to vibrate and cause sound waves *(1 mark)*.

7 a) A solenoid, or coil of wire (with an iron core) *(1 mark)*.
   b)

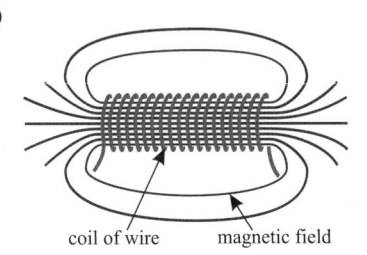

   coil of wire   magnetic field

   Inside the coil, the field is strong and uniform. Outside the coil, the field is the same as that of a bar magnet.
   (2 marks — 1 mark for showing by sketch or for saying that the field is uniform and strong inside the coil and 1 mark for showing by sketch or saying that the field is like that of a bar magnet outside the coil.)

   c) When the electromagnet is turned on, current flows through the coil of wire and produces a magnetic field *(1 mark)*. Iron is a magnetic material, so magnetism is induced in it and the bar is attracted to it *(1 mark)*. When the current stops, there is no longer a magnetic field around the electromagnet *(1 mark)* so the bar is no longer attracted to the electromagnet and drops *(1 mark)*.

8 a) Power = current × voltage or P = I × V *(1 mark)*
   b) P = I × V = 0.25 × 240 = **60 W**
   (2 marks for correct answer, otherwise 1 mark for substituting correct values into the equation.)
   c) If the transformer is 100 % efficient, input power = output power, so output power = 60 W.
   P = I × V so I = $\frac{P}{V} = \frac{60}{12} =$ **5 A**
   (3 marks for correct answer, otherwise 1 mark for the correct output power and 1 mark for substituting correctly into rearranged equation.)

9 a) A step-up transformer is used to increase the voltage of electricity supplied by the power stations to be very high *(1 mark)*. A higher voltage means less current for a given power ($V = I \times R$) and so less energy lost as heat *(1 mark)*. Step-down transformers are then used to bring the voltage of the supply back down to a safe level to be supplied to the consumer *(1 mark)*.

   b) i) $\frac{\text{input (primary) voltage}}{\text{output (secondary) voltage}} = \frac{\text{number of turns on primary}}{\text{number of turns on secondary}}$
      or $\frac{V_p}{V_s} = \frac{n_p}{n_s}$ *(1 mark)*
      ii) $\frac{V_p}{V_s} = \frac{n_p}{n_s}$ so $V_s = \frac{n_s}{n_p} \times V_p = 16 \times 25\,000 =$ **400 000 V**
      (4 marks available, otherwise 1 mark for saying $\frac{n_s}{n_p} = 16$, 1 mark for rearranging the equation correctly and 1 mark for substituting correctly into the equation.)

   c) If the current was direct, it wouldn't change so the magnetic field created by the primary coil wouldn't change *(1 mark)*. This means the magnetic field through the secondary coil wouldn't change *(1 mark)*, so no voltage would be induced across it *(1 mark)*.

Revision Summary for Section 6 (page 122)

18) The secondary voltage is unknown, so V_s should be on the top of the equation:
    $V_s \div V_p = N_s \div N_p$.
    So, $V_s \div 30 = 50 \div 10 = 5$
    and $V_s = 5 \times 30 = 150$ V

19) Using the equation $V_p I_p = V_s I_s$:
    $30\,000 \times I_p = 6000$
    (because $V \times I$ = power)
    So, $I_p = 6000 \div 30\,000 = 0.2$ A

Pages 128-129

Warm-Up Questions

1) The total number of protons and neutrons in the nucleus.
2) ion
3) They are large and heavy, so they collide with lots of atoms, causing ionisation.
4) beta (particles)
5) gamma (rays)
6) (Hans) Geiger and (Ernest) Marsden
7) An atom contains a small, positively charged nucleus where most of the mass of the atom is contained. The rest of the atom is mostly empty space.

Exam Questions

1 a) i)

Particle	Charge	Number present in an atom of iodine-131
Proton	positive	53
Neutron	zero	78
Electron	negative	53

(3 marks — 1 mark for each correct answer)

   ii) protons and neutrons *(1 mark)*
   b) Atoms with the same atomic number but a different mass number *(1 mark)*.
   Isotopes have the same number of protons but a different number of neutrons, so they have the same atomic number (no. of protons) but a different mass number (no. of protons and neutrons). The number of protons always equals the number of electrons in a neutral atom (i.e. not an ion).
   c) i) background radiation *(1 mark)*
      ii) Any two from: e.g. air / food / building materials / soils / rocks / radiation from space (cosmic rays) / living things
      (2 marks — 1 mark for each correct answer).
   d) gamma (rays) *(1 mark)*, alpha (particles) *(1 mark)*, beta (particles) *(1 mark)*

2 a) Beta (particles) *(1 mark)*, because it passes through the paper, but not the aluminium, so it is moderately penetrating in comparison to the other two *(1 mark)*.
   b) Geiger-Muller detector / photographic film *(1 mark)*

3 a) Gold (Au). A more positively charged nucleus (with a higher atomic number) will deflect the particles more *(1 mark)*.
   b) They will be deflected less *(1 mark)*.
   c) They will be deflected less *(1 mark)*.

4 a) i) $^{0}_{-1}e$
   (2 marks — 1 mark for each correct number.)
   ii) The atomic number increases by 1 *(1 mark)* and the mass number stays the same *(1 mark)*.
   b) i) The atomic number doesn't change *(1 mark)* and neither does the mass number *(1 mark)*.
   ii) $^{199}_{84}Po \rightarrow ^{195}_{82}Pb + ^{4}_{2}\alpha + ^{0}_{0}\gamma$
   (4 marks — 1 mark each for the α and the γ correct and 1 mark each for the mass and atomic numbers of Po.)

Pages 136-137

Warm-Up Questions

1) becquerels (Bq)
2) gamma (rays) and beta (particles)
3) Squirt a gamma source into the pipe, let it flow along, and go along the outside with a detector. If there's a crack in the pipe, the gamma source will collect outside the pipe, and your detector will show extra-high radioactivity at that point.
4) Because big movements in the ground could disturb the canisters the radioactive material is buried in and allow it to leak out. If this material gets into the groundwater it could contaminate the soil, plants, rivers, etc. and get into our drinking water.

Exam Questions

1. a) i) $2 \times 60 = 120$ seconds
      $120 \div 40 = 3$ half-lives
      $8000 \div 2 = 4000$, $4000 \div 2 = 2000$, $2000 \div 2 = $ **1000 Bq**
      (2 marks for the correct answer, otherwise 1 mark for calculating the number of half-lives.)
   ii) $8000 \div 2 = 4000$, $4000 \div 2 = 2000$, $2000 \div 2 = 1000$, $1000 \div 2 = 500$, $500 \div 2 = 250$, $250 \div 2 = 125$. So it takes 6 half-lives to drop to less than 200 Bq.
      $6 \times 40 = 240$ seconds
      $240 \div 60 = $ **4 mins**
      (3 marks for the correct answer, otherwise 1 mark for calculating the number of half-lives and 1 mark for calculating the number of seconds.)
   b) Paul. Sample size doesn't affect half-life but different isotopes do have different half-lives *(1 mark)*

2. a) E.g. When radiation enters the body, it can collide with molecules in body cells causing ionisation *(1 mark)* which can damage or destroy the molecules / cause cell damage/cell death/cancer/radiation sickness *(1 mark)*.
   b) i) Treatment (of cancer) using radiation *(1 mark)*.
      ii) E.g. radiotherapists may wear lead aprons/stand behind lead screens during procedures *(1 mark)*.
      iii) Any two from: E.g. always store radioactive material in a lead box when not in use *(1 mark)*. / Never allow skin contact with a radioactive source *(1 mark)*. / Always use tongs to hold radioactive sources *(1 mark)*. / Always hold radioactive sources at arm's length *(1 mark)*. / Keep radioactive sources pointed away from you *(1 mark)*.

3. a) The iodine-123 is absorbed in the same way that the patient's body normally absorbs iodine, but gives out radiation which can be detected outside the body *(1 mark)*. The patient is given iodine-123 and the amount of radiation emitted from the thyroid gland is monitored to check whether it is absorbing iodine properly *(1 mark)*.
   b) Alpha particles can't penetrate tissue/would be blocked by the body *(1 mark)*, so you couldn't detect them outside of the body *(1 mark)*. Alpha particles are also strongly ionising *(1 mark)* so they're dangerous to use as medical tracers *(1 mark)*.
   c) Technetium-99m because it's got a short half-life *(1 mark)*, which means it's easier to detect because its activity is higher/won't be very radioactive inside the patient for long *(1 mark)*.

4. One half-life: 1:20 000 000. Two half-lives: 1:40 000 000. Three half-lives: 1:80 000 000. $3 \times 5730 = $ **17 190 years**.
   (3 marks, otherwise 1 mark for correctly stating 3 half-lives and 1 mark for attempting to multiply the half-life by 3.)

5. a) E.g. Uranium-235/U-235 *(1 mark)*
   b) i) A slow-moving neutron gets absorbed by a uranium-235 nucleus causing it to split *(1 mark)*. The uranium nucleus will split to form two daughter nuclei *(1 mark)*, a small number of neutrons *(1 mark)* and a large amount of kinetic energy *(1 mark)*.
      ii) In a nuclear reactor, the neutrons released from each fission event collide with other uranium nuclei causing other fission events that release more neutrons *(1 mark)*. This is known as a chain reaction *(1 mark)*. The nuclear reactor contains a moderator that slows down the neutrons released from fission so that they can successfully collide with uranium nuclei *(1 mark)*.
   c) They limit the rate of fission by absorbing excess neutrons *(1 mark)*.

Revision Summary for Section 7 (page 138)

10) a) $^{131}_{53}I \longrightarrow {}^{131}_{54}Xe + {}^{0}_{-1}e$
    b) $^{241}_{95}Am \longrightarrow {}^{237}_{93}Np + {}^{4}_{2}He$
    c) $^{14}_{6}C \longrightarrow {}^{14}_{7}N + {}^{0}_{-1}e$

13) $400 \div 2 = 200$
    $200 \div 2 = 100$
    So, 1 day = 2 half-lives = 24 hours.
    Half-life of Cu-64 = 24 hours $\div 2 = 12$ hours.

Pages 143-166
Practice Paper — 1P

1. a) i) A and C *(1 mark)*
      ii) B *(1 mark)*
      iii) It will decelerate *(1 mark)*.
   b) i) Gravitational potential energy = mass × gravitational field strength × height or GPE = $m \times g \times h$ *(1 mark)*
      ii) GPE = $m \times g \times h = 1500 \times 10 \times 40 = 600\,000$ J = **600 kJ**
         (2 marks for correct answer in kJ, otherwise 1 mark for substituting the correct values into the correct equation.)
   c) An object that returns to its original shape once the forces on it causing a shape change have been removed *(1 mark)*.

2. a) If the magnetic field is moving or changing in relation to the coil of wire, a voltage is induced by electromagnetic induction *(1 mark)*.
   b) Any two from: increase the speed of rotation *(1 mark)*. / Increase the number of turns on the coil *(1 mark)*. / Increase the strength of the magnetic field *(1 mark)*.
   c) i) Efficiency = $\dfrac{\text{useful energy output}}{\text{total energy input}}$ *(1 mark)*
      ii) useful energy output = 180 MJ
         total energy output = useful energy output + wasted energy = 180 + 415 = 595 MJ
         total energy input = total energy output
         So efficiency = $\dfrac{\text{useful energy output}}{\text{total energy input}} = \dfrac{180}{595}$
         = **0.303 (to 3 s.f.) (or 30.3% (to 3 s.f.))**
         (3 marks available for correct answer as a decimal or a percentage, otherwise 1 mark for calculating the total energy output (and input) and 1 mark for substituting correctly into correct equation. Deduct 1 mark for incorrect number of s.f.)
   d) Current that is constantly changing direction *(1 mark)*.
   e) Any four marks from: Burning coal releases carbon dioxide into the atmosphere *(1 mark)* which contributes to climate change/global warming *(1 mark)*. / Burning coal releases sulfur dioxide into the atmosphere *(1 mark)* which causes acid rain *(1 mark)* which can harm trees, soils and wildlife *(1 mark)*. / Coal will eventually run out *(1 mark)*.

3. a) $E = I \times V \times t = 12 \times 230 \times 30 = $ **82 800 J**
      (2 marks for correct answer, otherwise 1 mark for substituting correct values into the correct equation.)
   b) The heater coils transfer energy to the water particles nearby (by conduction) and warm the water *(1 mark)*. The particles in the heated water move faster and further apart, so the water's density decreases *(1 mark)*. The warm water is less dense than the cooler water above it, so it rises through the tank by convection *(1 mark)*. The colder water sinks to the bottom of the tank where it is then heated *(1 mark)*.
   c) i) Any two from e.g. use a more precise thermometer *(1 mark)* / use a more precise stop watch *(1 mark)* / record results to a greater number of decimal places *(1 mark)*.
      ii) Take averages of her data for each wool jacket thickness *(1 mark)*.
      iii) E.g. the graph shows that for this beaker of water, the final temperature of the water increases with the thickness of the cotton wool jacket *(1 mark)*.

4. a) Stopping distance = thinking distance + braking distance
      = 9 + 14 = **23 m** *(1 mark)*
   b) So that an average value can be calculated / because any individual vehicle may have an extreme value of thinking distance or breaking distance depending on the vehicle or driver *(1 mark)*. This makes the data more reliable *(1 mark)*.
   c) Any five from: e.g. The thinking distance/reaction time is increased if the driver is: tired *(1 mark)* / under the influence of drugs/alcohol *(1 mark)* / old aged *(1 mark)* / inexperienced *(1 mark)*.
      The braking distance is increased: in poor weather conditions *(1 mark)* / if the surface of the road is slippy *(1 mark)* / if the car is heavier *(1 mark)* / if the brakes/tyres are worn/faulty *(1 mark)*.

5. a) a moon *(1 mark)*
   b) gravity *(1 mark)*

c) $v = \dfrac{2 \times \pi \times r}{T}$ where r is the distance from the satellite to the centre of the Earth.

so $r = \dfrac{v \times T}{2 \times \pi} = \dfrac{3080 \times (24 \times 60 \times 60)}{2 \times \pi}$

= 42 353 040.2... m = **42 400 000 m** (to 3 s.f.)

(3 marks for correct answer, otherwise 1 mark for rearranging the equation, 1 mark for correctly substituting into the equation.)

d) Similarities — any two from: e.g. Both are electromagnetic waves *(1 mark)* / both travel at the same speed in free space *(1 mark)* / both are used for communications *(1 mark)* / both are transverse waves *(1 mark)* / both can be reflected/refracted/diffracted *(1 mark)*.

Differences — any two from: e.g. They have different wavelengths *(1 mark)* / they have different frequencies *(1 mark)* / they have different energies *(1 mark)*.

6 a) Any two from: It can cause cell damage *(1 mark)* / cell death *(1 mark)* / tissue damage *(1 mark)* / cell mutations *(1 mark)* / cancer *(1 mark)* / radiation sickness *(1 mark)*.

b) Geiger-Muller detector *(1 mark)*.

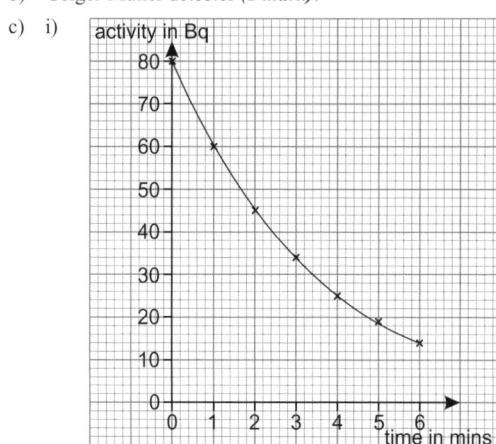

c) i) [graph of activity in Bq vs time in mins, curve from 80 Bq decaying through points over 6 minutes]

(5 marks available — 1 mark for a suitable scale chosen (more than half of the graph paper is used), 1 mark for a suitable curved line of best fit, 1 mark for the axes correctly labelled with variables and units, 2 marks for all the points plotted correctly to within half a square. Deduct up to 2 marks for incorrectly plotted points, 1 mark for each incorrect point plotted.)

ii) Half-life = **2.4 ± 0.1 min**

Draw a horizontal line from 40 Bq (half of the initial activity) on the activity axis across to the curve. Then draw a vertical line down to the time axis to find the value of the half-life.

(2 marks for correct answer otherwise 1 mark for attempting to use the graph correctly to find the half-life.)

d) Any four from: e.g. Some substances on Earth, such as air/food/building materials/soil/rocks *(1 mark)*. / Radiation from space/cosmic rays *(1 mark)*. / All living things contain radioactive material *(1 mark)*. / Nuclear waste *(1 mark)*. / Nuclear explosions that release radioactive material *(1 mark)*.

e) i) $^{226}_{88}\text{Ra} \rightarrow {}^{222}_{86}\text{N} + {}^{4}_{2}\alpha$ *(1 mark)*

ii) 88 *(1 mark)*

7 a) current *(1 mark)*

b) i) E.g. they have not ignored the anomalous point *(1 mark)*.

ii) Voltage = current × resistance or V = I × R *(1 mark)*

iii) V = 5 V, I = 1.4 A

V = I × R so $R = \dfrac{V}{I} = \dfrac{5}{1.4}$ = **3.6 ohms (Ω)** (to 2 s.f.)

(3 marks for the correct answer, otherwise one mark for correctly substituting into the correctly rearranged equation and 1 mark for the correct unit.)

c) Disagree. The graph shows that the gradient changes. The gradient is 1 ÷ resistance *(1 mark)* so the gradient changing shows that the resistance changes too *(1 mark)*.

8 a) clockwise *(1 mark)*

Use Fleming's left-hand rule and remember the magnetic field goes from north to south.

b) A current-carrying wire in a magnetic field experiences a force due to the motor effect *(1 mark)*. The force causes one side of the coil to move upwards and one side to move downwards, causing it to rotate *(1 mark)*.

c) Any two from: Increase the number of turns on the coil *(1 mark)*. / Increase the current in the wire *(1 mark)*. / Increase the magnetic field strength *(1 mark)*.

9 a) The force on piston A causes a pressure in the liquid *(1 mark)*. This pressure in the liquid is transmitted equally in all directions *(1 mark)*. The pressure of the liquid at piston B causes a force on piston B (equal to $F = P_A \times A_B$ where P_A is the pressure at piston A and A_B is the area of piston B) *(1 mark)*.

b) i) The pressure on piston A is equal to the pressure on piston B:

$P_A = P_B$. $P = \dfrac{F}{A}$ so:

P_A = Force on piston A ÷ Area of piston A = 25 ÷ 0.01 = 2500 N/m²,

so the pressure on piston B = P_B = 2500 N/m²
Force on piston B = F_B
$F_B = P_B \times$ Area of piston B = 2500 × 0.15 = **375 N**

(4 marks available — 1 mark for stating the pressure equation, 1 mark for correctly substituting the values for piston A into the equation, 1 mark for correctly calculating the pressure on piston A, 1 mark for correctly substituting into the correctly rearranged equation to find the force on piston B.)

ii) The pressure in a liquid increases with depth and the pistons aren't at the same depth *(1 mark)*.

10 a) The angle of incidence when a ray hits the edge of a fibre is greater than the critical angle *(1 mark)*, so the ray is totally internally reflected and almost none 'escapes' *(1 mark)*.

b) E.g. Shine a light ray at the block on a piece of paper and trace the block and the incident, refracted and emergent rays *(1 mark)*. Measure the angle of incidence *(1 mark)* and the angle of refraction *(1 mark)* at the air-material boundary. Use the equation $n = \dfrac{\sin i}{\sin r}$ to calculate the refractive index *(1 mark)*.

You could say lots of other things here. For example you could say that you'll repeat the experiment for different values of i, or that you'll take repeats at each value of i.

c) θ = critical angle (C).

$\sin C = \dfrac{1}{n}$ so $\theta = C = \sin^{-1}\left(\dfrac{1}{n}\right) = \sin^{-1}\left(\dfrac{1}{1.5}\right)$ = **42°** (to 2 s.f.)

(4 marks for correct answer, otherwise 1 mark for stating the equation for sin C, 1 mark for rearranging the equation correctly and 1 mark for correctly substituting into the equation.)

11 a) i) Total distance travelled = total area under the graph.

Splitting it into a rectangle (0-19 s) and a triangle (19-26 s):
Area under the graph = (19 × 15) + ((7 × 15) ÷ 2)
= **337.5 m**

(2 marks for the correct answer, otherwise 1 mark for indicating that the distance is represented by the area under the graph and showing working to calculate the area under the entire graph.)

ii) It increases *(1 mark)*, as the brakes transfer the kinetic energy of wheels into heat energy *(1 mark)*.

b) i) At point A when the skydiver first jumps, the downwards force of his weight due to gravity is pulling him down and there are no resistive forces acting upwards *(1 mark)*. As the skydiver's velocity increases, the resistive forces acting upwards increase *(1 mark)*. When the resistive forces acting upwards balance the force of his weight acting downwards *(1 mark)*, he reaches his terminal velocity and remains at a steady speed until point B *(1 mark)*.

ii) Opening the parachute causes the surface area of the skydiver to increase *(1 mark)*. This causes the resistive forces on the skydiver to increase, causing deceleration *(1 mark)*.

12 a) Brownian motion *(1 mark)*.

b) Small, light water particles travel around at high speeds *(1 mark)*. When they collide with heavier and larger pollen grains *(1 mark)* they cause them to move in a random path (Brownian motion) *(1 mark)*.

c) Particle theory *(1 mark)*.

13 a) The microwave oven emits microwaves *(1 mark)*. The microwaves penetrate a few centimetres into the food before being absorbed by the water molecules in the food *(1 mark)*. The energy is then conducted or convected to other parts of the food *(1 mark)*.

b) i) speed = frequency × wavelength or $v = f \times \lambda$ *(1 mark)*

ii) $v = f \times \lambda$ so $\lambda = \dfrac{v}{f} = \dfrac{3.0 \times 10^8}{2.5 \times 10^9}$ = **0.12 m**

(2 marks for correct answer, otherwise 1 mark for substituting into the correctly rearranged equation.)

c) i) Some microwaves are absorbed by molecules in the body and can heat human body tissue internally *(1 mark)*. Some people are worried that this might damage health *(1 mark)*.

ii) Disagree. Microwaves are more damaging than radio waves *(1 mark)*, but this is because they have a higher frequency than radio waves *(1 mark)* and so transfer more energy *(1 mark — note that no marks are awarded for agreeing)*.

d) E.g. satellite television *(1 mark)*/remote-sensing satellites *(1 mark)*/ satellite phones *(1 mark)*.

Pages 167-181

Practice Paper — 2P

1 a) i) The height of the wave, from the rest position to a crest. *(1 mark)*

   ii) The number of complete waves passing a certain point per second. *(1 mark)*

   b) The direction of oscillations is parallel to the direction of energy transfer for sound waves *(1 mark)*.

   c) The amplitude has decreased *(1 mark)*.

   d) Diffraction *(1 mark)* — the sound waves spread out, or bend, around the corner *(1 mark)*.

2 a) i) The paint drops all have the same charge and so repel each other, forming a fine spray *(1 mark)*.

   ii) The (negatively-charged) paint drops are repelled by each other but attracted to the (positively-charged) body panel *(1 mark)*, and so spread out across the panel, including to parts that are not directly facing the spray gun *(1 mark)*.

   b) E.g. during refuelling, friction causes electrons to be transferred between the fuel and the metal tanker *(1 mark)*. If the tank was made of an insulator, electrons transferred would be unable to move / be conducted away, and so a charge would build up on the tank *(1 mark)*. A build-up of charge can cause a spark — the fuel and its vapours are flammable, so this could cause a fire or explosion *(1 mark)*.

3 a) momentum = mass × velocity ($p = m \times v$) *(1 mark)*

   b) Skater A: $p = m \times v = 70 \times 9.0 =$ **630 kg m/s** *(1 mark)*
      Skater B: $p = m \times v = 50 \times 6.6 =$ **330 kg m/s** *(1 mark)*

   c) $p = m \times v \Rightarrow v = \dfrac{p}{m} = \dfrac{630 + 330}{70 + 50} =$ **8 m/s**
      (2 marks if answer correct, otherwise 1 mark for correct rearrangement of the equation and correct substitution of values into the equation.)

   d) i) Skater B exerts a force of 100 N in the opposite direction to the original force *(1 mark)*.

      ii) (Unbalanced) force = mass × acceleration (F = m × a) *(1 mark)*

      iii) $F = m \times a \Rightarrow a = \dfrac{F}{m} = \dfrac{100}{50}$
         = **2 metres per second squared (m/s²)**
         (3 marks if answer correct, otherwise 1 mark for correct rearrangement of the equation and correct substitution of values into the equation and 1 mark for the correct unit.)

4 a) 100 − 59.2 − 23.9 = **16.9%** *(1 mark)*

   b) Advantages — e.g. any two from:
      The reaction in the nuclear reactor doesn't produce any carbon dioxide emissions (i.e. it doesn't contribute to global warming/air pollution) *(1 mark)*.
      There is still a lot of nuclear fuel left in the ground *(1 mark)*.
      Nuclear reactions release more energy for the amount of fuel used compared to burning fossil fuels *(1 mark)*.
      Disadvantages — e.g. any two from:
      It takes longer/costs more to start up nuclear power stations than fossil fuel power stations *(1 mark)*.
      There's a risk with nuclear power of leaks of radioactive material or major catastrophe *(1 mark)*.
      Radioactive waste from nuclear power stations is very dangerous and difficult to dispose of *(1 mark)*.
      Decommissioning nuclear power stations is very expensive *(1 mark)*.

   c) i) E.g. ionising radiation can damage living cells and tissues *(1 mark)* and cause mutations in living organisms *(1 mark)*.

      ii) E.g. wearing full protective suits. *(1 mark)*

5 a) i) E.g. temperature/mass *(1 mark)*.

   ii) Control variables needs to be kept constant to make sure that any observed changes are due to just one variable being changed *(1 mark)*.

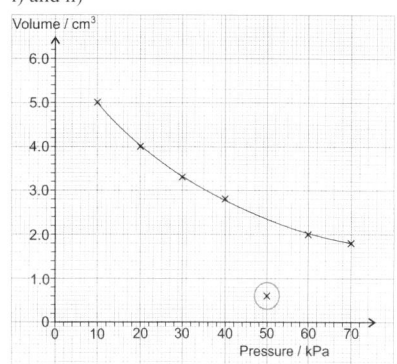

b) i) and ii)

(5 marks available for part i) — 1 mark for choosing a suitable scale (using at least half of the grid), 1 mark for correctly labelled axes with the correct units, 1 mark for plotting at least 6 correct points to the nearest half square, 1 further mark for correctly plotting all 7 points to the nearest half square, and 1 mark for an appropriate curve of best fit.)
(1 mark for part ii))

   iii) As pressure increases, the volume of the gas decreases / pressure is inversely proportional to volume *(1 mark)*.

   c) i) As temperature increases, the volume of the gas increases / temperature is proportional to volume *(1 mark)*.

      ii) Temperature = 25 + 273 = 298 K *(1 mark)*
         Reading from the graph, volume at 298 K = 6.1 cm³
         (1 mark, allow for error in calculation of temperature carried forward).

To convert from Celsius to Kelvin just add 273. To go from Kelvin to Celsius, subtract 273.

6 a) Step-up transformer *(1 mark)*

   b) i) $\dfrac{\text{input (primary) voltage}}{\text{output (secondary) voltage}} = \dfrac{\text{number of turns on primary}}{\text{number of turns on secondary}}$
      or $\dfrac{V_p}{V_s} = \dfrac{N_p}{N_s}$ *(1 mark)*

      ii) $\dfrac{V_p}{V_s} = \dfrac{N_p}{N_s} \Rightarrow N_s = \dfrac{N_p \times V_s}{V_p} = \dfrac{5000 \times 400}{25} =$ **80 000 turns**
         (3 marks if answer correct, otherwise 1 mark for correct rearrangement of the equation and 1 mark for correct substitution of values into the equation.)

   c) i) $V_p I_p = V_s I_s$ *(1 mark)*

      ii) $V_p I_p = V_s I_s \Rightarrow I_p = \dfrac{V_s I_s}{V_p} = \dfrac{400 \times 250}{25} =$ **4000 A**
         (2 marks if answer correct, otherwise 1 mark for correct rearrangement of the equation and correct substitution of values into the equation.)

   d) Step-up transformers are used to increase the voltage and decrease the current before the electricity is distributed *(1 mark)*. This reduces the amount of energy lost as heat (the higher the current, the larger the heating effect) *(1 mark)*. Step-down transformers are then used to reduce the voltage to usable and relatively safe levels before the electricity is provided to the consumer *(1 mark)*.

7 a) An electromagnet is a coil of wire connected to a voltage supply *(1 mark)*.

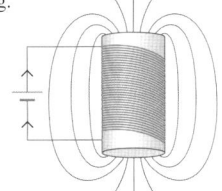

   b) i) E.g.

      (1 mark)

      ii) A magnetically soft iron core means the core stops being magnetic after the electromagnet is turned off (and so a metal load/object can be dropped) *(1 mark)*.

   c) i) moment = force × perpendicular distance from the line of action of the force to the pivot ($M = F \times d$) *(1 mark)*

      ii) total clockwise moment = total anticlockwise moment
         $M = F \times d$
         $5 \times 28\,000 = 10 \times$ weight of anvil
         $\Rightarrow$ weight of anvil = $\dfrac{5 \times 28\,000}{10} =$ **14 000 N**
         (3 marks if answer correct, otherwise 1 mark for showing the clockwise moment is equal to 5 × 28 000 and 1 mark for correct rearrangement of the equation and correct substitution of values into the equation.)

Working Out Your Grade

- Do both exam papers.
- Use the answers to mark each exam paper.
- Use the tables below to record your marks.

Paper 1

Q	Mark	Q	Mark
1		8	
2		9	
3		10	
4		11	
5		12	
6		13	
7			
Total			/120

Paper 2

Q	Mark	Q	Mark
1		5	
2		6	
3		7	
4			
Total			/60

- Add together your marks for the two papers to give a total mark out of 180.

Total Mark = Paper 1 Total + Paper 2 Total

Total Mark = ☐ / 180

- Look up your total mark in this table to see what grade you got.

Total Mark	Grade
139	A*
121	A
103	B
85	C
73	D
62	E
50	F
39	G
0	U

Important!

The grade boundaries above are given as a guide only.
Exam boards tinker with their boundaries each year, so any grade you get on these practice papers is no guarantee of getting that grade in the real exams — but it should give you a pretty good idea.

Index

A
absolute zero 106
acceleration 2-4, 15
accuracy 140
acid rain 93
air bags 20
air resistance 8, 11
alpha particles
    124-127, 130, 132, 134
alternating current (a.c.) 38
ammeters 38, 45
amplitude 54, 72
analogue signals 71
angle of incidence 63
angle of reflection 63
angle of refraction 66
anomalous results 141
atomic (proton) number 123, 126
atoms
  splitting 135
  structure 123, 127

B
background nuclear radiation 124
balanced forces 15
balancing nuclear equations 126
bar charts 141
beta particles 125, 126, 130, 132, 134
braking distance 18
broadband 58
Brownian motion 106

C
cameras 58
cancer treatment 133
carbon-14 123, 133
car safety features 20
categoric data 141
cavity wall insulation 87
centre of gravity 24
chain reactions 135
charge 46-50
chemical energy 77, 80
circuit breakers 34
circuits 35-38, 44-46
cladding 68
collisions
  momentum 19, 20
  particle 106, 107
conclusion 142
conduction 84, 85, 87
conductors (electrical) 35, 47-49
continuous data 141
control variables 139
convection 84-87
cosmic rays 124
critical angle 67, 68
crumple zones 20
current 35-41, 44-46

D
daughter nuclei 135
dependent variables 139, 141, 142
diffraction 56, 57, 72
digital signals 71
direct current (d.c.) 38
distance 1, 3, 4
distance-time graphs 3
double glazing 87
double insulation 33
drag 8, 9
draught-proofing 87
drawing graphs 141
dynamo effect 115

E
earthing 33
earth wire 33
efficiency 78-80
elastic deformation 27
elastic limit 27
elastic potential energy 77, 80
electrical conductors 33, 47-49
electrical energy 36, 46, 77, 80
electrical insulators 33, 47, 49
electrical power 35
electric motors 114
electromagnetic waves 56
  dangers 60
  uses 57-59
electromagnetism 112
electrons 46, 47, 123-125, 127
electrostatic force 8, 49
energy conservation 77
energy flow diagrams 78
energy transfer 36, 77-80
energy transformation diagrams 81
evaporation 105
experiments 139-142
  planning 142
extension (Hooke's law) 26, 27

F
fair tests 139
falling objects 11, 12, 91
Fleming's left-hand rule 113, 114
fluorescent lamps 59
forces 5, 8-12, 15-20, 23-29
fossil fuels 93
frequency 54, 60
friction 9
  static electricity 47
fuel filling 50
fuses 34, 35

G
galaxies 28
gamma rays 59, 60, 124-126, 130, 132-134
gases 103-107
Geiger-Muller detectors 124, 131
generators 116
geostationary satellites 29
geothermal energy 94
global warming 93
gold foil 127
gold-leaf electroscope 49
graph plotting 141
gravitational potential energy 77, 80, 91
gravity 5, 8, 11, 28, 29

H
half-life 130-132
hazards 140
heat transfer 80, 84-87
  uses 58
Hooke's law 26, 27
horseshoe magnets 113
hot water tank jacket 87
hydroelectricity 97

I
igneous rocks 133
immersion heaters 86
independent variables 139, 141, 142
induction
  electromagnetism 112
  magnetism 111
industrial tracers 132
infrared 58, 60
inkjet printers 50
insulating
  the home 87
  the human body 87
insulators (electrical) 33, 47-49
ionising radiation 60, 124, 125, 134
ions 124
isotopes 123
I-V graphs 39, 40

K
Kelvin scale of temperature 106
kinetic energy 77, 80, 91
  of a gas particle 106
kinetic theory 104

L
law of reflection 63
laws of motion 15, 16, 19
left-hand rule 113, 114
light 56, 58
light-emitting diodes 41
lightning 50
line graphs 141
lines of best fit 141
live wire 33
loft insulation 87
longitudinal waves 55, 72
loudness 72
loudspeakers 114

M
magnetic fields 111-117
magnetic materials 112
mains electricity 38, 118
mass 5
mass (nucleon) number 123, 125, 126
medical tracers 132
microwaves 56, 57, 60
Milky Way 28
moments 23
momentum 19, 20
motor effect 113, 114
movement energy 77
mutation of cells 60, 134

Index

N

natural length 26
neutral wire 33
neutrons 123, 125
  fission 135
night-vision equipment 58
non-renewable energy
      resources 93, 94
nuclear energy 77, 93,
    94, 134, 135
nuclear model of the atom 127
nuclear radiation 132-134
nuclei 123

O

optical fibres 58, 68
orbital speed 29
orbits 28, 29
oscilloscopes 72-74

P

parallel circuits 45
particle theory 106
period 54
photocopiers 50
photographic film 124
photography 58
pitch 73
plane mirror 64
plugs 33
plum pudding model 127
power 35, 36, 90
power rating 35
power stations 93-98, 135
precision 140
pressure (of a gas) 107
principle of moments 25
principle of the
     conservation of
     energy 77
protons 123, 125
pumped storage 98

R

radiation
  background 124
  electromagnetic 56-60
  nuclear 123-127,
    130-135
  thermal 84
radiators 86
radioactive dating 133
radioactive decay 124
radioactivity 123-127,
    130-135
radiotherapy 133
radio waves 56, 57
ray diagrams 64
reaction forces 8, 16
reflection 56, 63, 64, 72
refraction 56, 65-68, 72
refractive index 66-68
reliable results 139
renewable energy resources 93-97
repeat experiments 139
residual current circuit
     breakers (RCCBs) 34
resistance 35-41
resistors 35-41
resultant forces 15-17
Rutherford scattering 127

S

safety 140
Sankey diagrams 81
satellites 28, 29, 57
scalars 17
seat belts 20
series circuits 44
Snell's law 66-68
solar energy 96
sound energy 77, 80
sound waves 72-74
speed 1-4
  limits 18
  of a wave 54, 74
standard test circuit 38
stars 28
states of matter 104, 105
static electricity 47-50
sterilising food 59
stopping distance 18
stored energy 77

T

temperature
    84, 85, 106, 107
tension 8
terminal velocity 11, 12
thick curtains 87
thinking distance 18
thrust 8
tidal barrages 97
total internal reflection
    67, 68
transformers 117, 118
transverse waves 55
triangular prisms 65
turning forces 23, 24

U

ultraviolet 56, 59, 60
uncertainty 140
uniform magnetic fields 111
useful energy 78-80

V

valid results 139
Van de Graaff generators 49
variables 139
vectors 17, 19
velocity 1, 2, 4, 15, 19
velocity-time graphs 4
virtual image 64
visible light 56, 58
voltage 35-41, 46
voltage rating 35
voltmeters 38, 45
volume (of a gas) 107

W

watts 90
wavelength 54, 56
wave power 95
waves 54-60, 63-68, 71-74
weight 5, 8, 24
white light 65
wind farms 95
work done 89

X

X-rays 59